Ferries 2021

Europe's leading guide to the UK & Northern European ferry industry

Compiled by Nick Widdows

Ferry Publications

Europe's **leading** guide to the ferry industry

Contents...

Produced and designed by Ferry Publications trading as Lily Publications Ltd
PO Box 33, Ramsey, Isle of Man, British Isles, IM99 4LP.
Tel: +44 (0) 1624 898446 Fax: +44 (0) 1624 898449
www.ferrypubs.co.uk e-mail: info@lilypublications.co.uk
ISBN: 978-1911268-376

Europe's **leading** guide to the ferry industry

Introduction...

This is the thirty-third edition of this book, which first appeared in 1983 as the 24-page 'home published' *'Car Ferries from Great Britain and Ireland'*. The book aims to list every passenger/vehicle ferry in Great Britain and Ireland, ro-ro freight vessels which operate regular services between Great Britain and Ireland and to nearby Continental destinations and major passenger/vehicle ferries in other parts of Northern Europe. The coverage of Northern Europe is not fully comprehensive (to make it so would probably triple the size of the book) and does not include freight-only operations and vessels – although freight-only vessels have been included where the operators also run passenger services. Where operators use a mixture of ro-ro and container ships, I have only included the ro-ro ships. Exceptionally I have included the *Arx* of CLdN/Cobelfret Ferries and the *Elisabeth* of P&O as they operate to provide additional container capacity on ro-ro routes.

Each operator is listed alphabetically within sections – major operators, minor operators, freight-only operators, chain, cable and float ferries, passenger-only ferries, other North European passenger operators and vehicle/passenger vessels owned by companies not currently engaged in operating services. After details relating to each company's management, address, telephone numbers, email, website and services, there is a fleet list with technical data and then a potted history of each vessel with previous names and dates.

The Covid-19 pandemic has caused considerable disruption but I have assumed that 'normal' operations will eventually return except where a permanent change has been announced.

Nick Widdows

Whitstable, Kent

August 2020

Caroline Russ *(John Bryant)*

Foreword...

Twelve months ago, the foreword in Ferries 2020 reflected the prevailing optimism in the ferry industry, with much talk of new tonnage and only the prospect of a disorderly 'Brexit' clouding the horizon. The slow pace of progress in negotiations between Britain and the EU, with its profound impact on ferry operators, was much lamented. One year on, and this glacial progress continues to frustrate. Britain has now formally left the EU, but the scope of future fiscal and trading relationships remains unclear despite the backdrop of a final agreement deadline of 31 December 2020. A 'no deal' scenario would lead to a return to customs and immigration bureaucracy and attendant delays at ports streamlined to handle 'just in time' movements and ill-equipped to deal with freight congestion; any agreement would likely mean new administrative arrangements for traffic between Britain and Northern Ireland. None of this is good news for the transport industry.

Ferry companies are already gearing up to any potential new regime by taking steps to 'bypass' Britain, particularly for freight transits between Ireland and the rest of the EU, seeking to avoid the landbridge arrangements on which they have depended for so long. And the UK government is creating more permanent 'stacking' facilities in anticipation of freight traffic being delayed approaching the English Channel border. CLdN introduced a new route from Zeebrugge to Cork using one of their 'Kawasaki' class vessels from April 2020, with the service later extended to add Esbjerg to the weekly sailings. The company's Zeebrugge-Dublin service was expanded from two to three sailings weekly, to match the frequency of the Rotterdam-Dublin operation. This was not the limit of CLdN's post-Brexit ambitions. In June 2020, a new weekly service opened from Santander to Liverpool and Dublin utilising another of the 'Kawasaki' class vessels, which fitted in a round trip from Dublin to Liverpool in the middle of this schedule. The latter provided additional competition for P&O Ferries on this landbridge route, at a time when there has been much speculation about the financial health of the company. Meanwhile, Brittany Ferries will open a new direct route utilising the *Connemara* from Rosslare to Cherbourg in 2021, to supplement the Rosslare-Bilbao sailings which commenced in 2020. Rosslare is the preferred port for freight operators, but the company's Cork services will be also be enhanced by an additional mid-week sailing of the *Armorique* to Roscoff.

In the latter half of 2019 as the Brexit debate rumbled on, ferry operations continued as normal as a succession of negotiation deadlines were missed. Industry news was overwhelmingly positive; the third and fourth Laureline-class vessels *Sixtine* and *Hermine* entered service for CLdN, DFDS contemplated orders for two new ships on the North Shields-Ijmuiden route and P&O Ferries opened a new Calais-Tilbury route to bypass possible future congestion at Dover. In late September 2019, P&O Ferries announced their long-anticipated plans for two new vessels for their flagship Dover-Calais service, with the order being placed with the Guangzhou Shipyard in China. The *Humbria Seaways*, the second DFDS newbuild to head to Northern Europe, arrived in stormy conditions in February 2020 and soon found her North Sea services disrupted by the Covid-19 outbreak.

Away from Britain, the *Color Hybrid* entered service between Sandefjord and Strömstad for Color Line in August 2019, combining high quality passenger accommodation with spacious car deck capacity. Her status as the largest hybrid plug-in vessel yet constructed commanded attention, with 720 batteries giving the *Color Hybrid* the capability of sailing at 12 knots for up to an hour on battery power. Fjord Line's fast craft *Fjord Fstr* was launched in February 2020 at the Cebu shipyard in the Philippines; she is the largest aluminium craft (by volume) built by Austal and is destined for the Kristiansand-Hirtshals route. Following the successful introduction of the well-received fast craft *Express 4* during 2019, Molslinjen returned to Austal to place an order for a second craft for the Ystad-Rønne route, due to enter service in 2022. At 115m, this will be the largest craft yet built by Austal. Meanwhile,

Pride of Burgundy and Pride of Canterbury *(Bruce Peter)*

Grimaldi placed an order with the AVIC yard in China for two 'Superstar' class 230m ro-pax vessels, slated for delivery in 2023. The €230m order for a hybrid power cruise-ferry design by Knud E Hansen is expected to lead to their deployment on the Finnlines route from Kapellskär to Naantali via Långnäs. Destination Gotland's LNG powered ro-pax ferry *Visby* was joined by sister vessel the *Thjelvar* (later renamed the *Gotland*), which was delivered at the Guangzhou Shipyard in China in December 2019 and entered service in May 2020. Matt Davies reviews the *Visby* in this issue, in her previous guise whilst she was still named the *Visborg*.

Arguably the most important development was the appearance of the first Stena Line E-Flexers on the company's Irish Sea routes, with the welcome arrival of the *Stena Estrid* and *Stena Edda*; the first vessels of a design that will soon become a familiar sight across Europe. Andrew Cooke reviews crossings on the *Stena Estrid* and *Stena Edda* in this issue. Although the *Stena Estrid* suffered some early engine teething problems, the pair of vessels are set to be joined by the *Stena Embla* on the Birkenhead-Belfast route in early 2021. The march of the E-Flexers continued, as the Chinese shipyard resumed production with the laying of the keel for the sixth in the class, the *Salamanca*; Brittany Ferries' *Galicia* was expected in European waters as this volume went to press, ready for service on the company's UK-Spain routes. The *Côte d'Opale* was floated out at the Avic shipyard in May, already painted in DFDS livery, although not due to enter service on the Dover-Calais route until June 2021. Stena Line have since confirmed the start of construction work on the final two 'extended' E-Flexers, which will enter service from 2022.

Meanwhile, unhappiness with fast craft services to the Channel Islands was only partly assuaged by the takeover of Condor by a consortium comprised of the Columbia Threadneedle European Infrastructure Investment Fund and Brittany Ferries. Although the deal was confirmed early in 2020, future investment plans have yet to be revealed, with Covid-19 putting a blight on passenger carryings, forcing the company to implement severe staff cutbacks, and pushing back prospects for replacement of the *Commodore Clipper* and *Commodore Goodwill* and the deployment strategy of the *Condor Liberation*.

There were fewer problems in the Isle of Man, where the government's decision to nationalise the Isle of Man Steam Packet Company in 2018 helped sustain the company and its lifeline service during the pandemic. Plans for a new vessel to replace the *Ben-my-Chree* were

CONNEMARA

Connemara *(Andrew Wood)*

Côte D'Albâtre *(Darren Holdaway)*

W.B. Yeats *(Gordon Hislip)*

announced in July 2020 following much consultation. The new ro-pax is to be built at the Hyundai Mipo Dockyard in Ulsan, South Korea and is due to enter service in spring 2023.

Some European shipbuilders were already in trouble before the Covid-19 pandemic struck. Protracted delivery problems at the Flensburger Schiffbau-Gesselschaft & Co KG (FSG) shipyard in Germany led to the cancellation of the €165m new-build order for Irish Ferries' Holyhead-Dublin route, with work having not started on an order placed in January 2018. Delays in building Irish Ferries' *W.B. Yeats* had a knock-on impact on Brittany Ferries' new-build *Honfleur*. Although this vessel was in a more advanced state of construction, she was well behind schedule, having originally been slated to enter service in June 2019. Following repeated financial problems and the announcement of the bankruptcy of FSG, it came as little surprise when the order was cancelled, although there is a commitment at the shipyard to complete the vessel. The future of the partially constructed hull is uncertain. FSG claimed to have lost €25m on the contract to build the award-winning *W.B. Yeats* for Irish Ferries. Both ferry companies were said to be considering their options, but neither will have been too disappointed with the new build cancellations as they consider their future capacity requirements in a post-Covid-19 era.

Nationalisation of the Ferguson shipyard in Glasgow did little to speed up delivery of the *Glen Sannox*, the first of a two-ship order for CMAL. Although the first steel was cut on 7 April 2016 and the vessel was launched on 21 November 2017, the *Glen Sannox* is not expected to enter service on the Ardrossan-Brodick route until April 2022 following extensive issues with her design, outfitting and costs, not helped by the protracted dispute between shipyard and customer which led to the former's demise.

There seemed little that could displace Brexit from the main topic of conversation, until an avalanche of change was precipitated by the Covid-19 virus outbreak. The snail's pace of resolution of the 'Brexit' issue lay in stark contrast to the speed with which the pandemic posed, in a matter of weeks, an existential threat to the transport industry, it's suppliers and customers. The consequences of this worldwide outbreak have devastated ferry companies' finances and crippled prospects for the pattern of continued growth, putting many routes, vessels and jobs in jeopardy. The future has never been cloudier than at present.

The Covid-19 virus gave early warning of its potential to disrupt shipping when the plight of passengers on board the cruise vessels *Diamond Princess* and *Grand Princess* received extensive media attention. The reality of the unfolding situation took time to be fully appreciated in the countries of north west Europe, but international borders were quickly closed, and freedom of movement restricted as the virus spread. Many ferry operators had little choice other than to suspend passenger services for all but the most essential travel, with freight operations scaled down to match falling demand, as manufacturing and retail activity was heavily supressed. Vessel lay-ups accelerated as March progressed. This quickly posed grave threats to many operators, routes and services, and it was not long before companies as large as P&O Ferries were reportedly seeking substantial sums of government support to survive. Those operators with a balanced portfolio of freight and passenger revenues were better placed to weather the storm than those dependant on more seasonal passenger revenues, with cruise-ferry and fast craft operators proving particularly prone to financial problems following the loss of passenger income.

Many ferry services were judged as being essential 'lifeline' links, and became eligible to receive packages of government support through the crisis, illustrating their importance to the modern economy. Estonia, Finland, Ireland, Spain and the UK were amongst those who provided tranches of financial help, although this concept was not without challenge, with CLdN and Grimaldi in particular, being vocal about state support creating an 'unfair' competitive marketplace.

Some smaller island communities chose to close themselves off from the outside world in largely successful attempts to thwart the spread of the virus, continuing lifeline freight services but placing passenger services in hibernation; a return to normality for many of these services seems likely only in the very long term.

What began as a drop off in bookings for the second quarter of 2020 rapidly escalated to

Fridtjof Nansen *(John Bryant)*

become a full-scale operational close-down in a matter of days. With revenues drying up, companies were forced to take drastic steps to reduce their costs. Plans to suspend or close loss-making routes, redeploy fleet capacity, lay-up vessels, implement mass redundancy and furlough schemes, and slim down frequencies, were quickly announced. Widespread job losses were announced across the industry, with Condor, DFDS, P&O Ferries, Stena Line, Tallink, and Viking Line being prominent amongst those proposing a variety of cutbacks.

In the event, the rapid closedown of services proved to be a much easier process than subsequent re-opening. There was early optimism of something approaching a 'normal' summer for the passenger business, but the fragility of the recovery was soon evident as fresh outbreaks of Covid-19 infections grew in some of the more popular tourist destinations. Multiple efforts to re-start holiday businesses across Europe were thwarted as quarantine requirements were re-imposed on travellers. The UK government, for example, initially mandated a 14-day quarantine period for all people entering the country just as services were being re-introduced, then sought to relax the restrictions for selected countries where infection levels were low, before re-imposing restrictions at short notice on an individual country basis as infection rates grew again. None of this made life easy for ferry operators, as international travel was increasingly discouraged, and any hopes that there might be a sustained improvement in revenues were crushed. With the prospect of a second 'wave' of infection as the European autumn advances, the immediate outlook is bleak; the ferry industry is, of course, far from alone in this predicament, with the airline industry facing even greater challenges. The advance of the low-cost airline has also been curbed.

The new 'normal' experience for those able to enjoy ferry travel has been marked by substantial change, with operators required to operate vessels with reduced passenger capacity, whilst employing significantly enhanced health checks on intending travellers. The wearing of masks and adherence to social distancing arrangements, together with enhanced shipboard cleaning regimes, are now mandatory. The on-board experience is becoming more remote, less personal and contactless, with passenger journeys now more for essential rather than leisure purposes, in line with other public transport operations. These changes provide security and restore some confidence in response to the pandemic but do little to enhance the attractions of ferry travel and encourage use. Paradoxically, the Channel Tunnel might be expected to prosper from the comparative soulless isolation of their services.

Scandinavian ferry services were the first to re-open, having been closed from mid-March until late-May. Stena Line took quick action to permanently close their services from Frederikshavn to Oslo and from Sassnitz to Trelleborg, later declaring 950 redundancies across their Scandinavian network. DFDS added a call in Frederikshavn to their København-

Oslo service in an attempt to secure traffic abandoned by Stena Line. Viking Line closed their routes from Stockholm to Helsinki and Stockholm to Mariehamn until late June, concentrating traffic on the Turku route. Other operators took the opportunity to introduce new routes in a creative and experimental approach to the crisis. Fjordline operated a new Hirtshals-Kristiansand-Stavanger rotation, Tallink switched vessels from the Stockholm-Helsinki route to open up new services between Stockholm and Riga, Helsinki and Riga, and a duty-free focused route from Stockholm to Mariehamn and Visby. Whether these become permanent features of future schedules remains to be seen.

On the Norwegian Coastal route, Hurtigruten withdrew 14 of their 16-ship fleet from service, with traffic justifying only a basic lifeline operation. Although an enhanced service was introduced from mid-June, only six vessels were in service by late summer with the *Kong Harald, Lofoten, Nordkapp, Nordnorge*, and *Vesteralen* remaining in lay-up.

Passenger services around the British coast generally resumed around the end of June, but later government imposition of variable quarantine requirements frustrated demand. Guernsey and the Isle of Man remain in self-imposed isolation from visitors, although some resident travel is permissible. The approach of different operators varied. DFDS restored the majority of their fleet on the Dover Straits, but P&O Ferries left vessels in lay-up, operating a once-unthinkable three ship service through the peak season.

The travel business is facing a seismic change. Many operators face a difficult future, with 2020 summer revenues severely depleted and poor prospects through to summer 2021 and beyond. A long, slow recovery may be the most probable outcome, but it is likely to take a significant period for the ferry industry to return to previous traffic levels; some consolidation of operations seems inevitable. Freight revenues might be expected to recover in line with the return of the manufacturing sector, but the future of passenger services is more difficult to predict whilst the Covid-19 virus remains virulent.

The ferry industry has never faced a peacetime challenge comparable to the global Covid-19 pandemic. Twelve months ago, the vessel order book represented the largest tonnage of new vessels on record. Now the medium-term outlook for ferry operators remains shrouded in fog, as the industry adjusts to the 'new normal' whilst further outbreaks of the virus potentially escalate as colder weather advances. This 2021 edition of the 'Ferries' series provides an important snapshot of the state of play, at an historical milestone in the evolution of the ferry industry.

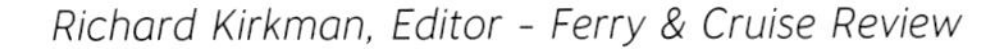
Richard Kirkman, Editor - Ferry & Cruise Review

Nils Holgersson *(Frank Lose)*

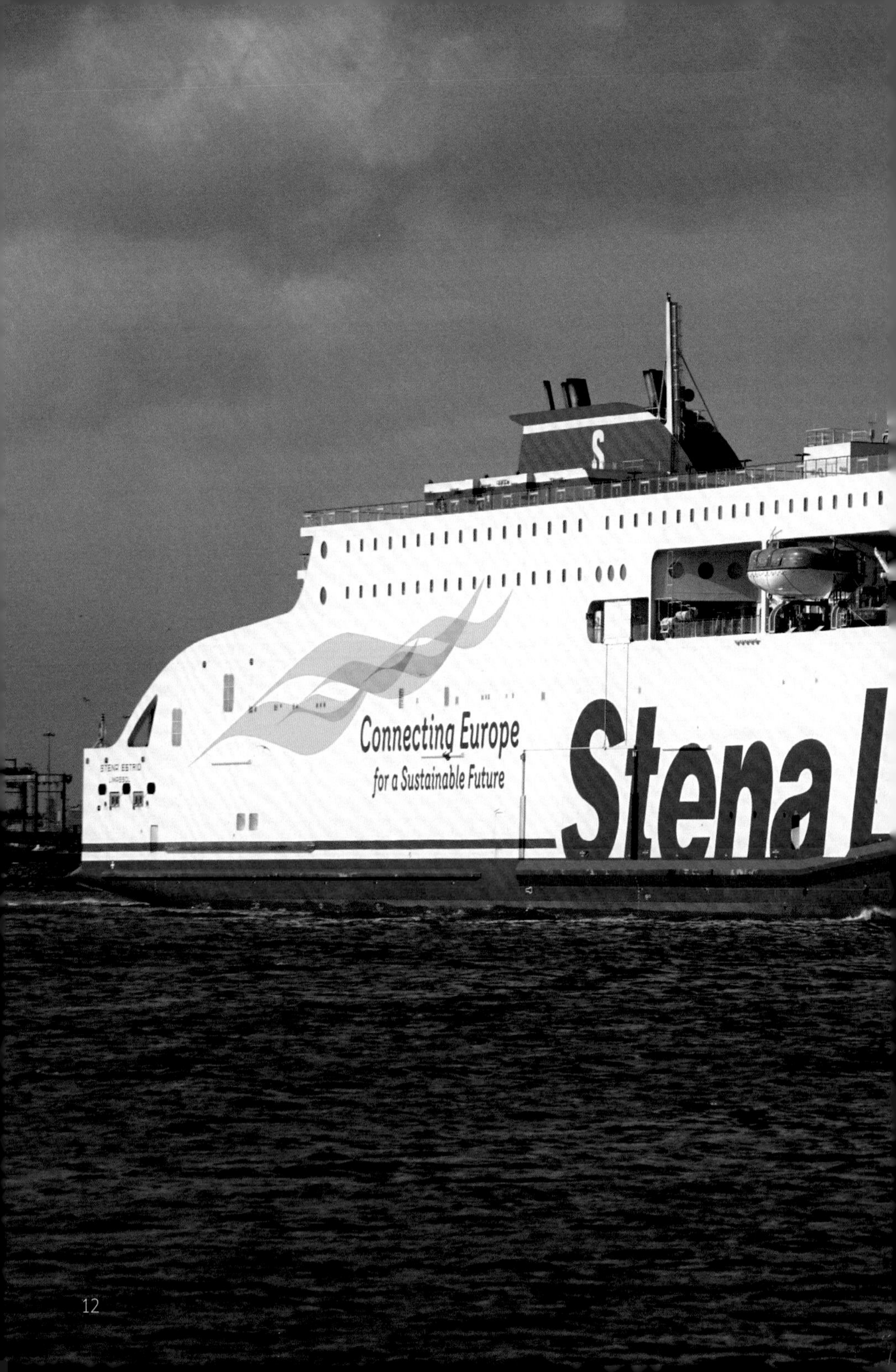
Connecting Europe
for a Sustainable Future
Stena L

Stena Estrid *(Andrew Cooke)*

STENA LINE'S NEW RO-PAX CONCEPT – THE E-FLEXER

Andrew Cooke sails with Stena Line on their new 'E Flexer' ships

Ferry operators constantly strive for the optimum in versatility and efficiency; Stena embarking upon this project in 2014 in search of the next generation in Ro-Pax design. Various design options were considered, resulting in the E-Flexer Class created jointly by Stena RoRo and Deltamarin for Stena Line's operations, as well as for the charter market. The project set out not only to design and build a class of vessel that was as environmentally friendly and efficient as possible but to also produce a flexible platform that would permit variable configurations for a diversity of routes from short day crossings to longer overnight services. The success of this aim is reflected in the routes that the vessels have been ordered for, ranging from the 90-minute Dover-Calais crossing to Brittany Ferries' Portsmouth to Spain routes with crossing times of 23 hours and over. The chosen hull form was found to be the most efficient at the 22 knot design speed, with indications that the hull was so efficient that the ship would be capable of maintaining a speed of 18 knots with just one engine and propeller in use. To further enhance flexibility, the E-Flexer design allows each ship to be built in differing lengths of 215m or 240m, with or without cabin accommodation. The chosen shipyard to undertake the newbuilds was AVIC Weihai (now China Merchants Jinling Shipbuilding (Weihai) Co. Ltd.). The choice of yard surprised many as it had limited experience with ferries at that stage.

The name E-Flexer was a perfect choice for a 'green,' efficient and flexible workhorse and the first order was placed on 11 March 2016 for a quartet of ships with options for 2 further pairs, since exercised with further options added. The first steel was cut for the initial ship on 26 August 2017 prior to fabricating the 304 blocks for the hull and superstructure. The keel laying ceremony took place on 2 February 2018 and, less than 8 months later, all sections were in place with the float-out following on 16 January 2019. The 175 passenger and 64 crew cabins were all prefabricated on site, lifted aboard and, thanks to their modular construction, wheeled in to position one by one and connected up, almost on a 'plug and play' basis. In line with the 'E' theme, all of the Stena Line examples of the class are being assigned with names beginning with that letter, plus the Stena prefix of course. These names are of a Nordic theme, the identities of the first trio of E-Flexers being chosen via a staff competition. Thank goodness 'Boaty McBoatface' does not start with E! So, *Stena Estrid* was the name bestowed upon Yard No. W0263, an appellation connected to Stena Line's Scandinavian heritage. Estrid is an Old Norse eastern-Nordic version of the name Astrid and means 'divinely beautiful' or 'beautiful goddess'. The second and third ships for Stena (actually the 2nd and 4th in the series) are named *Stena Edda* and *Stena Embla*. The third E-Flexer is going to Brittany Ferries on charter as the *Galicia* for Portsmouth-Spain.

The *Stena Estrid* went to sea for the first time on 5 September, followed by a three-day series of trials in October 2019. At design draught the ship achieved a speed of 22.4 knots, slightly exceeding the design specification. The *Stena Estrid* was delivered by the shipyard on 15 November 2019 and she sailed away from her birthplace on 22 November, bound for the Irish Sea, as sisters *Stena Edda*, *Galicia* and *Stena Embla* continued their respective fitting-out and build processes. A delivery voyage of over 10,000 nautical miles lay ahead for a crew of 27 under the command of Senior Master Matthew Lynch. On the homeward stretch to Holyhead the ship called in to Dublin on the evening of 22 December before reaching Wales the next morning. Following trials, storing and training, the 41,671t *Stena Estrid* undertook her maiden service voyage to Dublin on 13 January 2020 in the teeth of Storm Brendan. The 9,777t Deadweight/14,991t Net Tonnage ship replaced the 30,551gt and 2002 built *Stena Superfast X*, which is now on charter to Corsica Linea as the *A Nepita*, operating from Marseille. The 'Estrid's daily schedule is usually the 08.55 and 20.30 departures from Holyhead and the 14.50 and 02.15 sailings from Dublin.

The Stena E-Flexer series could total 11 if all current options are taken up with the sister ship to the *Stena Estrid*, the *Stena Edda* (W0264), being delivered exactly two months after her sister, arriving in Belfast Lough on 25 February and Birkenhead three days later. The *Stena Edda* entered

The ample promenade area on Deck 10 aboard *Stena Edda.* *(Andrew Cooke)*

The Stena Plus Lounge. *(Andrew Cooke)*

service with the 22.30 sailing between Birkenhead (Twelve Quays) and Belfast on 9 March, replacing the 27,510gt and 2005 built *Stena Lagan*. The third ship in the series, Yard No. W0267, will be delivered as Brittany Ferries' *Galicia* in autumn 2020. To reflect her long-haul role, Decks 7 & 8 are extended to increase passenger capacity and the car garage on Deck 7 will give way to cabins (341 overall). An exhaust scrubber will also be installed.

The fourth ship, W0266, will follow in early 2021 as the *Stena Embla*, joining the *Stena Edda* to increase the Belfast-Liverpool freight capacity by 20% overall. Yard No. W0268 is also due for delivery in 2021 as the *Côte D'Opale* for DFDS (Dover-Calais - equipped with a third bow thruster) and W0269 will arrive autumn 2021 as Brittany Ferries' LNG powered *Salamanca* for Portsmouth-Spain, modified in the same way as the *Galicia*. The 350m^3 LNG tanks mean she will have a smaller capacity of 2,758 lane metres as likewise her sister ship, W0270, to be delivered as Brittany Ferries' *Santona* in 2023. The steel cutting for the *Santona* began in November 2019. Yard Nos W0271 and W0272 are the 240m long variants with a 3,600 lane metre and 200 car capacity, 1,200 passengers and 263 cabins. These were originally scheduled for 2022 but, as with all dates, this may be subject to change. The naming ceremony was originally announced for the *Stena Estrid* at 30 March in Dublin. Alas, the Covid-19 pandemic meant that did not happen, along with any planned event for the *Stena Edda*. Hopefully the ceremonies will take place when some normality returns. The Taoiseach (Irish Prime Minister) Leo Varadkar and his partner Dr Matt Bennett had been invited to name the *Stena Estrid* but declined to be the Godparents of the new vessel.

Sampling the new era

In March, my wife and I took the opportunity to try the new E-Flexer ferries for ourselves, a trip timed to coincide with the service debut of the second in the series. Although arranged in February 2020, the day that we drove towards Holyhead coincided with the news that the world was beginning to shut down in response to the escalating Covid-19 pandemic. Although there were no travel restrictions in the UK and Republic of Ireland at this time, we had no idea how close that time actually was. The E-Flexer return trip began with the 08.55 departure from Holyhead of the *Stena Estrid*. We travelled by car but, owing to low traffic levels, were parked on the vast upper vehicle deck rather than on the Deck 7 dedicated car garage. At 214.50m in length, the *Stena Estrid* is the longest of the Ro-Pax ferries currently serving on the Irish Sea. Her waterline length is 202.50m with a beam of 27.80m, design draught of 6.40m and hull depth of 9.50m. Departure was observed from Deck 9 aft, one deck above where the builder's plate is on display. The crossing time to Dublin is 3 hours 15 minutes, ample time to see what the *Stena Estrid* had to offer. Incidentally, the name Estrid is of Old Norse origin meaning 'beautiful goddess' (Astridr, consisting of the elements 'Ass' meaning god and 'Fridr' meaning beautiful). This name is also a variation of Astrid. The standard E-Flexer Series of ships has 10 decks and the following outlines what is contained within that sleek and purposeful exterior:

Deck 1: The Tanktop and Deck 1 house the machinery spaces, storage tanks etc with the central section of Deck 1 providing a 345 lane metre capacity Freight Hold with a 4.80m clear-height. This is accessed via a fixed 3.50m wide ramp from the main vehicle deck. This ramp is covered by a hydraulic hatch cover when access is not required - ie when loading Deck 3 or at sea. The aft portion of Deck 1 is where the engine rooms can be found. Rather than having four main engines to propel the vessel, the E-Flexer ships need just two owing to their lower power requirements. Not only does this mean less fuel is consumed by the engines but it also means there is a lot less weight carried within the ship. The main engines are two Caterpillar MaK 12 M43C V12 4-stroke marine diesel engines, manufactured by Caterpillar Motoren Rostock GmbH, Rostock, Germany. The power output is 25,200kW. The 12 M43C engine series have a 500-514rpm speed range, a 430mm bore, a 610mm stroke and approximate dimensions of 8.25m long, 5.20m high and 2.90m wide. Each engine has an approximate dry weight of 95t. The twin engines drive two Caterpillar Feathering Controllable-Pitch MPP 1410f (PB58547) propellers via two Caterpillar Renk RSHL-112 gearboxes. Two WE Tech 2,600kW permanent magnet shaft generators are installed with variable frequency drive connected to a DC-link switchboard. So efficient is this electricity supply system that while the main engines are running the shaft generators attached to them can produce all the power required for the ship's systems, without the need to run the auxiliary generators. The system can supply power regardless of the main

The Living Room lounge, Deck 8. *(Andrew Cooke)*

The Sky Lounge/Bar on Deck 8. *(Andrew Cooke)*

Reception Area – Guest Services - on Deck 7. *(Andrew Cooke)*

One of the spacious stairways *(Andrew Cooke)*

Lounge area on Deck 7 adjacent to Guest Services. *(Andrew Cooke)*

Taste Self Service Restaurant on Deck 7. *(Andrew Cooke)*

engine speed. There are also three Wärtsilä 8L20 MGO/HFO Auxiliary Generators plus a Mitsubishi S12A2-M(P)TA Emergency Generator. Manoeuvrability is assisted by two Rolls-Royce 'high lift' rudders and two Wärtsila WTT24 CP 2,400kW transverse tunnel bow thrusters. A smoother ride for both passengers and freight is assisted by two retractable fin stabilisers. The *Stena Estrid* is the first new ferry built for Stena Line to comply with the Safe Return to Port (SRtP) regulations, which is designed to ensure that new passenger vessels of greater than 120m in length when involved in an emergency can return to port under their own power with passengers and crew still safely onboard.

Deck 3: This level is the main vehicle deck with a 1,320 lane metre capacity and a clear-height of 5.20m. As mentioned above, a hatch-covered ramp leads to the Hold Deck from here plus a 5.90m wide hoistable ramp that connects the main deck with the upper deck. The ship's twin-level-drive-through vehicle loading configuration is designed for efficient loading and unloading and allows for quicker turnarounds. Freight capacity on the E-Flexers is stated as being around 50% higher than comparable standard Ro-Pax ships currently in service, including the ship that the 'Estrid' replaces. The Deck 3 stern ramp/door has a clear-width of 17m, a length of 9.50m plus 2.50m flaps. The bow ramp/door has a clear-width of 5m, a length of 16.20m and 1.50m flaps. The bow shell doors are of the clam shell type. The ramp flaps fitted throughout the ship are MacGregor 'soft flaps' that greatly reduce the noise of vehicles travelling over them.

Deck 5: The upper vehicle deck offers a 1,435 lane metre capacity and a clear-height of 5.20m. Drive through access at the bow is via a hydraulic weather door with a clear-width of 5m and a 5.20m clear-height. There is an open weather deck section aft with a 17m wide access over the stern via gates. There are 100 reefer plugs fitted, 50 on Deck 3 and 50 on Deck 5 and, overall, Decks 1,3 & 5 offer a freight capacity of 3,100 lane metres (210 trucks). The vehicle deck ventilation system generates 10 air changes per hour in port and likewise whilst at sea.

Deck 7: Just under 50% of the aft section of this deck is set aside for a dedicated 1,800m^2 car garage with capacity for up to 120 cars. This area has a 2.20m clear-height (the extreme aft section is open-air) and is accessed via a hoistable 2.90m wide ramp from Deck 5. The location of the car garage allows passengers to simply walk from their vehicles to Guest Services and other amenities on Deck 7 forward, without needing to use staircases and lifts, thus accelerating turnaround times. The passenger accommodation on this level also includes a shop, Café Barista, lounge area and the large self-service Taste Restaurant located forward (with a décor of light wood finishes, blue carpeting & blue/brown upholstery and over 300 seats) that overlooks the bow, with a play area on the port side. Deck 7 also has a promenade deck on either side along with fully heated kennels on the starboard side.

Deck 8: The aft section of this deck is home to a portion of the 175 passenger cabins and, moving forward, small movie lounges on either side facing on to the Sky Lounge. This area could be described as the ship's centrepiece. The lighting is randomly adorned with small cherub Estrids and birds. As its name suggests, the Sky Bar has a large skylight atrium above it that ensures the area is bathed in daylight. Other areas of the passenger accommodation are punctuated with figures, sculptures and eye-catching ornaments, adding to the cruise-ferry ambience. Forward from here are Video Game & Children's Play Areas, the Living Room Lounge to port, the 170-seater Trucker's Lounge to starboard and the Stena Plus Lounge overlooking the bow (£16 per head supplement). Nestled behind the Stena Plus is the deliberately windowless Hygge Reclining Lounge. Hygge is a Danish term that means enjoying life, living in the moment and creating joy and cosiness wherever you are, and this lounge allows you to do just that. An £8 per person supplement is payable for this peaceful environment. The décor throughout Deck 8 follows the easy-on-the-eye theme of natural/light wood and shades of beige, brown, blue, grey, orange and red. The interior spaces in general are spacious, light, airy, easily catering for the 3 hour 15 minute crossing benefitting from the plentiful use of panoramic picture windows.

Deck 9: As with the deck below, the aft section is home to the remainder of the cabins (inside, outside categories & 6x deluxe cabins – catering for 684 passengers in total). Located forward of here is the accommodation for the 73 crew members (mode dependent), crew mess and crew cabins. Outside deck space is plentiful overall, on the stern of Deck 8 and 9, the promenade areas on Deck 7 and the expanse of Deck 10 either side and forward of the funnel. Amidships on Deck 10 is a helipad on its own pedestal. Whilst on board, it soon becomes apparent that the

Taste Self Service Restaurant on Deck 7. *(Andrew Cooke)*

Trucker's Restaurant/Lounge on Deck 8. *(Andrew Cooke)*

ship's accommodation for up to 1,000 passengers is neatly divided between day areas in the forward areas of Decks 7 & 8 and night/sleeping areas aft on Decks 8 & 9. All too soon we were approaching Dublin port and it was time to leave the *Stena Estrid*.

Two days later it was time to be welcomed by the 'factory-fresh' *Stena Edda* on her seventh day in service for the 10.30 Belfast-Liverpool (Birkenhead) sailing, a crossing of around 8 hours in duration. The ship takes her name from Edda, one of the first woman of ancient Norse mythology. The name means 'Petitioner', hence Eddorna, mother for the Icelandic folk tales. The connotation of each ship's name is shown in the central atrium stairway on Deck 7. On this voyage the car garage on Deck 7 was in use and the benefits of stepping from vehicle deck directly to passenger areas was all too clear. As with the voyage to Dublin, we travelled in the comfy and peaceful Stena Plus lounge, which features a variety of seating styles, a drink and snack buffet (pre-Covid-19 anyway), an at-seat food and beverage service and lovely views out

The *Stena Estrid* departs Dublin for Holyhead. *(Andrew Cooke)*

across the sea from the prime location of Deck 8 overlooking the bow. The Irish Sea was in a gentle spring-like mood for the voyage to Merseyside and, as we sailed past the eastern coast of the Isle of Man, there was also the opportunity to visit the bridge and meet Captain Greg Paciorek who, understandably, was very proud of his new ship. It will be very interesting to see how the short-sea and long-haul versions of the E-Flexer design compare with the first two members of the build, but Stena's new combination of a ro-ro workhorse and cruise ferry produces a very impressive result, one that has certainly brought a new era to Stena Line's Irish Sea services. The *Stena Embla* joins the 'Edda' in 2021 further lifting the Belfast service to another new level.

Andrew Cooke

VISBO
POWERED BY
LNG
VISBORG

Visborg *(Matt Davies)*

VOYAGE ON THE VISBORG

Matt Davies sails on the first of Destination Gotland's two new Chinese built ferries the Visborg, now renamed Visby, the fastest LNG ro-pax ferry in the world

In March 2019, the 32,447t LNG powered new ro-pax ferry *Visby* entered service with Destination Gotland in Sweden on the domestic route from Nynäshamn near Stockholm to Visby on the island of Gotland. The vessel, which is designated SF 1650 class (the number denoting passenger capacity), is the first of two sisters built for the Company by the Guangzhou Shipyard International Company Limited (GSI) at Guangzhou, southern China. Originally ordered back in 2014 for delivery in 2017, considerable construction delays were encountered due to the Chinese yard being new to LNG technology and it was December 2018 when the *Visby* was finally handed over. Second vessel the *Thjelvar* was delivered in China in December 2019 and entered service in May 2020.

The 28 knot pair, which are officially the fastest LNG powered ro-pax vessels in the world, are impressive, efficient and well-appointed but functional vessels and well worth the wait. Destination Gotland is no stranger to GSI, having gone to the yard for previous fast ro-paxes, the SF 1500 class *Visby* and *Gotland* delivered in 2002 and 2003. The pair ordered in 1999 and now almost 18 years old, also suffered from construction delays. Destination Gotland were however very satisfied and assured of GSI's build quality and value for money returned to them for the latest vessels with the basic concept of the SF1500 being copied with efficiency and environmental improvements added. GSI has also built tanker vessels for Destination Gotland's parent company.

Sweden's oldest passenger shipping company

Destination Gotland AB is subsidiary of Rederi AB Gotland and has been in existence since 1998 when awarded the Swedish Transport Administration contract to provide ferry services between the Swedish mainland and the island of Gotland, which although home to only 25,000 permanent residents, is a popular summer holiday destination for Scandinavians and sees many weekend commuters return from Stockholm where they live in the week. In 2014 the contract for the period between 2017 and 2027 was awarded and included a requirement to reduce emissions and improve environmental footprint through new vessels. Travellers to Gotland have doubled since 2003 and each year now sees 1.7 million passengers, 550,000 cars and 850,000 metres of cargo carried and up to 18 sailings a day operating in the high season. There are three routes; Nynäshamn – Visby with a crossing time of 3 hours 15 minutes and Oskarshamn – Visby with a crossing time of 2 hours 55 minutes, both of which operate year round and Västervik – Visby which operates mid-June and mid-August with a crossing time of 2 hours 30 minutes.

When set up, Destination Gotland was initially owned 75% by Rederi AB Gotland and 25% by Silja Line but parent Rederi AB Gotland took full control in 1999. Rederi AB Gotland, which trades as Gotlandsbolaget, was founded as Ångfartygsbolaget Gotland in 1865 and is Sweden's oldest passenger shipping company. It is owned by 2,700 shareholders with the majority being from Gotland. Gotlandsbolaget had operated ferry services to Gotland continuously until 1988, with operations being under a concession arrangement from 1970. In 1988 the contract was lost to new company Gotlandslinjen, set up by the Swedish Shipping Company Nordström & Thulin and it was 10 years later when Gotlandsbolaget took it back and operations recommenced under the Destination Gotland name. In addition to the ferry business, Gotlandsbolaget operates vessels on the charter market. It owns the ro-ro vessel *Gute*, five product tanker vessels and three offshore windfarm workboats. The Company also owns and operates a number of resort hotels on Gotland.

SF 1500 ro-pax and fast craft

Initially operating with temporary tonnage, Destination Gotland quickly ordered two new fast ro-pax vessels, the SF 1500 designated 195-metre-long and 29,746t *Visby* and *Gotland*. The pair have operated the Nynäshamn and Oskarshamn to Visby routes since delivered by GSI in 2002 and 2003. Each carries 1,500 passengers and 500 cars over 1,750 lane metres at speed of 28.5

The SF1500 class vessel the *Gotland* is seen at Visby. She was renamed the *Drotten* in February 2020. Sister SF1500 vessel the *Visby* is also to be renamed and will swap names with the *Visborg*. *(Matt Davies)*

The smaller of Destination Gotland's two fastcraft the *Gotlandia* laid up for the winter in *Visby*. *(Matt Davies)*

The second SF 1650 class vessel which was built as the *Thjelvar* entered service as the *Gotland* in May 2020. The vessel is seen arriving at Nynäshamn. *(Richard Seville)*

The SF 1650 class *Visborg* is seen arriving at Nynäshamn. The vessel is to be renamed the *Visby*. *(Matt Davies)*

knots. In addition, two fast ferries designated SF700, also built new for Destination Gotland, have been operated on a seasonal basis for many years; the 112 metre 700 passenger and 145 car capacity *Gotlandia* which was built by Alstom Leroux Naval, France in 1999 and capable of 35 knots and the larger 122-metre-long *Gotlandia II* which can carry 78- passengers and 160 cars which was built by Fincantieri at La Spezia, Italy in 2006 and capable of 32 knots.

Between 2007 and 2009, Destination Gotland briefly operated the *Gotlandia* on a summer link between Visby and the island of Öland which is linked to the Swedish mainland by bridge. Nowadays one of the fast craft, usually the *Gotlandia II* operates the summer Västervik to Visby route with the other used to provide additional sailings to Nynäshamn and Oskarshamn at peak times. The Västervik connection is relatively new, being launched in 2017 following the failure of new start-up company Gotlandsbåten AB who introduced the fast craft *Express* on a summer service in competition with Destination Gotland in 2016.

SF 1650 ro-pax newbuilds

The arrival of the first new SF 1650 class vessel the *Visborg* last year, did not result in the displacement of any of the existing Destination Gotland fleet. Instead overall capacity was increased by around 20% with additional summer sailings operating on the Nynäshamn and Oskarshamn routes during 2019. Following the arrival of the second SF 1650 vessel *Thjelvar* in early 2020, it is still not clear whether any of the fleet will be disposed of. The timetable for 2020, issued prior to the impact of Covid-19, sees both SF 1650 vessels operate the Nynäshamn route and one SF1500 vessel operate the Oskarshamn route from spring onwards. From late June sailing frequencies step up and the three vessels are scheduled to interwork both routes between Fridays and Mondays with the majority of Oskarshamn sailings and those midweek remaining in the hands of the SF 1500 vessel. A single fast craft were scheduled to operate between mid-June and mid-August. It was intended the other fastcraft and other SF 1500 would be timetable for additional peak sailings as bookings developed. As a result of the COVID-19 crisis summer 2020 operations have been conducted with both SF 1650 vessels and a single SF 1500 vessel. Both fastcraft have been laid up and the seasonal Västervik to Visby route has not operated..

Although *Visborg* was ordered in June 2014, construction work did not start until December 2015 with the vessel launched just under a year later in December 2016. Fitting out was somewhat protracted and it was April 2018 when sea trials were finally conducted. The *Visborg* was formally named in a ceremony at GSI in Guangzhou on 12 December 2017 with delivery made to Destination Gotland two days later. On 18 December 2018 the vessel set sail for Landskrona in Sweden sailing via Hong Kong, Singapore, Durban and Gran Canaria arriving just over a month later on 23 February 2019. After a two month stay at the Öresund Shipyard in Landskrona where final work was completed and remaining equipment installed, the *Visborg* entered service on the Nynäshamn - Visby route on 28 March 2019. Meanwhile sister *Thjelvar* which was ordered in July 2015 was launched in July 2017 and it was a further two and half years later in December 2019 when sea trials were conducted. She was then quickly delivered to Destination Gotland on 30 December 2019, departing Guangzhou on 10 January 2020 for Landskrona in Sweden where she arrived on 3 February 2020 for final works. Later the same month, the *Thjelvar* was renamed *Gotland* under which name she made her maiden voyage from Visby to Nynäshamn on 30 May 2020.

It has been a longstanding Rederi AB Gotland tradition that the two principal ferries serving Gotland have carried the names *Visby* and *Gotland* and in the past outgoing vessels have been renamed prior to introduction of new vessels. The renaming of the *Thjelvar* was therefore not a surprise and in order to release the name Gotland, the SF 1500 *Gotland* was renamed *Drotten* during February 2020. The *Visborg* is also set to be renamed later this year and will take the name *Visby* from the other SF 1500 vessel which will become the *Visborg*. What is surprising is that the *Visborg* and *Visby* did not change names prior to the introduction of the new *Visborg* in March 2019. The SF 700 fast craft *Gotlandia* was similarly renamed in 2003, having been built as the *Gotland*, she was renamed to allow the second SF 1500 to take the name.

Efficient and environmentally friendly

The SF 1650 was designed by OSK-ShipTech of Denmark using the concept of the SF 1500 which was designed by Knud E. Hansen also of Denmark. OSK acted as consulting naval architects from initial design concept through to delivery and also provided build supervision and support for GSI

The fastcraft ***Gotlandia II*** which normally operates the Västervik to Visby seasonal route. It has been suspended for 2020 due to the COVID-19 crisis. *(Matt Davies)*

The forward lounge on deck 7 of the ***Visborg*** which has reclining seats for 675. *(Matt Davies)*

The central section on the *Visborg* includes the self-service cafeteria and table seating. *(Matt Davies)*

Open seating and the children's play area in the central section of the *Visborg*. *(Matt Davies)*

The open aft section of the upper vehicle deck on the *Visborg*. On either side are fixed inclines leading to the stern ramps at main vehicle deck level. *(Matt Davies)*

Looking aft along the main vehicle deck of the *Visborg*. This deck has 1,130 lane metres and can accommodate 230 cars. *(Matt Davies)*

with whom a joint venture company, Guangzhou SinoDane Ship Design, has now been established to commercialise further high quality ro-pax designs based on Danish design and international standards. GSI is now building a new OSK and Sinodane designed ferry for Algerie Ferries, the *Badji Mokhtar III* for the delivery in summer 2021, two ro-pax and two double ended ferries for P&O's Dover - Calais service for delivery in 2023. In addition, four OSK designed ro-paxes were ordered jointly by Moby and GNV in early 2018 for delivery from 2020 onwards but delivery has now slipped to 2022. The yard is also building two Deltamarin designed ro-pax ferries for DFDS for delivery in 2021 and use in the Baltic. Interior design for the *Visborg* and *Thjelvar* was provided for OSK by the well-known Swedish ferry interior design Company Figura Arkitekter. The SF 1650 is a high capacity design with low fuel consumption and despite being some 1,200 tonnes larger and having greater capacity than the SF1500 offers a significant reduction in fuel consumption through an optimised hull form.

Power is provided by four Wärtsilä W12V50DF engines which give 46,800 KW output providing for a very fast service speed of 28.5 knots at 85% of power. There also two Wärtsilä 9L20DF generators for use when in port. Such a speed is something of a rarity these days for a ro-pax but it is required to shorten crossing times, thereby benefitting connectivity for Gotlanders and allowing the vessels to be intensively used. The engines are dual fuel allowing operation on either LNG or marine gas oil. There are two large 285 metre cubic capacity LNG tanks under the main vehicle deck forward of the engine room. As is now standard on new vessels, each Wärtsilä engine is located in a separate watertight and fire insulated engine room to significantly reducing the likelihood of both being disabled.

Although the Baltic's NOx Emission Control Area (NECA) does not take effect until 1 January 2021, the vessel is already sailing on LNG which reduces Co^2 emissions by 20% and sulphur emissions by 99%. Refuelling is undertaken in Visby by an LNG bunker tanker which moors alongside and when filled each SF 1650 can complete 10 return crossings prior to the next fill. Alternatively operating on marine gas oil the vessels have a range of 6,500 nautical miles. In the high season the vessels will bunker every day and in the low season twice per week. Thrusters and propellers are also from Wärtsilä; each vessel has 2 Wärtsilä CT250M Thrusters and 2 Wärtsilä Controllable Pitch propellers whilst gearboxes are Renk Aktiengesellschaft NDSHL-2400.

On-board the *Visborg*

In December last year, along with two other Ferry & Cruise Review correspondents, I made a round trip from Nynäshamn to Visby on *Visborg* to experience the new SF1600 vessel. Our trip was my first ever with Destination Gotland though my travelling companions had previously made crossings on the Company's SF 1500 vessels. Boarding as a foot passenger was an incredibly efficient and automated process with tickets simply being swiped airport style at turnstiles into a lounge from which an elevated walkway led straight to the vessel. Destination Gotland impressively turns around fully loaded vessels in just 45 minutes and literally as soon as the last foot disembarking passenger came off the gangway, the automatic gates immediately opened and the large assembled crowd boarded.

The *Visborg* is 32,447t and 199.9 metres in length and, as denoted by the class designation SF 1650, can carry 1,650 passengers. Vehicle capacity is 2,310 lane metres allowing 500 cars to be carried. Although only 4 metres longer than the SF 1500, an extra 150 passengers can be carried and lane metres have increased by 560 from 1,750 to 2,310 metres. The vessel is Ice Class 1A strengthened which is necessary for year round Baltic operation. The vehicle deck layout is simple and designed for fast and efficient loading and unloading. There are two 4.9 metre full height vehicle decks accessed directly from three stern ramps. The port and starboard side stern ramps lead directly via a fixed incline to the 1,130 lane metre upper vehicle deck on level 5 which can take 240 cars whilst the centre stern ramp provides the access to the 1,180 lane metre main vehicle deck on level 3 which can take 260 cars. Unusually for a ro-pax there are no mezzanine decks or internal ramps between the decks, nor is there a lower hold due to the space being used for the LNG tanks. At the bow, the main vehicle deck is accessed via bow doors whilst the upper vehicle deck is accessed through a port side door in the forward superstructure which connects with side loading ramps ashore in Visby where vessels berth bow in.

One of the pleasures of travelling with Destination Gotland is that every single passenger has their own allocated reclining seat with each having spacious leg room, a fold down table for food and drink and sight line of the many numerous TV screens dotted about. Each seat also has access to USB port, power socket and headphone socket for the TV. In total there are 1,658 reclining seats on-board and with the vessel having large panoramic windows throughout the lounges all feel light and airy. There are two categories of seating with the only real difference being the location and passengers have to select their seat when booking. The aft side lounges are the lowest price option, with seats in the forward lounges costing slightly more. In addition, passengers can choose seats in dedicated lounges for those with travelling with young children or pets.

The layout of the new SF 1600 vessels closely replicates the internal layout of the SF 1500 vessels but public space and free seating around the Cafeteria has been increased to better cater for those wanting to eat, the shop has been enlarged, a pet lounge added in place of some cabins and a small coffee bar counter is included in the upper forward lounge. In addition, a large sheltered seating area with café bar for summer use has been added outside, addressing the limited outside seating on the SF 1500 vessels.

Passenger accommodation is spread over two levels on deck 7 and deck 8. Deck 7 has a large full width reclining seat lounge forward with seating for 675 with mid-ships being a large open plan walk through area with table seating for 318 seating for 318. In the centre is is an information counter with adjoining cafe bar, children's play area and the self-service Cafeteria.

Moving aft, the accommodation is split with a port side walkway running through a reclining seat lounge to the Toddler Lounge and the starboard side walkway side running through the shop to the aft reclining seat lounge. Separating the port and starboard sides, are the galley and stores which lie in between. Deck 8 has a large full width reclining seat lounge forward with seating for 620 that includes a small café bar counter, mid-ships on the port side is a small lounge for those travelling with pets whilst the rest of the deck is given to cabins. There are 98 cabins in total with berths for 222 and they are normally used in day mode with upper bunks stowed and lower bunks set up as sofa seating. Deck 9 has the bridge forward with the remainder given over to crew use and comprising cabins, messrooms, a gym and sauna. In summer a crew of 70 operates reducing to 35 for the winter. Finally, at the highest level on deck 10, located between the funnel and forward mast is the sheltered outside seating area with a café bar counter and seating for 200.

Verdict

Overall, I found the *Visborg* to be a most pleasant vessel to travel on. The use of panoramic windows throughout the public areas makes the vessel light and airy. To me at least, the concept of everyone on-board having their own allocated seat and moving to catering areas when required worked well on a very busy crossing and prevented the usual experiences of scrambling to find a seat and risking losing it later, enduring table seating being blocked by people not eating and people sprawling out across several seats whilst others can't find anywhere to sit. It most certainly allows a very high passenger capacity to be carried without the vessel feeling unbearably full. Sailing in the low season, we were treated to the rare sight of the full Destination Gotland fleet all in port during our short stay in Visby, the capital of Gotland, with the *Visborg* and SF 1500 vessels *Visby* and *Gotland all* present as well as the fast craft *Gotlandia* and *Gotlandia II* which were both laid up for the winter.

Although only self-service meals are available on-board Destination Gotland's ferries, the quality of catering was exceptionally good and prices were reasonable and portions large. A wide variety of typically Swedish dishes are served and my meal of meatballs, sauce, lingonberry, mashed potato and warm cucumber salsa was delicious and far better than that in IKEA which I am also quite fond of! My fellow FCR travel companions were far less impressed than me with the concept used by Destination Gotland, finding their vessels including the new *Visborg* rather soulless and the experience much more akin to travelling on a fast ferry. To be fair to them, the vessel is essentially a series of high quality reclining seat lounges, all furnished in identical décor, though bright colours and attractive materials are used and the catering offer and outside deck space are good. But for me, the functionality and practicality works well and I am surprised that more ferry operators have not embraced the Destination Gotland concept.

Matt Davies

Visborg *(Destination Gotland)*

Spirit of France

Spirit of France *(George Holland)*

ROUND BRITAIN & IRELAND REVIEW 2019/2020

The following is a review of passenger and freight ferry activities during 2019 and the first half of 2020. Some events occurring in the first half of 2019 will have also been mentioned in 'Ferries 2020'.

EAST COAST & THAMES

In mid-June 2019, the contract to convey Stora Enso paper and card traffic from Göteborg to Zeebrugge passed to DFDS Seaways. For the last five years it had been carried by SOL Continent Line, using the *Schieborg* and *Slingeborg*, chartered from Wagenborg of The Netherlands. DFDS purchased these vessels, renaming them *Gothia Seaways* and *Belgia Seaways* respectively. The *Fionia Seaways* was added to the route, enabling six departures to be operated per week. In late 2019, agreement was reached with CNdL to co-ordinate their services from January 2020, each operator being commercial responsible for its own traffic but buying capacity on each other's ships. Initially DFDS ran then two ex-Wagenborg vessels, with the *Begonia Seaways* operating one round trip per week from Göteborg and CLdN provided a *Laureline* class vessel. In April, the DFDS contribution changed to a single ship - the *Hollandia Seaways*.

In Autumn 2019, DFDS Seaways announced plans to revitalise their North Shields - IJmuiden route by replacing the 1980s built *King Seaways* and *Princess Seaways* with two twenty first century vessels owned by Moby Lines of Italy - the *Moby Wonder* of 2001 and *Moby Aki* of 2005, to become the *Amsterdam Seaways* and *Newcastle Seaways* respectively. Sadly this never took place as the banks holding mortgages on Moby's vessels refused to back the deal, which involved a swap of ships and a additional cash payment to the Italian operator. On 22 March 2020 DFDS suspended the route due to the Covid-19 pandemic but it resumed on 15 July.

The *Hollandia Seaways*, third of DFDS Seaways' Nanjing built 'jumbo' ferries, and the first to come to Northern Europe, arrived at Vlaardingen on 21 November after a seven week voyage from China. She was placed on the Göteborg - Gent service. The fourth newbuild, the *Humbria Seaways* arrived 2 February and entered service the following Saturday on the Vlaardingen - Immingham route. Her arrival allowed the *Tulipa Seaways* to move to Vlaardingen - Felixstowe and the charter of the *Fionia Seaways* to end. She was then chartered to Finnlines, renamed the *Fionia Sea*. Numbers 5 and 6, the *Flandria Seaways* and *Scandia Seaways* should enter service in the autumn and early winter respectively.

In January 2019 the *Finlandia Seaways* replaced a container vessel on the DFDS Seaways service from Immingham to Western Norway but this only lasted a few weeks until she was in turn replaced by a side-loading pallet carrier. However, in April a ro-ro service was re-instated using the chartered *Trader*.

After relieving the *Stena Europe* on the Irish Sea all summer (see Irish Sea), in October 2019 the *Stena Nordica* was chartered to the UK Department for Transport and moved to Rotterdam to provide extra capacity to relieve Dover in the event of a 'no-deal Brexit' at the end of the month. This never happened and although she was used by Stena Line during the winter refit period she spent most of the time laid up at the Dutch port.

During winter 2020, Stena Line increased capacity on its North Sea routes by replacing the 2,133 lane metre *Misana* and *Misida* on the Rotterdam - Killingholme route by two vessels chartered from Alternative Transport of Turkey, the 3,663-lanemetre *Hatche* and *Qezban*.

Following the loss of the Göteborg - Zeebrugge Stora Enso traffic, SOL Continent Line's parent company, Swedish Orient Line, formed a joint venture with Wallenius Lines of Sweden - Wallenius SOL. They continued to operate two services from the Baltic to Antwerpen, Zeebrugge and Tilbury. Four new LNG powered 420 trailer ro-ros were ordered from the Yantai CIMC Raffles Shipyard, Yantai, China for delivery in 2021.

Vespertine *(Rob de Visser)*

Stena Nordica *(Rob de Visser)*

In November 2019 CLdN sold the *Cymbeline* to Navigmag of Chile. This left just one remaining of the original four 'super-Bazias' class vessels built in China in the early nineties which started the company's use of names ending in 'ine'.

In February 2019 CLdN took delivery of the *Laureline*, the first of four 50,443 ton vessels built by Hyundai Mipo at Ulsan, South Korea, and she entered service in March. Sister vessel *Ysaline* entered service in June. Numbers three and four, the *Sixtine* and *Hermine*, entered service in the autumn. Similar in may ways to the larger *Celine* and *Delphine*, which were delivered in 2017 and early 2018, they are shorter and have one deck less. In July 2019 the option for a further two vessels of the type was exercised; these will be LNG powered and a new refuelling facility at Zeebrugge is to be built. An order for two similar vessels from the Uljanik Shipyard in Pula, Croatia was cancelled because of the shipyard's failure to deliver. In January 2019 the *Meleq* of Alternative Transport (Ekol) of Turkey was chartered; in January 2020 she was purchased and transferred to the Maltese flag.

Three of the four *Mazarine* class vessels, built in 2009 and 2010, had an extra deck added over winter 2019/20 but, due to the Covid-19 crises it was decided to defer work on the fourth vessel, the *Peregrine*.

In March 2019 P&O Ferries chartered the *Wilhelmine* of CLdN and she was initially deployed on the Teesport – Rotterdam service. This enabled the charter of the German registered *Wega*, a 749-TEU containership built in 1996, which had been introduced in August 1998 to supplement the smaller *Estraden*.

On 3 April 2020 the Hull – Zeebrugge vessel, the *Pride of York* was laid up and on 24 April she was joined in lay up by the *Pride of Bruges*. The service was replaced by a six day per week freight service operated on alternate days by the *Norsky*, moved from the Zeebrugge – Tilbury route and the container ship *Elisabeth*. The *Norsky* was initially replaced by the *Estraden*, switched from the Zeebrugge – Teesport service (which then became a single ship operation) but a month later she changed places with the Rotterdam – Teesport vessel, the *Wilhelmine* of CLdN.

On 25 May 2020, P&O's Tilbury – Zeebrugge service started using the new Tilbury 2 river berth, on the site of the old power station; previously the service used the inner docks. Finnlines, Transfennica and Wallenius SOL continue to use the docks.

New vessels for the historic Woolwich Free Ferry, operated by Briggs Marine, were delivered from Remontowa, Gdansk, Poland in November 2018 but did not enter service until February 2019. The *Ben Woollacott* and *Dame Vera Lynn* have 210 lane metres of vehicle deck space. In January 2020 Transport for London announced that the route would be taken 'in house' at the end of the year from the present contractor, Briggs Marine.

In March 2019, MBNA Thames Clippers took delivery of the *Venus Clipper*, built by the Wight Shipyard at Cowes, Isle of Wight.

EASTERN CHANNEL

Despite continuing to have no ferry services, the port of Ramsgate was very much in the headlines during early 2019 when Seaborne Freight, a company which had for some time been promising to resume ferry operations at the port, was awarded a contract to provide additional freight services to Oostende to relieve Dover in the event of a no-deal 'Brexit' (withdrawal of the UK from the EU) at the end of March. Controversy arose because the company had no vessels and no experience of running a service. In the event financial and technical backing from Arklow Shipping of Ireland was withdrawn, the company backed out and 'Brexit' was deferred. Some work was undertaken on dredging the port but subsequently the local council decided that it should no longer be kept 'ferry ready'. During 2019 and early 2020 deliveries of new Citroën and Peugeot cars were made to the port by the vessels of UECC and LD Seaplane, but they were using the port as a backup to Sheerness.

In September 2019 P&O Ferries ordered two double ended ferries from Guangzhou Shipyard International, Guangzhou, China for the Dover – Calais service. They are due enter service in 2023. They will be the first double-ended ferries built for a non-domestic route from the UK and at 230 metres in length they will be the longest to ever cross the Channel. Initial drawings

European Seaway *(Frank Lose)*

Commodore Clipper *(Darren Holdaway)*

Normandie *(Brian D. Smith)*

European Causeway and Stena Superfast VIII *(George Holland)*

would indicate the lack of a 'Dover Skywalk'. Whether foot passengers will be bused aboard or not carried at all is yet to be confirmed. For the first time since the 'Free Enterprise' series vessels, passengers will enjoy open deck space at the forward and aft ends. An option exists for two further sister ships. They are expected to replace the ageing 'Super European' class vessels built in the early 1990s.

Also in September, P&O Ferries launched a new Calais - Tilbury freight service with the chartered *Caroline Russ*. The aim was to by-pass Dover and any post-Brexit problems which might have arisen there. However, like many attempts to launch trailer services from France to the UK, the service failed to attract much traffic and was ceased at the end of the year.

Chaos at Dover at the end of March and December 2019 did not materialise due to the deferment of Brexit and signing of a withdrawal agreement and a one year transitional period. Despite many strikes and protests by in France during 2019 in opposition to President Macron's reforms, the port of Calais remained open, although there were occasions when French immigration staff at Dover decided to impose more stringent passport checks without adequate staffing to do this. This resulted in major delays to passengers arriving at the port, although the operation of ferries was not affected. Also during 2019 all P&O's Dover based vessels were transferred to Cypriot registry.

Whilst 2020 might have been expected to be another quiet year, the Covid-19 crisis changed all that. The reaction of the two operators was markedly different. In March, DFDS withdrew the *Calais Seaways* from the Calais service but maintained a full service on the Dunkerque route. The *Calais Seaways* returned to traffic on 6 July. Cuts to P&O's service were more drastic, with the *Pride of Burgundy* and *Pride of Canterbury* laid up at Leith and the freighter *European Seaways*, already in 'warm lay-up' at Tilbury, remaining in that state. At the time of going to print, the situation remained the same, with just three vessels in service at Dover. Large job cuts were announced, affecting routes from both Hull and Dover.

WESTERN CHANNEL AND SOLENT

In 2016 Brittany Ferries ordered a new vessel from FSG in Flensburg for delivery in 2019. However, the *Honfleur* as she is called was seriously delayed and in 2020 all work stopped. In June 2020, it was announced that the order had been cancelled. However, the building of three 'e-flexer' vessels chartered from Stena RoRo, one arriving in September in 2020, the second in 2021 and the third in 2023 has continued apace. The first of these vessels is to be named *Galicia*, the second *Salamanca* and the third *Santoña*.

The *Baie de Seine* completed her final voyage for Brittany Ferries on 13th March and was returned to owners DFDS, who restored her to her previous name, *Sirena Seaways* and transferred her to the Baltic.

The Covid-19 pandemic caused all Brittany Ferries routes to become 'freight only' and several vessels were laid up. Passenger services were gradually resumed in July.

In March 2020 Brittany Ferries, jointly with Columbia Threadneedle Investments, assumed control of Condor Ferries from its Australian owners. Due to severe entry restrictions imposed by the Channel islands governments, Condor catamaran services were suspended from March; services resumed in July but only serving Jersey. The *Commodore Clipper* and *Commodore Goodwill* continued to operate, primarily for freight.

Following the delivery of Wightlink's new *Victoria of Wight* in August 2018, in January 2019 the *St. Cecilia* was sold to an Italian operator. This left just one vessel, the *St Faith*, of British Rail Sealink design (albeit built under Sea Containers ownership) operating in UK waters. In June 2019 a 50% share in the company was sold to Fiera Infrastructure Inc of Canada.

During the Covid-19 emergency, the hourly Portsmouth - Fishbourne service was maintained, but passengers were encouraged to remain in their vehicles, initially on some sailings and then on all. The Lymington - Yarmouth service and the Portsmouth - Ryde Fastcat service were suspended, the former resuming on 17th July.

In April 2019 Red Funnel took delivery of a new vessel from Camell Laird, Birkenhead. Unlike the 'Raptor' class, the *Red Kestrel* is a freight only vessel with a passenger capacity of twelve.

IRISH SEA

In November 2019 the *AF Michela*, renamed the *Kerry*, was chartered to Brittany Ferries and placed on the Cork - Santander route. The *Connemara* then operated as a refit relief vessel on services from the UK to France. At the end of February 2020, the Irish port was changed to Rosslare and the Spanish one to Bilbao.

Irish Ferries' new 54,975t ferry, the *W B Yeats*, entered service in January 2019. Over the summer period she operated mainly between Dublin and Cherbourg. The order for a second, even larger vessel, from the same yard - FSG at Flensburg, Germany, to replace the *Epsilon* on the Dublin - Holyhead route was cancelled before production had started due to delays and the bankruptcy of the shipyard. Early in 2019, Irish Ferries announced that the services from Rosslare to Roscoff and Cherbourg operated by the *Oscar Wilde* would not operate during 2019. The vessel was subsequently sold to Mediterranean Shipping Company SA of Italy.

In March 2019 Stena Line sent the 38 year old *Stena Europe* to Turkey for a major life-extension refit, expected to take three months, she eventually returned to the Fishguard - Rosslare route in August. The *Stena Nordica* was moved from the Karlskrona - Gdynia route to cover while she was away.

In January 2019 the first e-flexer, the *Stena Estrid*, replaced the *Stena Superfast X* on the Holyhead - Dublin route. However, in May she was taken out of service for repairs to be conducted on one of her engines and was alongside at Cairnryan for six weeks before she returned to service in June. The ever-versatile *Stena Nordica* substituted. Sister vessel *Stena Edda* entered service on the Birkenhead - Belfast service in March, replacing the *Stena Lagan* which was sent to Turkey for lengthening (although this was delayed due to the Covid-19 pandemic). In February 2019 the *Stena Forerunner* returned to the North Sea and was placed on the Rotterdam - Killingholme service, being replaced at Birkenhead by sister vessel *Stena*

Clansman *(George Holland)*

Forecaster. She withdrawn in early June due to a decline in traffic and the increased freight capacity provided by the *Stena Edda*.

In July 2019, Seatruck's *Clipper Ranger* was chartered to *CTMA* of Canada for one year, with an option to buy; in December, they purchased her.

In March 2019 P&O Ferries moved the freighter *Mistral* from the North Sea to the Liverpool - Dublin service, initially as refit cover but later as permanent replacement for the ro-pax *European Endeavour* which was sold to Eckerö Line of Finland and renamed the *Finbo Cargo*. The *Mistral* operated on the *European Endeavour's* schedules which had previously been available to car passengers but, with only twelve passengers allowed, this facility was withdrawn. In December Seatruck's *Clipper Pennant* was chartered to P&O Ferries to replace the *Mistral*. A fourth ship was introduced onto the route in July 2020 in the form of the *Misida*, like the *Mistral*, chartered from Godby Shipping.

CLdN increased their involvement with The Irish Republic by launching two new routes in spring 2020. In April a weekly Zeebrugge - Cork service was introduced followed in June by a weekly service from Santander in Spain to Liverpool and Dublin - the first CLdN service to not serve a Belgian or Dutch port.

In July, the Isle of Man Steam Packet company announced that they had ordered a new vessel from the Hyundai Mipo Shipyard in Ulsan, South Korea to replace the *Ben-My-Chree* in 2023, although this ship will be retained as a back-up vessel.

SCOTLAND

Caledonian MacBrayne had another difficult summer trying to cope with increasing traffic, an aging fleet and continuing delays in the two ships being built by Ferguson's at Port Glasgow. The introduction of Road Equivalent Tariff (RET) in 2017 and the increasing popularity of the Scottish Islands for tourists created a situation where island residents could not take their vehicles - cars and trucks - onto the mainland. The second factor caused a number of breakdowns which necessitated unwelcome shuffling of vessels and, with no reserve vessels, cancellations and disruption to people's travel plans. After her launch in late 2017 very little progress was made on the *Glen Sannox*, as the builders and the owners, Caledonian Maritime Assets argued about the impact of changes made to the design since the contract was awarded. The second hull remains un-launched and, whilst it is hoped that the *Glen Sannox* might be delivered in 2020, there is no certainty about this. Since the order of these two vessels, no further orders have been placed.

The transfer of the Gourock - Kilcreggan for Strathclyde Partnership for Transport to Transport Scotland and the operation form Clyde Marine to Caledonian MacBrayne did not take place in autumn 2019 as expected but eventually happened in April 2020. The vessel used, the *Cruiser*, has been chartered to Caledonian MacBrayne.

In April 2020 Orkney Ferries acquired the small Norwegian Passenger ferry, the *Nordic Sea* to replace the 1973 built *Golden Mariana* on the Westray - Papa Westray route.

In 2019, Orkney operator, Pentland Ferries, took delivery of the *Alfred*, an 85m catamaran. The new vessel, 25m longer than the existing craft, was built at the Strategic Marine Shipyard, Vũng Tàu, Vietnam.

At the end of October 2019, Serco secured the contact to operate the *Northlink* services to Orkney and Shetland for another eight years.

Nick Widdows

A **guide** to using this book

Sections Listing is in seven sections. ***Section 1*** – Services from Great Britain and Ireland to the Continent and between Great Britain and Ireland (including services to/from the Isle of Man and Channel Islands), ***Section 2*** – Domestic services within Great Britain and Ireland, ***Section 3*** – Freight-only services from Great Britain and Ireland and domestic routes, ***Section 4*** – Minor vehicle ferries in Great Britain and Ireland (chain and cable ferries etc), ***Section 5*** – Major passenger-only operators, ***Section 6*** – Major car ferry operators in Northern Europe, ***Section 7*** – Companies not operating regular services possessing vehicle ferries which may be chartered or sold to other operators.

Order The company order within each section is alphabetical. Note that the definite article and words meaning 'company' or 'shipping company' (eg. 'AG', 'Reederei') do not count. However, where this is part of a ship's name it does count. Sorting is by normal English convention eg. 'Å' is treated the same as 'A' and comes at the start, not as a separate character which comes at the end of the alphabet as is the Scandinavian convention. Where ships are numbered, order is by number whether the number is expressed in Arabic or Latin digits.

Listing of Ships When a ship owned by a company listed in this book is on charter to another company listed, then she is shown under the company which operates her. When a ship owned by a company listed in this book is on charter to another company not listed, then she is shown under the company which owns her.

IMO Number All ships of 100t or greater (except vessels solely engaged in fishing, ships without mechanical means of propulsion (eg. chain ferries), pleasure yachts, ships engaged on special service (eg. lightships), hopper barges, hydrofoils, air cushion vehicles, floating docks and structures classified in a similar manner, warships and troopships, wooden ships) are required to be registered by the International Maritime Organisation (IMO), an agency of the United Nations. The seven digit number (the final digit is a check digit) is retained by the ship throughout her life, however much the vessel is rebuilt. This number is now required to be displayed on the ship externally and on top so that it can be read from the air. The scheme is administered by Lloyd's Register-Fairplay, who maintain a database of all ships in excess of 100t (with some exceptions), not just those classified through them. Some vessels which do not qualify for an IMO number have a Lloyd's number in the same series.

Company Information This section gives general information regarding the status of the company. That is, nationality, whether it is public or private sector and whether it is part of a larger group.

Management The Managing Director and Marketing Director or Manager of each company are listed. Where these posts do not exist, other equivalent people are listed. Where only initials are given, that person is, as far as is known, male.

Address This is the address of the company's administrative headquarters. In the case of some international companies, British and overseas addresses are given.

Telephone and Fax Numbers are expressed as follows: + [*number*] (this is the international dialling code which is dialled in combination with the number dialled for international calls (00 in the UK, Ireland and most other European countries); it is not used for calling within the country), ([*number*]) (this is the number which precedes area codes when making long-distance domestic calls – it is not dialled when calling from another country or making local calls (not all countries have this)), [*number*] (this is the rest of the number including, where appropriate, the area dialling code). UK '08' numbers are sometimes not available from overseas and the full number must be dialled in all circumstances.

Internet Email addresses and **Website** URLs are given where these are available; the language(s) used is shown. The language listed first is that which appears on the home page when accessed from a UK based computer; the others follow in alphabetical order. In a few cases Email facility is only available through the Website. To avoid confusion, there is no other punctuation on the Internet line.

Routes operated After each route there are, in brackets, details of **1** normal journey time, **2** regular vessel(s) used on the route (number as in list of vessels) and **3** frequencies (where a number per day is given, this relates to return sailings). In the case of freight-only sailings which operate to a regular schedule, departure times are given where they have been supplied. Please note that times are subject to quite frequent change and cancellation.

Winter and Summer In this book, Winter generally means the period between October and Easter while Summer means Easter to October. The peak Summer period is generally June, July and August. In Scandinavia, the Summer peak ends in mid-August whilst in the UK it starts rather later and generally stretches into the first or second week of September. Dates vary according to operator.

Terms The following words mean ***'shipping company'*** in various languages: Redereja (Latvian), Rederi (Danish, Norwegian, Swedish), Rederij (Dutch), Reederei (German) and Zegluga (Polish). The following words mean ***'limited company':*** AB - Aktiebolaget (Swedish) (Finnish companies who use both the Finnish and Swedish terms sometimes express it as Ab), AG - Aktiengesellschaft (German), AS - Aksjeselskap (Norwegian), A/S - Aktie Selskabet (Danish), BV - Besloten Vennootschap (Dutch), GmbH - Gesellschaft mit beschränkter Haftung (German), NV - Naamloze Vennootschap (Dutch), Oy - (Finnish), Oyj - (Finnish (plc)) and SA - Société Anonyme (French).

Spelling The convention now used in respect of town and country names is that local names are used for towns and areas of countries (eg. Göteborg rather than Gothenburg) and English names for countries (eg. Germany rather than Deutschland). Many towns in Finland have both Finnish and Swedish names; we have used the Finnish name except in the case of Åland which is a Swedish-speaking area. In the case of Danish towns, the alternative use of 'å' or 'aa' follows local convention. The following towns, islands and territories, which have alternative English names, are expressed using their local names - the English name is shown following: Antwerpen/Anvers - Antwerp, Funen - Fyn, Génova - Genoa, Gent - Ghent, Gothenburg - Göteborg, Hoek van Holland - Hook of Holland, Jylland - Jutland, København -Copenhagen, Oostende - Ostend, Porto - Oporto, Sevilla - Seville, Sjælland - Sealand and Venezia - Venice.

Types of Ferry

These distinctions are necessarily general and many ships will have features of more than one category.

Car Ferry Until about 1970, most vehicle ferries were primarily designed for the conveyance of cars and their passengers and foot passengers. Little regard was paid to the conveyance of lorries and trailers, since this sort of traffic had not begun to develop. Few vessels of this type are still in service.

Multi-purpose Ferry From about 1970 onwards vehicle ferries began to make more provision for freight traffic, sharing the same ship with passengers and cars. Features usually include higher vehicle decks, often with retractable mezzanine decks, enabling two levels of cars or one level of freight and coaches, and separate facilities (including cabins on quite short crossings) for freight drivers.

Cruise Ferry In the 1980s the idea of travelling on a ferry, not just to get from A to B but for the pleasure of the travel experience, became more and more popular and ferries were built with increasingly luxurious and varied passenger accommodation. Such vessels also convey cars and freight but the emphasis is on passenger accommodation with a high level of berths (sometimes providing berths for all passengers).

Ro-pax Ferry A vessel designed primarily for the carriage of freight traffic but which also carries a limited number of ordinary passengers. Features generally include a moderate passenger capacity – up to about 500 passengers – and a partly open upper vehicle deck. Modern ro-pax vessels are becoming increasingly luxurious with facilities approaching those of a cruise ferry.

Ro-ro Ferry A vessel designed for the conveyance of road freight, unaccompanied trailers and containers on low trailers (known as 'Mafis' although often made by other manufacturers) and new cars. Some such vessels have no passenger accommodation but the majority can accommodate up to 12 passengers – the maximum allowed without a passenger certificate. On routes where there is a low level of driver-accompanied traffic (mainly the longer ones), ordinary passengers, with or without cars, can sometimes be conveyed. On routes with a high level of driver-accompanied traffic, passenger capacity will sometimes be higher but facilities tend to be geared to the needs of freight drivers eg. lounge with video, high level of cabins on routes of three hours or more. Technically such vessels are passenger ferries (having a passenger certificate).

Con-ro Many ro-ro vessels are capable of having ISO (International Standards Organisation) containers crane-loaded on the upper 'weather' deck. In this book the term con-ro applies only to vessels whose upper deck can only take containers and has no vehicle access.

Fast Ferry Streamlined vessel of catamaran or monohull construction, speed in excess of 30 knots, water jet propulsion, generally aluminium-built but some have steel hulls, little or no freight capacity and no cabins.

Timescale Although the book goes to press in August 2019, I have sought to reflect the situation as it will exist in September 2019 with regard to the introduction of new ships or other known changes. Vessels due to enter service after September 2019 are shown as '**Under Construction**'. This term does not necessarily man that physical work has started but an order has been placed with a shipyard. The book is updated at all stages of the production process where this is feasible, although major changes once the text has been paginated are not possible; there is also a 'Late News' section on page xx for changes which cannot be incorporated into the text.

List of vessels

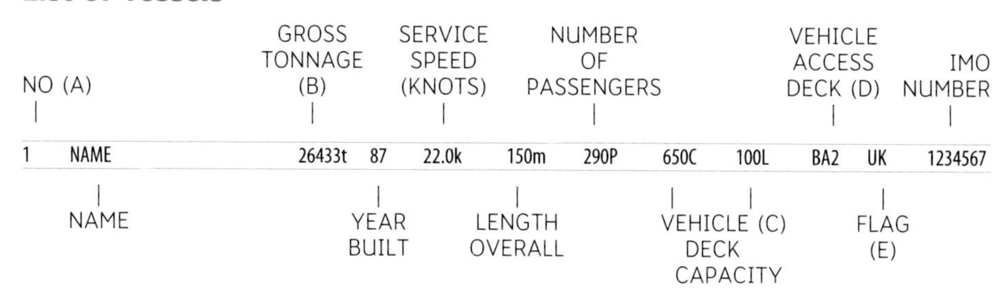

(A) >> = fast ferry, • = vessel laid up, F = freight-only vessel (max 12 passengers), F+ = freight-only vessel (with passenger certificate), p = passenger-only vessel.

(B) C = Cars, L = Lorries (**15m**), T = Trailers (**13.5m**), r = can also take rail wagons, - = No figure quoted.

(C) B = Bow, A = Aft, S = Side, Q = Quarterdeck, R = Slewing ramp, 2 = Two decks can be loaded at the same time, C = Vehicles must be crane-loaded aboard, t = turntable ferry.

(D) The following abbreviations are used:

In the notes ships are in CAPITAL LETTERS, shipping lines and other institutions are in *italics*.

AX = Åland Islands
BE = Belgium
BM = Bermuda
BS = Bahamas
CA = Canada
CY = Cyprus
DE = Germany
DK = Denmark
EE = Estonia
ES = Spain
FI = Finland
FO = Faroe Islands
FR = France
GR = Greece
IM = Isle of Man
IR = Republic of Ireland
IT = Italy
LT = Lithuania
LV = Latvia
MT = Malta
NL = Netherlands
NO = Norway
PT = Portugal
SG = Singapore
SE = Sweden
TR = Turkey
UK = United Kingdom

Capacity In this book, capacities shown are the maxima. Sometimes vessels operate at less than their maximum passenger capacity due to reduced crewing or to operating on a route on which they are not permitted to operate above a certain level. Car and lorry/trailer capacities are the maximum for either type. The two figures are not directly comparable. Some parts of a vessel may allow cars on two levels to occupy the space that a trailer or lorry occupies on one level, some may not; some parts of a vessel with low headroom may only be accessible to cars. All figures have to be approximate.

Ownership The ownership of many vessels is very complicated. Some are actually owned by finance companies and banks, some by subsidiary companies of the shipping lines, some by subsidiary companies of a holding company of which the shipping company is also a subsidiary and some by companies which are jointly owned by the shipping company and other interests like a bank, set up specifically to own one ship or a group of ships. In all these cases the vessel is technically chartered to the shipping company. However, in this book, only those vessels chartered from one shipping company to another or from a ship-owning company unconnected with the shipping line are recorded as being on charter. Vessels are listed under the current operator rather than the owner. Charter is 'bareboat' (without crew) unless otherwise stated. If chartered with crew, vessels are 'time-chartered'.

Gross Tonnage This is a measure of enclosed capacity rather than weight, based on a formula of one gross ton = 100 cubic feet. Even small alterations can alter the gross tonnage. Under old measurement systems, the capacity of enclosed car decks was not included but, under the 1969 Convention, all vessels laid down after 1982 have been measured by a new system which includes enclosed vehicle decks as enclosed space, thereby considerably increasing the tonnage of vehicle ferries. Under this Convention, from 1st January 1995 all vessels were due to be re-measured under this system. Tonnages quoted here are, where possible, those given by the shipping companies themselves.

The following people are gratefully thanked for their assistance with this publication, many of them in ferry companies in the UK and abroad: John Bryant, Andrew Cooke, Andrew Wood, Matthew Davies, Darren Holdaway, George Holland, Richard Kirkman, Frank Lose, Peter Therkildsen, Ian Smith (Camrose Media), and Gomer Press Ltd.

Whilst every effort has been made to ensure that the facts contained here are correct, neither the publishers nor the writer can accept any responsibility for errors contained herein. We would, however, appreciate comments from readers, which we will endeavour to reflect in the next edition which we plan to publish in summer 2021.

PONT-AVEN

Pont-Aven *(Frank Lose)*

SECTION 1 – GB AND IRELAND – MAJOR PASSENGER OPERATORS

BRITTANY FERRIES

THE COMPANY *Brittany Ferries* is the trading name of *BAI SA*, a French private sector company and the operating arm of the *Brittany Ferries Group*. The UK operations are run by *BAI (UK) Ltd*, a UK private sector company, wholly owned by the *Brittany Ferries Group*.

MANAGEMENT CEO Christophe Mathieu, **Commercial Directors, Passengers** Simon Johnson, Joëlle Croc, Florence Gourdon, **Commercial Director, Freight** Simon Wagstaff, **Director, UK** John Napton.

ADDRESS Millbay Docks, Plymouth, Devon PL1 3EW.

TELEPHONE Reservations *All Services* +44 (0)330 159 7000, **Freight – Administration & Enquiries** +44 (0)330 159 5000, **Reservations** +44 (0)330 159 5000.

INTERNET Websites *Passenger* www.brittanyferries.com *(English, French, Spanish, German)*, ***Freight*** www.brittanyferriesfreight.co.uk *(English)*

ROUTES OPERATED Conventional Ferries *All year* Plymouth – Roscoff (6 hrs (day), 7 hrs – 9 hrs (night); ***ARMORIQUE, PONT-AVEN***; up to 2 per day (Summer), 1 per day (Winter)), Poole – Cherbourg (4 hrs 15 mins; ***BARFLEUR***; 1 per day), Portsmouth – St Malo (8 hrs 45 mins (day), 10 hrs 45 mins (night); ***BRETAGNE***; (1 per day), Portsmouth – Caen (Ouistreham) (6 hrs (day), 6 hrs – 8 hrs (night); ***NORMANDIE, MONT ST MICHEL***; 3 per day), Portsmouth – Le Havre (5 hrs 30 mins (day), 9 hrs (night); ***CONNEMARA***, ***ÉTRETAT***; 1 per day), Portsmouth – Santander (Spain) (24 hrs; ***CAP FINISTÈRE, PONT-AVEN***; up to 3 per week), Portsmouth – Bilbao (Spain) (24/32 hrs; ***CAP FINISTÈRE***; up to 3 per week, Rosslare – Bilbao (52 hrs; ***KERRY (2020), ÉTRETAT (2021)***; 2 per week), ***Summer only*** Plymouth – Santander (Spain) (19 hrs 30 mins; ***PONT-AVEN***; 1 per week (April – October)), Cork – Roscoff (14 hrs-16 hrs 30 mins; ***ARMORIQUE, PONT-AVEN***; 2 per week), Rosslare – Roscoff (15 hrs; ***KERRY***; 1 per week), **Fast Ferry *Summer only*** Portsmouth – Cherbourg (3 hrs; ***NORMANDIE EXPRESS***; up to 2 per day (May-September)). **Freight-only service** Poole – Bilbao (31 hrs; ***MN PELICAN***; 2 per week). ***From March 2021*** Rosslare – Cherbourg (17hrs; ***ÉTRETAT***; 1 per week).

Note: Sailings to France and Spain operated by the KERRY and ÉTRETAT are branded 'économie'.

1	ARMORIQUE	29468t	09	23.0k	167.0m	1500P	470C	65L	BA2	FR	9364980
2	BARFLEUR	20133t	92	19.0k	158.0m	1212P	590C	112T	BA2	FR	9007130
3	BRETAGNE	24534t	89	19.5k	151.0m	1926P	580C	84T	BA	FR	8707329
4	CAP FINISTÈRE	32728t	01	28.0k	203.9m	1608P	1000C	140T	BA	FR	9198927
5	CONNEMARA	26500t	07	24.0k	186.5m	800P	170C	140L	BA	FR	9349760
6	ÉTRETAT	26500t	08	23.5k	186.5m	800P	185C	120L	A	FR	9420423
7	KERRY	24418t	01	24.0k	186.5m	1000P	75C	120L	BA	CY	9243447
8F	MN PELICAN	12076t	99	20.0k	154.5m	12P	-	115T	A2	FR	9170999
9	MONT ST MICHEL	35592t	02	21.2k	173.0m	2200P	880C	166T	BA2	FR	9238337
10	NORMANDIE	27541t	92	20.5k	161.0m	2120P	600C	126T	BA2	FR	9006253
11»	NORMANDIE EXPRESS	6581t	00	40.0k	97.2m	900P	260C	-	A	FR	8814134
12	PONT-AVEN	41748t	04	26.0k	184.3m	2400P	650C	85L	BA	FR	9268708

ARMORIQUE Built by STX Europe, Helsinki, Finland for *Brittany Ferries* to operate between Plymouth and Roscoff.

BARFLEUR Built as the BARFLEUR by Kvaerner Masa-Yards, Helsinki for the *Truckline* (freight division of *Brittany Ferries*) Poole – Cherbourg service to replace two passenger vessels and to inaugurate a year-round passenger service. In 1999 the *Truckline* branding was dropped for passenger services and she was repainted into full *Brittany Ferries* livery. In 2005 operated partly Cherbourg – Poole and partly Cherbourg – Portsmouth but in 2006 returned to operating mainly to Poole. In February 2010, she was laid up. The conventional car ferry service ended the following month. In February 2011 she resumed service on the Poole – Cherbourg route. In

MN Pelican *(Andrew Cooke)*

Barfleur *(Kevin Mitchell)*

Étretat *(Miles Cowsill)*

Cap Finistère *(Darren Holdaway)*

Connemara *(George Holland)*

Bretagne *(Darren Holdaway)*

September 2011 she was withdrawn again. In April 2012 chartered to *DFDS Seaways* to operate between Dover and Calais and renamed the DEAL SEAWAYS. In November 2012 returned to *Brittany Ferries* and renamed the BARFLEUR. Resumed the Poole - Cherbourg service in March 2013, replacing the COTENTIN but offering a service for both freight and passengers.

BRETAGNE Built by Chantiers de l'Atlantique, St Nazaire for the Plymouth - Santander and Cork - Roscoff services (with two sailings per week between Plymouth and Roscoff). In 1993 she was transferred to the Portsmouth - St Malo service. In 2004 also operated between Portsmouth and Cherbourg. In 2005 operated between Plymouth and Roscoff. In 2006 returned to the Portsmouth - St Malo route.

CAP FINISTÈRE Built as the SUPERFAST V by Howaldtswerke Deutsche Werft AG, Kiel, Germany for *Attica Enterprises* (now *Attica Group*) for use by *Superfast Ferries* of Greece. Initially operated between Patras and Ancona and in January 2007 switched to the Patras - Igoumenitsa - Bari route. In 2008 the route became Patras - Igoumenitsa - Ancona. In 2010 sold to *Brittany Ferries*, renamed the CAP FINISTÈRE and in March placed on the Portsmouth - Santander service, also operating some sailings between Portsmouth and Cherbourg. In 2011 began operating also between Portsmouth and Bilbao and only operated between Portsmouth and Cherbourg during the winter period.

CONNEMARA Built by CN Visentini, Porto Viro, Italy. Whilst under construction, sold to *Stena RoRo* of Sweden and provisionally named the STENA AUSONIA. However, before delivery a charter was arranged with *Balearia* of Spain and she was delivered as the BORJA. Operated between Barcelona and Palma (Majorca). In February 2010 the charter ended and she was laid up at Rotterdam. In April 2010 chartered to *Ave Line* and renamed the BALTIC AMBER. In October 2010 chartered to *DFDS Seaways* to replace the fire-damaged LISCO GLORIA. In March 2011 chartered to *LD Lines* to operate between Marseilles and Rades (Tunisia). In April she was moved to the Saint Nazaire (Nantes) - Gijon route. In June 2011 renamed the NORMAN ASTURIAS. In October 2011 the charter was ended but resumed the following month. Also operated between Poole, Santander and Gijon. In September 2014 chartered to *Intershipping*, Morocco and operated between Algeciras and Tangiers. In February 2016 chartered to *Anek Lines* of Greece, renamed the ASTERION and placed on the Patras - Igoumenitsa - Venezia route. In April 2018 chartered to *Brittany Ferries*, renamed the CONNEMARA and inaugurated a new twice weekly Cork - Santander service, with an additional service to Roscoff. In November 2019 transferred from the Cypriot to the French flag and operated on other routes.

ÉTRETAT Built as the NORMAN VOYAGER by CN Visentini, Porto Viro, Italy for *Epic Shipping* of the UK and chartered to *LD Lines*. Operated between Le Havre and Portsmouth and Le Havre and Rosslare. In September 2009 sub-chartered to *Celtic Link Ferries*. Initially operated between Cherbourg and Portsmouth and Cherbourg and Rosslare but the Portsmouth service was abandoned in November 2009. In October 2011 returned to *LD Lines* and placed on the St Nazaire - Gijon route. In November moved to the Portsmouth - Le Havre service and, following the establishment of the joint *LD Lines/DFDS* venture, the charter was transferred to *DFDS Seaways*. In April 2012 sold to *Stena RoRo*; she continued to be chartered to *DFDS*. In March 2014 chartered to *Brittany Ferries* and placed on the new 'économie' services between Portsmouth and Le Havre and Portsmouth and Santander. Renamed the ENTREAT.

KERRY Built as the CARTOUR by CN Visentini, Porto Viro, Italy. In September 2001 sold to *Levantina Trasporti* of Italy and in October chartered to *Caronte & Turist* of Italy and operated between Messina and Salerno. In October 2007, sold to *Vinashin Ocean Shipping Co* of Vietnam and renamed the VINASHIN PRINCE. In December, renamed the HOA SEN and operated between Ho Chi Min City and Hanang Bay. In May 2014 sold to a UK subsidiary of *Stena RoRo* and renamed the STENA EGERIA. Chartered to *Yantai Bohai International Ferry* of China and operated between Yantai and Pyeongtaek. In October 2017 chartered to *Adria Ferries* of Albania and operated between Durres (Albania) and Ancona (Italy). She was renamed the AF MICHELA. In November 2019 to renamed the KERRY and chartered to *Brittany Ferries* to replaced the CONNEMARA on the Cork - Santander/Roscoff service.

MN PELICAN Built as the TRANS BOTNIA for *SeaTrans ANS* of Norway. Hull constructed by Santierul Naval, Galatz, Romania and vessel completed by Fosen Mekaniske Verksteder, Frengen,

Norway. Chartered to *Transfennica* for service between Finland and Western Europe. In June 2006 sold to *Maritime Nantaise* of France. In January 2007 renamed the MN PELICAN. Placed on long term charter to the *French MOD*. In 2015 placed on the charter market. In January 2016 time chartered to *Brittany Ferries*.

MONT ST MICHEL Built by Van der Giessen de Noord, Krimpen aan den IJssel, Rotterdam for *Brittany Ferries*. Used on the Portsmouth – Caen route.

NORMANDIE Built by Kvaerner Masa-Yards, Turku, Finland for *Brittany Ferries*. Used on the Portsmouth – Caen route.

NORMANDIE EXPRESS Incat Evolution 10 catamaran built as the INCAT TASMANIA. In November 2000 chartered to *TranzRail* of New Zealand and renamed THE LYNX. Placed on the Wellington – Picton service. In July 2003 replaced by 1997-built Incat 86m craft INCAT 046, given the marketing name 'The Lynx' and laid up. In Spring 2005 chartered to *Brittany Ferries* to operate on their Cherbourg – Portsmouth and Caen – Portsmouth services and renamed the NORMANDIE EXPRESS. In 2007 purchased by *Brittany Ferries*. In 2015 operated to Cherbourg and Le Havre but since then has only operated to Cherbourg.

PONT-AVEN Built by Jos L Meyer Werft, Papenburg, Germany for *Brittany Ferries* to operate on the Plymouth – Roscoff, Plymouth – Santander and Cork – Roscoff routes.

Under Construction

13	GALICIA	42000t	20	22.0k	214.5m	1000P	300C	180L	BA2	FR	9856189
14	SALAMANCA	42000t	21	22.0k	214.5m	1000P	300C	180L	BA2	FR	9867592
15	SANTOÑA	42000t	23	22.0k	214.5m	1000P	300C	180L	BA2	FR	9886847

GALICIA Built by CMI Jinling Weihai Shipyard, Weihai, China for *Stena RoRo*. Before delivery she will be fitted with scrubbers to run on fuel oil. Upon delivery to be chartered to *Brittany Ferries* for five years. Expected to enter service in March 2021.

SALAMANCA Under construction by CMI Jinling Weihai Shipyard, Weihai, China for *Stena Line*. Designed to run on LNG. Upon delivery to be chartered to *Brittany Ferries* for five years.

SANTOÑA Under construction by CMI Jinling Weihai Shipyard, Weihai, China for *Stena Line* (9th in the series). Designed to run on LNG. Upon delivery to be chartered to *Brittany Ferries* for five years.

CALEDONIAN MACBRAYNE

THE COMPANY *Caledonian MacBrayne* is the trading name of *CalMac Ferries Ltd*, a subsidiary of *David MacBrayne Limited*, a Scottish registered company, wholly owned by the Scottish Ministers. The majority of *CalMac Ferries* vessels are owned by *Caledonian Maritime Assets Limited*, a separate company which is also owned by the Scottish Ministers.

MANAGEMENT Managing Director Robbie Drummond, **Director of Operations** Robert Morrison **Group Director of Communications and Community Engagement** Stuart Wilson

ADDRESS Ferry Terminal, Gourock PA19 1QP.

TELEPHONE Administration +44 (0)1475 650100, **Vehicle Reservations** +44 (0)800 066 5000.

FAX Administration +44 (0)1475 650336, **Vehicle Reservations** +44 (0)1475 635235.

INTERNET Email enquiries@calmac.co.uk **Website** www.calmac.co.uk *(English)*,

ROUTES OPERATED All-year vehicle ferries (frequencies are for Summer – services are listed alphabetically by mainland port or larger island port where service is between two islands). Ardmhor (Barra) – Eriskay (40 mins; ***LOCH ALAINN***; up to 5 per day), Ardrossan – Brodick (Arran) (55 mins; ***CALEDONIAN ISLES, ISLE OF ARRAN***; up to 6 per day), Colintraive – Rhubodach (Bute) (5 mins; ***LOCH DUNVEGAN***; frequent service), Kennacraig – Port Askaig (Islay) (2 hrs 5 mins; ***FINLAGGAN, HEBRIDEAN ISLES***; up to 4 per day), Kennacraig – Port Ellen (Islay) (2 hrs 20 mins; ***FINLAGGAN, HEBRIDEAN ISLES***; service currently suspended due to harbour works), Largs – Cumbrae Slip (Cumbrae) (10 mins; ***LOCH RIDDON, LOCH SHIRA***; every 30 or 15 mins), Leverburgh (Harris) – Berneray (1 hr 10 mins; ***LOCH PORTAIN***; 3-4 per day), Lochaline – Fishnish (Mull) (15 mins; ***LOCHINVAR***; up to 14 per day), Mallaig – Armadale (Skye) (23 mins; ***LOCHNEVIS*** (Winter) ***LOCH FYNE, LORD OF THE ISLES*** (Summer); up to 9 per day (2 in Winter)), Mallaig – Lochboisdale (South Uist) (3 hrs 30 mins; ***LORD OF THE ISLES***; 1 per day), Oban – Castlebay (Barra) (5 hrs); ***ISLE OF LEWIS***; 1 per day), Oban – Coll – Tiree (2 hrs 45 min to Coll 3 hrs 50 min to Tiree via Coll; ***CLANSMAN***; 1 per day), Oban – Colonsay (2 hrs 15 mins; ***CLANSMAN***; 5 per week), Oban – Craignure (Mull) (45 mins; ***CORUISK, ISLE OF MULL***; up to 7 per day), Oban – Lismore (50 mins; ***LOCH STRIVEN***; up to 5 per day), Sconser (Skye) – Raasay (15 mins; ***HALLAIG***; up to 11 per day), Tarbert (Loch Fyne) – Portavadie (25 mins; ***ISLE OF CUMBRAE***; up to 12 per day), Tayinloan – Gigha (20 mins; ***LOCH RANZA***; up to 10 per day), Tobermory (Mull) – Kilchoan (35 mins; ***LOCH TARBERT***; up to 7 per day), Uig (Skye) – Lochmaddy (North Uist) (1 hr 45 mins; ***HEBRIDES***; 1 or 2 per day), Uig (Skye) – Tarbert (Harris) (1 hr 40 mins; ***HEBRIDES***; 1 or 2 per day), Ullapool – Stornoway (Lewis) (2 hrs 45 mins; ***LOCH SEAFORTH***; up to 3 per day (one freight only)), Wemyss Bay – Rothesay (Bute) (35 mins; ***ARGYLE, BUTE***; hourly).

All-year passenger and restricted vehicle ferries (frequencies are for Summer) Gallanach (near Oban) – Kerrera (5 mins; ***CARVORIA***; up to 12 per day), Fionnphort (Mull) – Iona (5 mins; ***LOCH BUIE***; frequent), Mallaig – Eigg – Muck – Rum – Canna – Mallaig (round trip 7 hrs (all islands); ***LOCHNEVIS***; at least 1 sailing per day – most islands visited daily). **Note** Although these services are operated by vehicle ferries special permission is required to take a vehicle and tourist cars are not normally conveyed. **Summer-only vehicle ferries** Ardrossan – Campbeltown (2 hrs 30 mins; ***ISLE OF ARRAN***; 3 per week), Claonaig – Lochranza (Arran) (30 mins; ***CATRIONA***; up to 9 per day), Kennacraig – Port Askaig – Colonsay – Oban (3 hrs 35 mins; ***HEBRIDEAN ISLES***; 1 per week). **Winter-only vehicle ferry** Tarbert (Loch Fyne) – Lochranza (Arran) (1 hr; ***varies***; 1 per day). **All-year passenger-only ferries** Gourock – Dunoon (20 mins; ***ALI CAT, ARGYLL FLYER, CORUISK (winter only)***; 1 or 2 per hour, Gourock – Kilcreggan (13 mins; ***CHIEFTAIN***; approx hourly).

1p	ALI CAT	78t	99	8.5k	19.8m	250P	0C	0L	-	UK	
2	ARGYLE	2643t	07	14.0k	69.0m	450P	60C	-	BAS	UK	9365178
3p	ARGYLL FLYER	300t	01	19.5k	29.9m	227P	0C	0L	-	UK	9231016
4	BUTE	2612t	05	14.0k	69.0m	450P	60C	-	AS	UK	9319741
5	CALEDONIAN ISLES	5221t	93	15.0k	94.3m	1000P	120C	10L	BA	UK	9051284
6	CARVORIA	9t	17	8.0k	12.0m	12P	1C	0L	B	UK	
7	CATRIONA	499t	16	9.0k	43.5m	150P	23C	2L	BA	UK	9759862
8p	CHIEFTAIN	60t	07	8.6k	19.5m	1-0P	0C	0L	-	UK	
9	CLANSMAN	5499t	98	16.5k	99.0m	638P	90C	6L	BA	UK	9158953
10	CORUISK	1599t	03	14.0k	65.0m	250P	40C	-	BA	UK	9274836
11	FINLAGGAN	5626t	11	16.5k	89.9m	550P	88C	-	BA	UK	9482902
12	HALLAIG	499t	13	9.0k	43.5m	150P	23C	2L	BA	UK	9652832
13	HEBRIDEAN ISLES	3040t	85	15.0k	85.1m	494P	68C	10L	BAS	UK	8404812
14	HEBRIDES	5506t	00	16.5k	99.0m	612P	110C	6L	BA	UK	9211975
15	ISLE OF ARRAN	3296t	84	15.0k	85.0m	446P	68C	8L	BA	UK	8219554
16	ISLE OF CUMBRAE	201t	77	8.5k	37.7m	139P	18C	-	BA	UK	7521625
17	ISLE OF LEWIS	6753t	95	18.0k	101.2m	680P	123C	10L	BA	UK	9085974
18	ISLE OF MULL	4719t	88	15.0k	90.1m	962P	80C	20L	BA	UK	8608339
19	LOCH ALAINN	396t	98	10.0k	43.0m	150P	24C	-	BA	UK	9147722
20	LOCH BHRUSDA	246t	96	8.0k	35.4m	150P	18C	-	BA	UK	9129483
21	LOCH BUIE	295t	92	9.0k	35.5m	250P	9C	-	BA	UK	9031375
22	LOCH DUNVEGAN	549t	91	9.0k	54.2m	200P	36C	-	BA	UK	9006409
23	LOCH FYNE	549t	91	9.0k	54.2m	200P	36C	-	BA	UK	9006411
24	LOCH LINNHE	206t	86	9.0k	35.5m	199P	12C	-	BA	UK	8512308
25	LOCH PORTAIN	950t	03	10.5k	50.0m	200P	32C	-	BA	UK	9274824
26	LOCH RANZA	206t	87	9.0k	35.7m	199P	12C	-	BA	UK	8519887
27	LOCH RIDDON	206t	86	9.0k	35.5m	199P	12C	-	BA	UK	8519875
28	LOCH SEAFORTH	8478t	14	19.2k	116.0m	700P	143C	20L	BA	UK	9665437

Loch Fyne *(George Holland)*

Lochnevis *(George Holland)*

Eilean Arainn
www.calmac.co.uk
Caledonian MacBray

Isle of Arran *(George Holland)*

Catriona *(Miles Cowsill)*

Clansman *(Miles Cowsill)*

29	LOCH SHIRA	1024t	07	13.0k	43.0m	250P	24C	-	BA	UK	9376919
30	LOCH STRIVEN	206t	86	9.0k	35.7m	199P	12C	-	BA	UK	8512293
31	LOCH TARBERT	211t	92	9.0k	34.5m	149P	18C	-	BA	UK	9039389
32	LOCHINVAR	523t	14	9.0k	43.5m	150P	23C	2L	BA	UK	9652844
33	LOCHNEVIS	941t	00	13.0k	49.1m	190P	14C	-	A	UK	9209063
34	LORD OF THE ISLES	3504t	89	16.0k	84.6m	506P	56C	16L	BAS	UK	8710869

Note In the following list, Gaelic names are shown in parenthesis.

ALI CAT Catamaran built for *Solent & Wight Line Cruises* of Ryde, Isle of Wight. She operated a passenger service from Cowes to Hamble and Warsash and cruises from Cowes. At times chartered to *Wightlink* to cover for their fast catamarans. In 2002 chartered to *Red Funnel Ferries* who had contracted with *Caledonian MacBrayne* to operate passenger-only services between Gourock and Dunoon in the morning and evening peaks. In June 2011 purchased by and operated by *Argyll Ferries*. In January 2019, operation was transferred to *Caledonian MacBrayne*.

ARGYLE *(EARRA-GHÀIDHEAL)*, BUTE *(EILEAN BHÒID)* Built by Stocznia Remontowa, Gdansk, Poland to operate on the Wemyss Bay - Rothesay route.

ARGYLL FLYER Built as the QUEEN OF ARAN II by OCEA, Les Sables d'Olonne, France for *Inis Mór Ferries*. In 2007 sold to *Aran Island Ferries* and renamed the BANRION CHONAMARA. In June 2011 sold to *Argyll Ferries*, renamed the ARGYLL FLYER and replaced the car ferry SATURN on the Gourock - Dunoon service. In January 2019, operation was transferred to *Caledonian MacBrayne*.

CALEDONIAN ISLES *(EILEANAN CHALEDONIA)* Built by Richards Shipyard, Lowestoft, UK for the Ardrossan - Brodick (Arran) service.

CARVORIA Built by Malakoff Limited, Lerwick, Shetland for *Caledonian Maritime Assets* and chartered to *Caledonian MacBrayne* to replace the chartered GYLEN LADY on the Gallanach - Kerrera service.

CATRIONA Built by Ferguson Marine Engineering, Port Glasgow. Near sister vessel of the HALLAIG and LOCHINVAR. Operates on the Claonaig - Lochranza service during the summer and other routes during the winter.

CHIEFTAIN Built as the SEABUS by Voyager Boatyard, Millbrook, Plymouth for Clyde Marine Services, Scotland and operated on the ferry service between Gourock, Kilgreggan and Helensburgh on behalf of Strathclyde Partnership for Transport. In 2013 the contract to operate this service was awarded to *Clydelink* (Gourock - Kilcreggan only) and she was transferred to private hire and excursion work. In January 2014 she was renamed the CHIEFTAIN. In May 2018 the contract returned to *Clyde Marine Services* and she returned to this route. In June 2020 the service came under auspices of *Transport Scotland* and the contract was transferred to *Caledonian MacBrayne*; the CHIEFTAIN was chartered to them.

CLANSMAN *(FEAR-CINNIDH)* Built by Appledore Shipbuilders Ltd, Appledore, UK to replace the LORD OF THE ISLES on the Oban - Coll and Tiree and Oban - Castlebay and Lochboisdale services in the summer. She also serves as winter relief vessel on the Stornoway, Tarbert, Lochmaddy, Mull/Colonsay and Brodick routes.

CORUISK *(COIR' UISG')* Built by Appledore Shipbuilders Ltd, Appledore, UK to operate on the Mallaig - Armadale route during the summer. During the winter she operates on the Gourock - Dunoon passenger service during peak periods and when the usual vessels cannot sail due to adverse weather. Since summer 2016 she has operated as second vessel on the Oban - Craignure service.

FINLAGGAN *(FIONN LAGAN)* Built by Stocznia Remontowa, Gdansk, Poland for the Kennacraig - Islay service.

HALLAIG *(HALLAIG)* Built by Ferguson Shipbuilders, Port Glasgow, UK to replace the LOCH STRIVEN on the Sconser - Raasay service. The vessel has both diesel and battery electric propulsion and can be 'plugged in' to a land supply on Raasay overnight.

HEBRIDEAN ISLES *(EILEANAN INNSE GALL)* Built by Cochrane Shipbuilders, Selby UK for the Uig – Tarbert/Lochmaddy service. She was used initially on the Ullapool – Stornoway and Oban – Craignure/Colonsay services pending installation of link-span facilities at Uig, Tarbert and Lochmaddy. She took up her regular role in May 1986. From May 1996 she no longer operated direct services in summer between Tarbert and Lochmaddy, this role being taken on by the new Harris – North Uist services of the LOCH BHRUSDA. In 2001 she was replaced by the HEBRIDES and transferred to the Islay service. In Autumn 2002 she operated between Scrabster and Stromness for *NorthLink Orkney and Shetland Ferries* before port modifications at Scrabster enabled the HAMNAVOE to enter service in Spring 2003. She then returned to the Islay service. She also relieved on the *NorthLink* Pentland Firth service between 2004 and 2007.

HEBRIDES *(INNSE GALL)* Built by Ferguson Shipbuilders Ltd, Port Glasgow, UK for the Uig – Tarbert and Uig – Lochmaddy services.

ISLE OF ARRAN *(EILEAN ARAINN)* Built by Ferguson Ailsa, Port Glasgow, UK for the Ardrossan – Brodick service. In 1993 transferred to the Kennacraig – Port Ellen/Port Askaig service, also undertaking the weekly Port Askaig – Colonsay – Oban summer service. From then until 1997/98 she also relieved on the Brodick, Coll/Tiree, Castlebay/Lochboisdale, Craignure and Tarbert/Lochmaddy routes in winter. In 2001 she was replaced by the HEBRIDEAN ISLES and became a reserve for the larger vessels. She has operated on the two-ship Islay service in summer since 2003; this service is now all-year-round. Following the delivery of the FINLAGGAN in May 2011 she became a spare vessel, and operates extra services between Ardrossan and Brodick and Ardrossan and Campbeltown during the peak summer period.

ISLE OF CUMBRAE *(EILEAN CHUMRAIGH)* Built by Ailsa Shipbuilding Ltd, Troon, UK for the Largs – Cumbrae Slip (Cumbrae) service. In 1986 she was replaced by the LOCH LINNHE and the LOCH STRIVEN and transferred to the Lochaline – Fishnish (Mull) service. She used to spend most of the winter as secondary vessel on the Kyle of Lochalsh – Kyleakin service; however, this ceased following the opening of the Skye Bridge in 1995. In 1997 she was transferred to the Colintraive – Rhubodach service. In Summer 1999 she was transferred to the Tarbert – Portavadie service. In May 2015 replaced by the new LOCHINVAR and laid up. In summer 2016 returned to the Tarbert – Portavadie service.

ISLE OF LEWIS *(EILEAN LEÒDHAIS)* Built by Ferguson Shipbuilders Ltd, Port Glasgow, UK for the Ullapool – Stornoway service. In February 2015 replaced by the new LOCH SEAFORTH. Now operates between Oban and Castlebay (Barra).

ISLE OF MULL *(AN T-EILEAN MUILEACH)* Built by Appledore Ferguson, Port Glasgow, UK for the Oban – Craignure (Mull) service.

LOCH ALAINN *(LOCH ÀLAINN)* Built by Buckie Shipbuilders Ltd, Buckie, UK for the Lochaline – Fishnish service. Launched as the LOCH ALINE but renamed the LOCH ALAINN before entering service. After a brief period on the service for which she was built, she was transferred to the Colintraive – Rhubodach route. In 1998 she was transferred to the Largs – Cumbrae Slip service. In 2007 moved to the Ardmhor (Barra) – Eriskay service. She relieves the larger 'Loch' class vessels in the winter, with her own service covered by the LOCH BHRUSDA.

LOCH BHRUSDA *(LOCH BHRÙSTA)* Built by McTay Marine, Bromborough, Wirral, UK to inaugurate a new Otternish (North Uist) – Leverburgh (Harris) service. In 2001 the service became Berneray – Leverburgh. In 2003 she moved to the Eriskay – Barra service, previously operated by *Comhairle Nan Eilean Siar* vessels. In 2007 she became a spare vessel on the Clyde. In summer 2016 operated between Mallaig and Armadale. Note 'Bhrusda' is pronounced "Vroosta".

LOCH BUIE *(LOCH BUIDHE)* Built by J W Miller & Sons Ltd, St Monans, Fife, UK for the Fionnphort (Mull) – Iona service to replace the MORVERN (see *Arranmore Island Ferry Services*) and obviate the need for a relief vessel in the summer. Due to height restrictions, loading arrangements for vehicles taller than private cars are stern-only. Only islanders' cars and service vehicles (eg mail vans, police) are carried; no tourist vehicles are conveyed.

LOCH DUNVEGAN *(LOCH DÙNBHEAGAN)* Built by Ferguson Shipbuilders Ltd, Port Glasgow, UK for the Kyle of Lochalsh – Kyleakin service. On the opening of the Skye Bridge in October 1995 she was withdrawn from service and offered for sale. In Autumn 1997, she returned to service

Loch Alainn *(Miles Cowsill)*

Lord of the Isles *(Miles Cowsill)*

on the Lochaline - Fishnish route. In 1998 she was due to be transferred to the Colintraive - Rhubodach route but this was delayed because of problems in providing terminal facilities. She operated on the Clyde and between Mallaig and Armadale during the early summer and spent the rest of that summer laid up. In 1999 she was transferred to the Colintraive - Rhubodach route.

LOCH FYNE *(LOCH FINE)* Built by Ferguson Shipbuilders Ltd, Port Glasgow, UK for the Kyle of Lochalsh - Kyleakin service (see the LOCH DUNVEGAN). In Autumn 1997, she also served on the Lochaline - Fishnish route and was transferred to this route as regular vessel in 1998. In summer 2017 transferred to the Mallaig - Armadale route.

LOCH LINNHE *(AN LINNE DHUBH)* Built by Richard Dunston (Hessle) Ltd, Hessle, UK. Until 1997 she was used mainly on the Largs - Cumbrae Slip (Cumbrae) service and until Winter 1994/95 she was usually used on the Lochaline - Fishnish service during the winter. Since then she has relieved on various routes in winter. In Summer 1998 she operated mainly on the Tarbert - Portavadie route. In 1999 she was transferred to the Tobermory - Kilchoan service in summer.

LOCH PORTAIN *(LOCH PORTAIN)* Built by McTay Marine, Bromborough, Wirral, UK (hull constructed in Poland) to replace the LOCH BHRUSDA on the Berneray - Leverburgh service.

LOCH RANZA *(LOCH RAONASA)* Built by Richard Dunston (Hessle) Ltd, Hessle, UK for the Claonaig - Lochranza (Arran) seasonal service and used a relief vessel in the winter. In 1992 she was replaced by the LOCH TARBERT and transferred to the Tayinloan - Gigha service.

LOCH RIDDON *(LOCH RAODAIN)* Built by Richard Dunston (Hessle) Ltd, Hessle, UK. Until 1997 she was used almost exclusively on the Colintraive - Rhubodach service. In 1997, she was transferred to the Largs - Cumbrae Slip service. In January 2014 she became regular vessel on the Oban - Lismore service. However, after problems with using the slipways, she became the second vessel on the Largs - Cumbrae Slip service.

LOCH SEAFORTH *(LOCH SHIPHOIRT)* Built by Flensburger Schiffbau-Gesellschaft, Flensburg, Germany for the Stornoway - Ullapool service, replacing the ISLE OF LEWIS and freight vessel CLIPPER RANGER.

LOCH SHIRA *(LOCH SIORA)* Built by Ferguson Shipbuilders, Port Glasgow, UK for the Largs - Cumbrae Slip route.

LOCH STRIVEN *(LOCH SROIGHEANN)* Built by Richard Dunston (Hessle) Ltd, Hessle, UK. Used mainly on the Largs - Cumbrae Slip service until 1997. In Winter 1995/96 and 1996/97 she was used on the Tarbert - Portavadie and Claonaig - Lochranza routes. In 1997 she took over the Sconser - Raasay service. In winter 2014 replaced by the HALLAIG. In summer 2014 transferred to the Oban - Lismore route.

LOCH TARBERT *(LOCH AN TAIRBEIRT)* Built by J W Miller & Sons Ltd, St Monans, Fife, UK for the Claonaig - Lochranza service. Now a relief vessel.

LOCHINVAR *(LOCH AN BARR)* As the HALLAIG. Initially operated on the Tarbert - Portavadie route. In summer 2016 transferred to Mallaig - Armadale and in summer 2017 to the Lochaline - Fishnish route.

LOCHNEVIS *(LOCH NIBHEIS)* Built by Ailsa Shipbuilding, Troon, UK to replace the LOCHMOR on the Mallaig - Small Isles service and the winter Mallaig - Armadale service. Although a vehicle ferry, cars are not normally carried to the Small Isles; the ro-ro facility is used for the carriage of agricultural machinery and livestock and it is possible to convey a vehicle on the ferry from which goods can be unloaded directly onto local transport rather than transhipping at Mallaig.

LORD OF THE ISLES *(RIGH NAN EILEAN)* Built by Appledore Ferguson, Port Glasgow, UK to replace the CLAYMORE on the Oban - Castlebay and Lochboisdale services and also the COLUMBA (1420t, 1964) on the Oban - Coll and Tiree service. Now in the winter she operates as a relief vessel. In summer she operates between Mallaig and Lochboisdale and also between Mallaig and Armadale.

Under Construction

35	GLEN SANNOX	5000t	22	16.5k	102.4m	1000P	127C	16L	BA	UK	9794513
36	NEWBUILDING	5000t	23	16.5k	102.4m	1000P	127C	16L	BA	UK	9794525

GLEN SANNOX *(GLEANN SHANNAIG)*, NEWBUILDING Under construction by Ferguson Marine Port Glasgow Ltd for *Caledonian Maritime Assets* (CMAL) and to be chartered to *Caledonian MacBrayne*. The GLEN SANNOX will operate on the Ardrossan - Brodick service and the second vessel is likely to operate between Uig and Harris and North Uist. Construction has been heavily delayed and delivery date is uncertain.

CONDOR FERRIES

THE COMPANY *Condor Ferries Ltd* is a Channel Islands' private sector company owned by the Condor Group, Guernsey which is owned by *Brittany Ferries* and Columbia Threadneedle Investments.

MANAGEMENT Chief Executive Officer Paul Luxon, **Executive Director – Commercial** Greg Yeoman, **Executive Director – Operations** Elwyn Dop, **Executive Director – Freight** Steve Champion-Smith, **Finance Director** Steven Broomfield, **Executive Director – People and Culture** Rebecca Gilbert **Head of Sales and Marketing** Justin Amey, **Trade Sales Manager** Jonathan Godson.

ADDRESS Head Office New Jetty Offices, White Rock, St Peter Port, Guernsey GY1 2LL, **Sales and Marketing** Condor House, New Harbour Road South, Hamworthy, Poole BH15 4AJ.

TELEPHONE Administration *Guernsey* +44 (0)1481 728620, ***Poole*** +44 (0)1202 207207, **Passenger Reservations** +44 (0)345 609 1026, **Freight Reservations** +44 (0)1481 728620.

INTERNET Email *Passenger* contactcentre@condorferries.co.uk **Freight** freight@condorferries.co.uk **Website** www.condorferries.com *(English)* www.condorferries.fr *(French)*,

ROUTES OPERATED *COMMODORE CLIPPER (Conventional Passenger and Freight Ferry)* Portsmouth to Guernsey (from 7 hrs) and Jersey (from 9 hrs) daily except Sun. ***Fast Ferries CONDOR LIBERATION***; Poole - Guernsey (3 hrs) and Jersey (4 hrs 30 min); 1 per day (operates on a seasonal basis; less frequent during off-peak seasons), ***CONDOR RAPIDE***; Guernsey (1 hr 55 min) and Jersey (1 hr 25 mins) to St Malo (1 per day). ***Freight Ferry COMMODORE GOODWILL***; Portsmouth - Guernsey - Jersey (10 hrs 30 min; 1 per day), Guernsey - Jersey - St Malo (13 hrs; 1 per week).

1	COMMODORE CLIPPER	14000t	99	18.0k	129.1m	500P	100C	92T	A	BS	9201750
2F	COMMODORE GOODWILL	11166t	96	17.3k	126.4m	12P	-	92T	A	BS	9117985
3»	CONDOR LIBERATION	6307t	10	39.0k	102.0m	873P	245C	12L	A	BS	9551363
4»	CONDOR RAPIDE	5007t	97	40.5k	86.6m	870P	200C	-	A	BS	9161560

COMMODORE CLIPPER Ro-pax vessel built by Van der Giessen de Noord, Krimpen aan den IJssel, Rotterdam for *Commodore Ferries* to operate between Portsmouth and the Channel Islands. She replaced the ISLAND COMMODORE, a freight-only vessel. Her passenger capacity is normally restricted to 300 between the Channel Islands and the UK but is increased to 500 between Jersey and Guernsey.

COMMODORE GOODWILL Built by Koninklijke Scheldegroep BV, Vlissingen, The Netherlands for *Commodore Ferries*.

CONDOR LIBERATION Austal 102-metre Trimaran built speculatively by Austal Ships Pty, Fremantle, Australia as AUSTAL HULL 270. Laid up. In August 2014 sold to *Condor Ferries*. During autumn and early winter 2014/15 she was modified by Austal Ships in their shipyard at Balamban, Cebu, Philippines and in March 2015 renamed the CONDOR LIBERATION and placed on the Poole - Channel Islands service.

CONDOR RAPIDE Incat 86m catamaran built at Hobart, Tasmania, Australia as the INCAT 045. Chartered to *Transport Tasmania* of Australia and operated between Melbourne (Victoria) and Devonport (Tasmania). In 1999 she was chartered to the *Royal Australian Navy*, renamed the

Condor Liberation *(Andrew Cooke)*

Princess Seaways *(Richard Kirkman)*

HMAS JERVIS BAY and took part in moving Australian troops from Darwin to Dili (East Timor) as part of the United Nations operation. She operated over 75 trips between the two points carrying personnel and equipment for the United Nations Transitional Administration in East Timor (UNTAET). The charter ended in May 2001 and she was renamed the INCAT 045 and laid up. In Spring 2003 she was chartered to *Traghetti Isole Sarde (TRIS)* of Italy, renamed the WINNER and operated between Genoa and Palau (Sardinia). In Autumn 2003 the charter ended, she resumed the name INCAT 045 and was laid up at Portland, Dorset. In 2004 chartered to *SpeedFerries* and renamed the SPEED ONE. In May 2008 purchased by *SpeedFerries*. In November 2008 the services ceased and the company went into administration. She was laid up at Tilbury. In May she was sold at auction to *Epic Shipping* of the UK and renamed the SEA LEOPARD. In April 2010 sold to *Condor Ferries* and renamed the CONDOR RAPIDE. Entered service in May 2010.

DFDS SEAWAYS

THE COMPANY *DFDS Seaways* is a business unit within *DFDS A/S*, a Danish private sector company. Services from Dover, Newhaven and Marseilles are operated by *DFDS Seaways France* which was inaugurated in March 2013 following the establishment of a *DFDS Seaways/LD Lines* joint venture in November 2012. It is 82% owned by *DFDS* and 18% by *Louis Dreyfus Armateurs*. The Newhaven - Dieppe route is branded as *Transmanche Ferries*, operating under a franchise awarded by *Syndicat Mixte de L'Activité Transmanche* in Dieppe. In June 2018 *DFDS* acquired *UN RoRo* of Turkey. The Mediterranean fleet is outside the scope of this book.

MANAGEMENT President and CEO DFDS A/S Torben Carlsen, **Executive Vice President Shipping Division** Peder Gellert Pedersen, **Managing Director, DFDS Seaways PLC** Sean Potter, **Senior Vice President South** Kell Robdrup, **Head of English Channel Business Area** Filip Hermann, **Head of Passenger Business Area** Thorsted Hansen.

ADDRESS (UK) DFDS A/S, Whitfield Court, White Cliffs Business Park Whitfield, Dover CT16 3PX.

TELEPHONE Administration +44 (0)1304 874001. **Passenger Reservations *Dover- Calais*** 0871 574 7235, +44 (0)208 127 8303, ***Newcastle - Ijmuiden*** 0871 522 9955, +44 330 333 0245, ***Newhaven - Dieppe*** 0800 917 1201, +33 232 144 729, **Freight Reservations** see website.

INTERNET Websites *Passenger* www.dfdsseaways.co.uk *(various)* ***Freight*** freight.dfdsseaways.com *(English)* ***Corporate*** www.dfds.com *(English)*

ROUTES OPERATED *Passenger ferries* Newcastle (North Shields) - IJmuiden (near Amsterdam, The Netherlands) (15 hrs; ***KING SEAWAYS, PRINCESS SEAWAYS***; daily). **ROUTES OPERATED** Dover - Dunkerque (2 hrs; ***DELFT SEAWAYS, DOVER SEAWAYS, DUNKERQUE SEAWAYS***; 12 per day), Dover - Calais (1 hr 30 mins; ***CALAIS SEAWAYS, CÔTE DES FLANDRES, CÔTE DES DUNES***; 15 per day), Newhaven - Dieppe (4 hrs; ***CÔTE D'ALBÂTRE, SEVEN SISTERS***; up to 3 per day, ***Freight ferries*** Esbjerg - Immingham (18 hrs; ***ARK DANIA, ARK GERMANIA***; 6 per week), Cuxhaven - Immingham (19 hrs; ***BRITANNIA SEAWAYS, PETUNIA SEAWAYS***; 5 per week), Göteborg - Immingham (26 hrs (direct), *45 hrs (via Brevik (Fri)); ***FICARIA SEAWAYS, FREESIA SEAWAYS, MAGNOLIA SEAWAYS***; 5 per week), Brevik - Immingham (25 hrs (direct), 42 hrs (via Göteborg); ***FICARIA SEAWAYS, FREESIA SEAWAYS, MAGNOLIA SEAWAYS***; 2 per week), Göteborg - Brevik (Norway) - Gent (Belgium) (Göteborg 32 hrs, Brevik 32 hrs; ***BEGONIA SEAWAYS, PRIMULA SEAWAYS***; 6 per week (1 per week via Brevik), Göteborg - Zeebrugge (34 hrs; ***HOLLANDIA SEAWAYS, CLdN LAURELINE CLASS***; 6 per week) (joint timetable with *CLdN*), Vlaardingen - Immingham (14 hrs; ***GARDENIA SEAWAYS, HUMBRIA SEAWAYS***; 8 per week), Vlaardingen - Felixstowe (7 hrs;***, SELANDIA SEAWAYS, SUECIA SEAWAYS, TULIPA SEAWAYS***; 3 per day), Zeebrugge - Immingham - Halden (Norway) - Fredrikstad - Zeebrugge (***TRANSPORTER***; weekly circuit). *DFDS Seaways* also operates services in the Baltic (see section 7) and Mediterranean (which are outside the scope of this book). Note: vessels are often switched between routes.

1F	ARK DANIA	33313t	14	20.0k	195.2m	12P	-	206T	A	DK	9609964
2F	ARK GERMANIA	33313t	14	20.0k	195.2m	12P	-	206T	A	DK	9609952
3F	BEGONIA SEAWAYS	37722t	04	22.5k	230.0m	12P	-	340T	AS	DK	9262089

4F	BELGIA SEAWAYS	21005t	00	18.0k	183.4m	12P	-	180T	A	LT	9188245
5F	BRITANNIA SEAWAYS	24196t	00	21.1k	197.5m	12P	-	200T	AS	DK	9153032
6	CALAIS SEAWAYS	28833t	91	21.0k	163.6m	1850P	600C	100L	BA2	FR	8908466
7	CÔTE D'ALBÂTRE	18425t	06	22.0k	112.0m	600P	300C	62L	BA	FR	9320128
8	CÔTE DES DUNES	33796t	01	25.0k	186.0m	1500P	700C	120L	BA2	FR	9232527
9	CÔTE DES FLANDRES	33940t	05	25.0k	186.0m	1500P	700C	120L	BA2	FR	9305843
10	DELFT SEAWAYS	35923t	06	25.5k	187.0m	780P	200C	120L	BA2	UK	9293088
11	DOVER SEAWAYS	35923t	06	25.8k	187.0m	780P	200C	120L	BA2	UK	9318345
12	DUNKERQUE SEAWAYS	35923t	05	25.8k	187.0m	780P	200C	120L	BA2	UK	9293076
13F	FICARIA SEAWAYS	37939t	04	22.5k	230.0m	12P	-	340T	AS	DK	9320568
14F	FINLANDIA SEAWAYS	11530t	00	20.0k	162.2m	12P	-	140T	A	LT	9198721
15F	FREESIA SEAWAYS	37722t	04	22.5k	230.0m	12P	-	340T	AS	DK	9274848
16F	GARDENIA SEAWAYS	32000t	17	21.0k	209.6m	12P	-	262T	A2	LT	9809095
17F	GOTHIA SEAWAYS	21005t	00	18.0k	183.4m	12P	-	180T	A	LT	9188233
18F	HOLLANDIA SEAWAYS	60465t	19	21.0k	237.4m	12P	-	480T	A2	DK	9832585
19F	HUMBRIA SEAWAYS	60465t	20	21.0k	237.4m	12P	-	480T	A2	DK	9832597
20	KING SEAWAYS	31788t	87	20.0k	161.6m	1400P	600C	104T	BA	DK	8502406
21F	MAGNOLIA SEAWAYS	32289t	03	22.5k	199.8m	12P	-	280T	AS	DK	9259496
22F	PETUNIA SEAWAYS	32289t	04	22.5k	199.8m	12P	-	280T	AS	DK	9259501
23F	PRIMULA SEAWAYS	37985t	04	22.5k	229.8m	12P	-	340T	AS	DK	9259513
24	PRINCESS SEAWAYS	31356t	86	18.5k	161.0m	1600P	600C	100T	BA	DK	8502391
25F	SELANDIA SEAWAYS	24196t	98	21.0k	197.5m	12P	-	206T	A	DK	9157284
26	SEVEN SISTERS	18425t	06	22.0k	112.0m	600P	300C	62L	BA	FR	9320130
27F	SUECIA SEAWAYS	24196t	99	21.0k	197.5m	12P	-	206T	AS	DK	9153020
28F	TRANSPORTER	6620t	91	16.5k	122.0m	0P	-	90T	A	FI	8820858
29F	TULIPA SEAWAYS	32000t	17	21.0k	209.6m	12P	-	262T	A2	LT	9809100

ARK DANIA, ARK GERMANIA Built by P+S Werften GmbH, Stralsund, Germany. They are used for the German/Danish joint ARK Project providing NATO transport but are also available for *DFDS* use and charter when not required. They have a crane for loading containers on the weather deck. In December 2012 the order for these vessels was cancelled due to late delivery. Following negotiations with the shipyard it was agreed that they would be completed under a new contract which was signed in February 2013. Both vessels were delivered to *DFDS* in April 2014, the ARK GERMANIA almost complete, the ARK DANIA still incomplete. The latter vessel was towed to the Fayard shipyard, Odense, to be completed. The ARK GERMANIA entered service a few days after delivery, the ARK DANIA in November 2014.

BEGONIA SEAWAYS Built as the TOR BEGONIA by Flensburger Schiffbau-Gesellschaft, Flensburg, Germany for *DFDS Tor Line*. Operates on the Göteborg – Immingham/Brevik route. In Summer 2009 lengthened by 30m by MWB Motorenwerke Bremerhaven AG, Germany. In July 2012 renamed the BEGONIA SEAWAYS.

BELGIA SEAWAYS, GOTHIA SEAWAYS Built as the SLINGEBORG and SCHIEBORG by Flender Werft AG, Lübeck, Germany for *Wagenborg* of The Netherlands and time-chartered to *Cobelfret Ferries* to operate on the *Stora Enso* (a paper and card manufacturer)/*Cobelfret Ferries* service between Zeebrugge and Göteborg. In November 2014 the arrangement between *Stora Enso* and *Cobelfret Ferries* ended and they were chartered to *SOL Continent Line* who took over the operation of the service. In June 2019 the service was taken over by *DFDS Seaways* and both vessels were purchased by that company. They were renamed the BELGIA SEAWAYS and GOTHIA SEAWAYS respectively.

BRITANNIA SEAWAYS Built as the TOR BRITANNIA by Fincantieri-Cantieri Navali Italiani SpA, Ancona, Italy for *DFDS Tor Line*. Operated on the Göteborg – Immingham route until 2004 when she was transferred to the Esbjerg – Immingham route. In January 2010 chartered to *Norfolkline* to operate between Vlaardingen and Felixstowe. In May 2011 renamed the BRITANNIA SEAWAYS.

CALAIS SEAWAYS Built as the PRINS FILIP by NV Boelwerf SA, Temse, Belgium for *Regie voor Maritiem Transport (RMT)* of Belgium for the Oostende – Dover service. Although completed in 1991, she did not enter service until May 1992. In 1994 the British port became Ramsgate. Withdrawn in 1997 and laid up for sale. In 1998 she was sold to *Stena RoRo* and renamed the

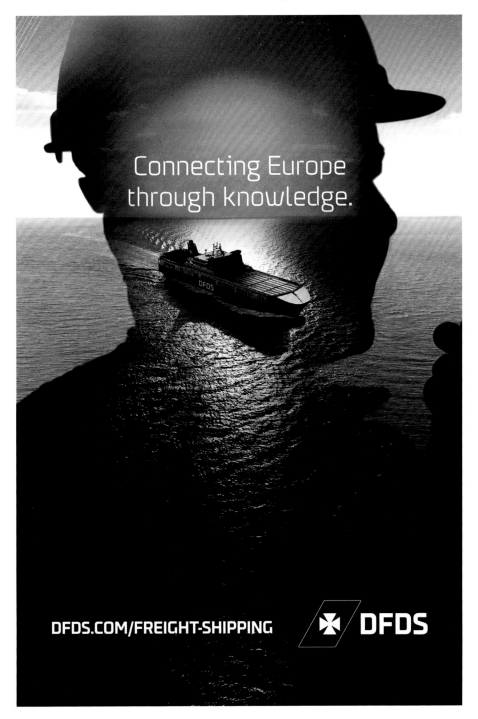

Calais Seaways *(Frank Lose)*

Côte des Dunes *(Frank Lose)*

STENA ROYAL. In November 1998 she was chartered to *P&O Ferries* to operate as a freight-only vessel on the Dover - Zeebrugge route. In Spring 1999 it was decided to charter the vessel on a long-term basis and she was repainted into *P&O Stena Line* (later *P&O Ferries*) colours and renamed the P&OSL AQUITAINE. In Autumn 1999 she was modified to make her suitable to operate between Dover and Calais and was transferred to that route, becoming a passenger vessel again. In 2002 renamed the PO AQUITAINE and in 2003 the PRIDE OF AQUITAINE. In September 2005 sold to *LD Lines* and renamed the NORMAN SPIRIT. In October, inaugurated a Le Havre - Portsmouth service, replacing that previously operated by *P&O Ferries*. In November 2009 moved to the Dover - Boulogne route. In March 2010 chartered to *TransEuropa Ferries*, placed on the Oostende - Ramsgate service (as part of a joint venture) and renamed the OSTEND SPIRIT. In May 2011 returned to the Portsmouth - Le Havre route and renamed the NORMAN SPIRIT. In November 2011 chartered to *DFDS Seaways* to add extra capacity to their Dover - Dunkerque route. In February 2012 transferred to the new Dover - Calais route, joint with *DFDS Seaways*. Ownership transferred to *DFDS Seaways* in late 2012. In March 2013 refurbished, repainted into *DFDS Seaways* colours and renamed the CALAIS SEAWAYS. In 2021 to be replaced by the new CÔTE D'OPALE.

CÔTE D'ALBÂTRE Built by Astilleros Barreras SA, Vigo, Spain for *Transmanche Ferries* to operate between Newhaven and Dieppe. In February 2009 she was moved to the Boulogne - Dover and Dieppe - Dover routes for *LD Lines*. In September 2009 moved to the Le Havre - Portsmouth route. The vessel has had periods laid up when not required on the Newhaven - Dieppe route.

CÔTE DES DUNES Built as the SEAFRANCE RODIN by Aker Finnyards, Rauma, Finland for *SeaFrance*. Launched in November 2001. In November 2011 laid up. In June 2012 sold to *Eurotransmanche*. In July 2012 renamed the RODIN. In August 2012 chartered to *MyFerryLink* and resumed operation between Calais and Dover. In July 2015 chartered to *DFDS Seaways* after *MyFerryLink* operations ceased. After a prolonged occupation by former *MyFerryLink* workers. *DFDS Seaways* took possession in early September and in November 2015 she was renamed the CÔTE DES DUNES. She re-entered service on the Dover - Calais route in February 2016. In June 2017 purchased by *DFDS Seaways*.

CÔTE DES FLANDRES Built as the SEAFRANCE BERLIOZ by Chantiers de l'Atlantique, St Nazaire for *SeaFrance*. Launched in March 2005. In November 2011 laid up. In June 2012 sold to *Eurotransmanche*, a *Groupe Eurotunnel* company. In July 2012 renamed the BERLIOZ. In August 2012 chartered to *MyFerryLink* and resumed operation between Calais and Dover. In July 2015 chartered to *DFDS Seaways* after *MyFerryLink* operations ceased. After a prolonged occupation by former *MyFerryLink* workers, *DFDS Seaways* took possession in early September and, in November 2015, she was renamed the CÔTE DES FLANDRES. She re-entered service on the Dover - Calais route in February 2016. In June 2017 purchased by *DFDS Seaways*.

DELFT SEAWAYS, DOVER SEAWAYS, DUNKERQUE SEAWAYS Built as the MAERSK DELFT, DOVER SEAWAYS and MAERSK DUNKERQUE by Samsung Heavy Industries, Koje (Geoje) Island, South Korea for *Norfolkline* to operate between Dover and Dunkerque. In July and August 2010 renamed the DELFT SEAWAYS, DOVER SEAWAYS and DUNKERQUE SEAWAYS.

FICARIA SEAWAYS Built as the TOR FICARIA by Flensburger Schiffbau-Gesellschaft, Flensburg, Germany for *DFDS Tor Line*. Operated on the Göteborg - Immingham/Brevik service. In Summer 2009 lengthened by 30m by MWB Motorenwerke Bremerhaven AG, Germany. In July 2011 renamed the FICARIA SEAWAYS. In March 2015 placed on the Vlaardingen - Immingham service.

FINLANDIA SEAWAYS Launched as the FINNMAID but renamed the FINNREEL before delivery. Built by Jinling Shipyard, Nanjing, China for the *Macoma Shipping Group* and chartered to *Finnlines*. In 2008 sold to *DFDS Lisco* and in January 2009 delivered, chartered to *DFDS Tor Line* and renamed the TOR FINLANDIA. Operated on the Immingham - Rotterdam route until January 2011 when she was transferred to the Rosyth - Zeebrugge route. In May 2012 moved to the Cuxhaven - Immingham service but returned in July. In December 2012 renamed the FINLANDIA SEAWAYS. In October 2013 moved to the Kiel - St Petersburg service. In April 2014 returned to the Rosyth - Zeebrugge route. In April 2018 she had a serious engine room fire and the route closed. She returned to service in November 2018 on the Immingham - Cuxhaven service.

Dunkerque Seaways *(John Bryant)*

Hollandia Seaways *(Peter Therkildsen)*

Selandia Seaways *(Frank Lose)*

King Seaways *(Frank Lose)*

FREESIA SEAWAYS Built as the TOR FREESIA by Flensburger Schiffbau-Gesellschaft, Flensburg, Germany for *DFDS Tor Line*. Operates on the Göteborg – Immingham/Brevik service. In Summer 2009 lengthened by 30m by MWB Motorenwerke Bremerhaven AG, Germany. In August 2012 renamed the FREESIA SEAWAYS.

GARDENIA SEAWAYS, TULIPA SEAWAYS Built by Flensburger Schiffbau-Gesellschaft, Flensburg, Germany for the Siem Industries Inc (owners of FSG). They are bareboat chartered to *DFDS Seaways* for five years with an option to purchase at the end of the charter period. Operate between Vlaardingen and Immingham.

HOLLANDIA SEAWAYS, HUMBRIA SEAWAYS Built by Jinling Shipyard, Nanjing, China.

KING SEAWAYS Built as the NILS HOLGERSSON by Schichau Seebeckwerft AG, Bremerhaven, Germany for *Rederi AB Swedcarrier* of Sweden for their service between Trelleborg and Travemünde, joint with *TT-Line* of Germany (trading as *TT-Line*). In 1992 purchased by *Brittany Ferries* for entry into service in Spring 1993. After a major rebuild, she was renamed the VAL DE LOIRE and introduced onto the Plymouth – Roscoff, Plymouth – Santander and Cork – Roscoff routes. In 2004 transferred to the Portsmouth – St Malo and Portsmouth – Cherbourg services. In 2005 operated mainly Portsmouth – St Malo. In 2006 sold to *DFDS*, renamed the KING OF SCANDINAVIA and placed on the Newcastle – IJmuiden route. In January 2011 renamed the KING SEAWAYS.

MAGNOLIA SEAWAYS Built as the TOR MAGNOLIA by Flensburger Schiffbau-Gesellschaft, Flensburg, Germany for *DFDS Tor Line*. In July 2011 renamed the MAGNOLIA SEAWAYS.

PETUNIA SEAWAYS Built as the TOR PETUNIA by Flensburger Schiffbau-Gesellschaft, Flensburg, Germany for *DFDS Tor Line*. In July 2011 renamed the PETUNIA SEAWAYS.

PRIMULA SEAWAYS Built as the TOR PRIMULA by Flensburger Schiffbau-Gesellschaft, Flensburg, Germany for *DFDS Tor Line*. In July 2010 renamed the PRIMULA SEAWAYS. In July 2016 lengthened by 30m by MWB Motorenwerke Bremerhaven AG, Germany.

PRINCESS SEAWAYS Built by Schichau Seebeckwerft AG, Bremerhaven, Germany as the PETER PAN for *TT-Line* for the service between Travemünde and Trelleborg. In 1992 sold to *TT Line* of Australia (no connection) for use on their service between Port Melbourne (Victoria) and Devonport (Tasmania) and renamed the SPIRIT OF TASMANIA. In 2002 sold to *Nordsjøferger K/S* of Norway and renamed the SPIR. After modification work she was, in 2003, renamed the FJORD NORWAY and chartered to *Fjord Line*. Placed on the Bergen – Egersund – Hanstholm route. In 2005 placed on the Bergen – Stavanger – Newcastle route, but operated once a week to Hanstholm. In October 2006 sold to *DFDS* and renamed the PRINCESS OF NORWAY, remaining on the Newcastle – Norway service but no longer serving Hanstholm. In May 2007 moved to the Newcastle – IJmuiden route. In February 2011 renamed the PRINCESS SEAWAYS.

SELANDIA SEAWAYS Built as the TOR SELANDIA by Fincantieri-Cantieri Navali Italiani SpA, Ancona, Italy for *DFDS Tor Line*. Operated on the Göteborg – Immingham route until 2004 when she was moved to the Göteborg – Gent route. In 2005 she moved to the Göteborg – Harwich route. In July the UK terminal moved to Tilbury. In August 2010 renamed the SELANDIA SEAWAYS. Currently operates on the Rotterdam – Felixstowe route.

SEVEN SISTERS Built by Astilleros Barreras SA, Vigo, Spain for *Transmanche Ferries* to operate between Newhaven and Dieppe. In recent years generally held as a reserve vessel. In March 2014 transferred to the *DFDS Seaways* Portsmouth – Le Havre service. She continues to carry *Transmanche Ferries* branding. In 2015 returned to the Newhaven – Dieppe service as second vessel, continuing to operate for *DFDS Seaways*. The vessel has had periods laid up when not required on the Newhaven – Dieppe route.

SUECIA SEAWAYS Built as the TOR SUECIA by Fincantieri-Cantieri Navali Italiani SpA, Ancona, Italy for *DFDS Tor Line*. Operated on the Göteborg – Immingham route until 2004 when she was transferred to the Esbjerg – Immingham route. Later transferred to the Danish flag. In March 2010 chartered to *Norfolkline* to operate between Vlaardingen and Felixstowe and continued on the route when it was taken over by *DFDS*. In June 2011 renamed the SUECIA SEAWAYS.

TRANSPORTER Built as the HAMNÖ by Brodogradiliste "Sava", Macvanska Mitrovica, Yugoslavia (fitted out by Fosen Mekaniske Verksteder of Rissa, Norway) for *Rederi AB Gustav Erikson* of Finland and chartered to *Transfennica* for service between Finland and Germany. In 1995 the owning company became *United Shipping* and in 2002 *Birka Cargo AB*. In 2000 she was chartered to the *Korsnäs Paper Group* to carry their traffic from Gävle (Sweden) to Chatham and Terneuzen (The Netherlands). In 2002 she was renamed the BIRKA TRANSPORTER. In April 2004 chartered to *Grimaldi Lines* of Italy to operate between Marseille and Tunis and in 2010 to *Holmen Paper Ab* of Sweden. In April 2013 ownership was transferred to *Eckerö Shipping Ab* of Finland and in June she was renamed the TRANSPORTER. In January 2016 she was sold to *Naviera Benzu Sl* of Spain. In March 2019 she was sold back to *Eckerö Shipping* and in April she was chartered to *DFDS Seaways* to operate on the Zeebrugge - Immingham - Halden - Fredrikstad service.

Under Construction

30	CÔTE D'OPALE	42000t	21	22.0k	214.5m	1000P	300C	180L	BA2	FR	9858321
31F	FLANDRIA SEAWAYS	60465t	20	21.0k	237.4m	12P	-	480T	A2	DK	9860142
32F	SCANDIA SEAWAYS	60465t	21	21.0k	237.4m	12P	-	480T	A2	DK	9864681

CÔTE D'OPALE Under construction by CMI Jinling Weihai Shipyard, Weihai, China for *Stena RoRo*. Designed to run on either methanol or LNG but before delivery she will be fitted with scrubbers to run on fuel oil. Upon delivery to be chartered to *DFDS Seaways* for ten years to operate between Dover and Calais. It is assumed she will be French flagged when delivered.

FLANDRIA SEAWAYS, SCANDIA SEAWAYS Under construction by Jinling Shipyard, Nanjing,

IRISH FERRIES

THE COMPANY *Irish Ferries* is a Republic of Ireland private sector company, part of the *Irish Continental Group*. It was originally mainly owned by the state-owned *Irish Shipping* and partly by *Lion Ferry AB* of Sweden. *Lion Ferry* participation ceased in 1977 and the company was sold into the private sector in 1987. Formerly state-owned *B&I Line* was taken over in 1991 and from 1995 all operations were marketed as *Irish Ferries*.

MANAGEMENT Irish Continental Group Chief Executive Office Eamonn Rothwell, **Irish Ferries Limited Managing Director** Andrew Sheen.

ADDRESS PO Box 19, Ferryport, Alexandra Road, Dublin 1, D01 W2F5, Republic of Ireland.

TELEPHONE Administration +353 (0)1 607 5700, **Reservations *Ireland*** +353 (0)818300 400, ***Rosslare Harbour*** +353 (0)53 913 3158, ***Holyhead*** +44 (0)8717 300200, ***Pembroke Dock*** +44 (0)8717 300500, ***National*** 44 (0)8717 300400, ***24 hour information*** +353 (0)818300 400 (Ireland) or 44 (0)8717 300400 (UK).

FAX Administration & Reservations *Dublin* +353 (0)1 607 5660, ***Rosslare*** +353 (0)53 913 3544.

INTERNET Email info@irishferries.com **Website** www.irishferries.com *(English, French, German, Italian)*

ROUTES OPERATED Conventional Ferries Dublin - Holyhead (3 hrs 15 mins; ***EPSILON, ULYSSES, W. B. YEATS***; 2-4 per day), Rosslare - Pembroke Dock (4 hrs; ***ISLE OF INISHMORE***; 4 per day), Dublin - Cherbourg (17-19 hrs; ***W. B. YEATS***; up to 4 per week). **Fast Ferry** Dublin - Holyhead (1 hr 49 min; ***DUBLIN SWIFT***; 2 per day).

1»	DUBLIN SWIFT	8403t	01	35.0k	101.0m	900P	200C	16T	BA	CY	9243227
2	EPSILON	26375t	11	24.0k	177.5m	500P	500C	190T	A	IT	9539054
3	ISLE OF INISHMORE	34031t	97	21.3k	182.5m	2200P	802C	152T	BA2	CY	9142605
4	ULYSSES	50938t	01	22.0k	209.0m	1875P	1342C	241L	BA2	CY	9214991
5	W. B. YEATS	54975t	18	22.5k	194.8m	1850P	1216C	165L	BA2	CY	9809679

DUBLIN SWIFT Austal Auto-Express 101 catamaran built by Austal Ships Pty, Fremantle, Australia as the WESTPAC EXPRESS. Chartered through a number of third party companies to the *US Marine Corps* as a support vessel. In 2015 returned to *Austal Ships*. In May 2016 sold to the

DSG
DIXON
EPSILON

Epsilon and **W.B. Yeats** *(Gordon Hislip)*

DUBLIN
ROSSLARE
HOLYHEAD
PEMBROKE
CHERBOURG
Leading the way
IRISH FERRIES
Irish Ferries are proud to maintain the highest maritime and customer standards.
We operate the finest fleet on the Irish Sea, including our new cruise ferry W.B. Yeats awarded 'Ferry of the Year 2019' at the Ferry Shipping Summit, along with the 'Ferry Concept Award' and the 'Interior Architecture Award' at the SHIPPAX Industry Awards.
Combining our modern fleet with optimum schedules and the best value fares for drivers, passengers and freight customers alike, makes Irish Ferries Ireland's leading ferry company.
N538
IRISH FERRIES

Irish Continental Group. Chartered to *Sealift Inc* of the USA and continued to be operated for the *US Marine Corps*. In November 2017 charter ended; laid up in Belfast. In March 2018 renamed the DUBLIN SWIFT and in April replaced the JONATHAN SWIFT on the Holyhead - Dublin route.

EPSILON Built as the CARTOUR EPSILON by CN Visentini, Porto Viro, Italy. Chartered to *Caronte & Tourist SPA* of Italy. In November 2013 chartered to *Irish Ferries*. In February 2014 renamed the EPSILON. In March 2019 purchased by *Caronte & Tourist SPA* of Italy. Charter to *Irish Ferries* continued.

ISLE OF INISHMORE Built by Van der Giessen de Noord, Krimpen aan den IJssel, Rotterdam for *Irish Ferries* to operate on the Holyhead - Dublin service. In 2001 replaced by the ULYSSES and moved to the Rosslare - Pembroke Dock route.

ULYSSES Built by Aker Finnyards, Rauma, Finland for *Irish Ferries* for the Dublin - Holyhead service.

W. B. YEATS Built by Flensburger Schiffbau-Gesellschaft, Flensburg, Germany. Operates between Dublin and Cherbourg in the summer and Dublin and Holyhead in the winter. Entered Service on the Dublin to Holyhead Service on 22 January 2019 and then transfer to Dublin to Cherbourg Service on 14 March. She has also provided relief on the Rosslare - Pembroke route when the ISLE OF INISHMORE is in dry dock.

ISLE OF MAN STEAM PACKET COMPANY

THE COMPANY The *Isle of Man Steam Packet Company Limited* is an Isle of Man-registered company owned by the Isle of Man Government.

MANAGEMENT Chief Executive Officer Mark Woodward.

ADDRESS Imperial Buildings, Douglas, Isle of Man IM1 2BY.

TELEPHONE Administration +44 (0)1624 645645, **Reservations** +44 (0)1624 661661

FAX Administration +44 (0)1624 645627.

INTERNET Email iom.reservations@steam-packet.com **Website** www.steam-packet.com *(English),*

ROUTES OPERATED Conventional Ferries *All year* Douglas (Isle of Man) - Heysham (3 hrs 30 mins; ***BEN-MY-CHREE***; up to 2 per day), Douglas - Belfast (5 hours; ***BEN-MY-CHREE***; occasional). **Fast Ferries *March-October*** Douglas - Liverpool (2 hrs 40 mins; ***MANANNAN***; up to 2 per day), Douglas - Belfast (2 hrs 55 mins; ***MANANNAN***; up to 2 per week), Douglas - Dublin (2 hrs 55 mins; ***MANANNAN***; up to 2 per week), Douglas - Heysham (2 hrs; ***MANANNAN***; occasional), **Freight Ferry** Douglas - Heysham (3 hrs 30 mins; ***ARROW***; as required).

1F	ARROW	7606t	98	15.0k	122.3m	12P	-	84T	A	IM	9119414
2	BEN-MY-CHREE	12747t	98	18.0k	124.9m	630P	275C	90T	A	IM	9170705
3»	MANANNAN	5743t	98	43.0k	96.0m	865P	200C	-	A	IM	9176072

ARROW Built as the VARBOLA by Astilleros de Huelva SA, Huelva, Spain for the *Estonian Shipping Company*. On completion, chartered to *Dart Line* and placed on the Dartford - Vlissingen route. In 1999 she was renamed the DART 6. At the end of August 1999, the charter was terminated and she was renamed the VARBOLA. She undertook a number of short-term charters, including *Merchant Ferries*. In 2000 long-term chartered to *Merchant Ferries* to operate between Heysham and Dublin. In 2003 the charter ended and she was chartered to *Dart Line* to replace the DART 9; she was placed initially on the Dartford - Vlissingen route but later transferred to the Dartford - Dunkerque route. Later sub-chartered to *NorseMerchant Ferries* and placed on the Heysham - Dublin route. In 2004 the charter transferred to *NorseMerchant Ferries*. In 2005 sold to *Elmira Shipping* of Greece and renamed the RR ARROW. In October 2007 sold to *Seatruck Ferries* but the charter to *Norfolkline* continued. Renamed the ARROW. In June 2009 returned to *Seatruck Ferries*. In April 2014 long term chartered to *IOMSP*. When not required she is sub-chartered to other operators.

Ben-my-Chree *(Miles Cowsill)*

Hamnavoe *(Miles Cowsill)*

BEN-MY-CHREE Built by Van der Giessen de Noord, Krimpen aan den IJssel, Rotterdam for the *IOMSP Co* and operates between Douglas and Heysham. Additional passenger accommodation was added at her spring 2004 refit. In 2005 her passenger certificate was increased from 500 to 630. She operates some sailings between Douglas and Belfast in the summer.

MANANNAN Incat 96m catamaran built at Hobart, Tasmania. Initially chartered to *Transport Tasmania* of Australia and operated between Port Melbourne (Victoria) and Georgetown (Tasmania). In 1999 chartered to *Fast Cat Ferries* of New Zealand and operated between Wellington (North Island) and Picton (South Island) under the marketing name 'Top Cat'. In 2000 she was laid up. In 2001 she was chartered to the *US Navy* and renamed the USS JOINT VENTURE (HSV-X1). In 2008 the charter was terminated and she was renamed the INCAT 050. Later purchased by *IOMSP*. Following conversion back to civilian use she was renamed the MANANNAN and entered service in May 2009.

Under Construction

4	NEWBUILDING	-	23	-	-	-	-	-	BA	IM	-

NEWBUILDING Under construction by Hyundai Mipo Dockyard, Ulsan, South Korea. She will replace the BEN MY CHREE on the Douglas - Heysham service, which will become a back-up vessel. No technical details are available at the time of going to press but she is likely to be between 130 metres and 142 metres long and have a passenger and vehicle capacity a bit bigger than the BEN-MY-CHREE.

NORTHLINK FERRIES

THE COMPANY *NorthLink Ferries* is a UK based company, wholly owned by *Serco Group plc*. The service is operated on behalf of Scottish Ministers.

MANAGEMENT Managing Director Stuart Garrett, **Customer Service Director** Peter Hutchinson.

ADDRESS Ferry Terminal, Ferry Road, Stromness, Orkney KW16 3BH.

TELEPHONE Customer Services 0845 6000 449, (International +44 (0)1856 885500), **Freight Reservations** 0845 6060 449.

FAX +44 (0)1856 851795.

INTERNET Email info@northlinkferries.co.uk **Website** www.northlinkferries.co.uk *(English),*

ROUTES OPERATED *Passenger Ferries* Scrabster - Stromness (Orkney) (1 hr 30 min; ***HAMNAVOE***; up to 3 per day), Aberdeen - Lerwick (Shetland) (direct) (12 hrs; ***HJALTLAND, HROSSEY***; 3 northbound/4 southbound per week), Aberdeen - Kirkwall, Hatston New Pier (Orkney) (5 hrs 45 mins) - Lerwick (14 hrs; ***HJALTLAND, HROSSEY***; 4 northbound/3 southbound per week). ***Freight Ferries*** Aberdeen - Kirkwall (Orkney) (12 hrs; ***HELLIAR, HILDASAY***; 4 per week), Aberdeen - Lerwick (Shetland) (***HELLIAR, HILDASAY***; 4 per week).

1	HAMNAVOE	8780t	02	19.3k	112.0m	600P	95C	20L	BA	UK	9246061
2F	HELLIAR	7800t	98	17.0k	122.3m	12P	-	86T	A	IM	9119397
3F	HILDASAY	7606t	99	17.0k	122.3m	12P	-	84T	A	IM	9119426
4	HJALTLAND	11720t	02	24.0k	125.0m	600P	150C	30L	BA	UK	9244958
5	HROSSEY	11720t	02	24.0k	125.0m	600P	150C	30L	BA	UK	9244960

HAMNAVOE Built by Aker Finnyards, Rauma, Finland for *NorthLink Orkney and Shetland Ferries Ltd* to operate on the Scrabster - Stromness route. Did not enter service until Spring 2003 due to late completion of work at Scrabster to accommodate the ship. *Caledonian MacBrayne's* HEBRIDEAN ISLES covered between October 2002 and Spring 2003. Initially owned by the *Royal Bank of Scotland*, she was acquired by *Caledonian Maritime Assets Ltd* (owned by *Transport Scotland*) in May 2018.

HELLIAR Built as the LEHOLA by Astilleros de Huelva SA, Huelva, Spain for the *Estonian Shipping Company*. Initially used on *ESCO* Baltic services. In 1998 chartered to *Czar Peter Line* to operate between Moerdijk (The Netherlands) and Kronstadt (Russia). In 1999 chartered to *Delom* of

France to operate between Marseilles and Sete and Tunis. In 2000 she returned to *ESCO*, operating between Kiel and Tallinn. In 2003 chartered to *Scandlines AG* and transferred to subsidiary *Scandlines Estonia AS*. Operated Rostock - Helsinki - Muuga initially and later Rostock - Helsinki. Service finished at the end of 2004 and in 2005 she was chartered to *P&O Ferries* to operate between Hull and Rotterdam and Hull and Zeebrugge. In 2005 sold to *Elmira Shipping* of Greece. Later renamed the RR TRIUMPH. In 2006 transferred to *P&O Irish Sea* to operate between Liverpool and Dublin. In 2007 chartered to *Balearia* of Spain and operated from Barcelona. In December 2007 purchased by *Seatruck Ferries* and renamed the TRIUMPH. In Spring 2008 she was sub-chartered to *Condor Ferries* to cover for the refit period of the COMMODORE GOODWILL. In June 2008 placed on the Liverpool - Dublin route and in July renamed the CLIPPER RACER. In February 2009 replaced by the new CLIPPER PACE. In April 2009 again chartered to *Balearia*. In January 2011 chartered to *NorthLink Ferries* and renamed the HELLIAR. In June 2017 sold to *CF Clip Helliar LLC*; the charter continued. In March 2019 purchased by *Caledonian Maritime Assets Ltd* (owned by *Transport Scotland*).

HILDASAY Built as the LEILI by Astilleros de Huelva SA, Huelva, Spain for the *Estonian Shipping Company*. Used on Baltic services. In 2002 chartered to *Crowley Maritime* of the USA and renamed the PORT EVERGLADES EXPRESS. In 2004 resumed the name LEILI and chartered to *NorseMerchant Ferries* to operate between Birkenhead and Dublin. In July 2005 moved to the Heysham - Belfast route and at the same time sold to *Elmira Shipping* of Greece and renamed the RR SHIELD. In 2007 sold to *Attica Group* of Greece and renamed the SHIELD. In January 2008 sold to *Seatruck Ferries* but continued to be chartered to *Norfolkline*. In June 2009 returned to *Seatruck Ferries*. In January 2009 chartered to *NorthLink Orkney and Shetland Ferries* and renamed the HILDASAY. In June 2017 sold to *CF Clip Hildasay LLC*; the charter continued. In March 2019 purchased by *Caledonian Maritime Assets Ltd* (owned by *Transport Scotland*).

HJALTLAND, HROSSEY Built by Aker Finnyards, Rauma, Finland for *NorthLink Orkney and Shetland Ferries* to operate on the Aberdeen - Kirkwall - Lerwick route when services started in 2002. Initially owned by the *Royal Bank of Scotland*, they were acquired by *Caledonian Maritime Assets Ltd* (owned by *Transport Scotland*) in May 2018.

ORKNEY FERRIES

THE COMPANY *Orkney Ferries Ltd* (previously the *Orkney Islands Shipping Company*) is a British company, an arms-length organisation of *Orkney Islands Council*.

MANAGEMENT Ferry Services Manager Andrew Blake.

ADDRESS Shore Street, Kirkwall, Orkney KW15 1LG.

TELEPHONE Administration +44 (0)1856 872044, **Reservations** +44 (0)1856 872044.

FAX Administration & Reservations +44 (0)1856 872921.

INTERNET Email info@orkneyferries.co.uk **Website** www.orkneyferries.co.uk *(English)*,

ROUTES OPERATED Kirkwall (Mainland) to Eday (1 hr 15 mins), Rapness (Westray) (1 hr 25 mins), Sanday (1 hr 25 mins), Stronsay (1 hr 35 mins), Papa Westray (1 hr 50 mins), North Ronaldsay (2 hrs 30 mins) ('North Isles service') (timings are direct from Kirkwall - sailings via other islands take longer; ***EARL SIGURD, EARL THORFINN, VARAGEN***; 1/2 per day except Papa Westray which is twice weekly and North Ronaldsay which is weekly), Pierowall (Westray) - Papa Westray (25 mins; ***NORDIC SEA***; up to six per day (Summer service - passenger-only)), Kirkwall - Shapinsay (25 mins; ***SHAPINSAY***; 6 per day), Houton (Mainland) to Lyness (Hoy) (35 mins; ***HOY HEAD***; 5 per day), and Flotta (35 mins; ***HOY HEAD***; 4 per day) ('South Isles service') (timings are direct from Houton - sailings via other islands take longer), Tingwall (Mainland) to Rousay (20 mins; ***EYNHALLOW***; 6 per day), Egilsay (30 mins; ***EYNHALLOW***; 5 per day) and Wyre (20 mins; ***EYNHALLOW***; 5 per day) (timings are direct from Tingwall - sailings via other islands take longer), Stromness (Mainland) to Moaness (Hoy) (25 mins; ***GRAEMSAY***; 2/3 per day) and Graemsay (25 mins; ***GRAEMSAY***; 2/3 per day) (passenger/cargo service - cars not normally conveyed).

1	EARL SIGURD	771t	90	12.5k	45.0m	190P	26C	-	BA	UK	8902711

2	EARL THORFINN	771t	90	12.5k	45.0m	190P	26C	-	BA	UK	8902723
3	EYNHALLOW	104t	87	10.5k	28.8m	95P	11C	-	BA	UK	8960880
4p•	GOLDEN MARIANA	33t	73	9.5k	15.2m	40P	0C	-	-	UK	
5	GRAEMSAY	90t	96	10.0k	20.6m	73P	2C	-	C	UK	
6	HOY HEAD	358t	94	11.0k	53.5m	125P	24C	3L	BA	UK	9081722
7p	NORDIC SEA	69t	12	10.0k	21.5m	40P	0C	0L	C	UK	
8	SHAPINSAY	199t	89	10.0k	32.6m	91P	16C	-	B	UK	8814184
9	THORSVOE	385t	91	10.6k	35.0m	122P	16C	-	BA	UK	9014743
10	VARAGEN	928t	88	14.5k	49.9m	144P	33C	5L	BA	UK	8818154

EARL SIGURD, EARL THORFINN Built by McTay Marine, Bromborough, Wirral, UK to inaugurate ro-ro working on the 'North Isles service'.

EYNHALLOW Built by David Abels Boat Builders, Bristol, UK to inaugurate ro-ro services from Tingwall (Mainland) to Rousay, Egilsay and Wyre. In 1991 she was lengthened by 5 metres, to increase car capacity.

GOLDEN MARIANA Built by Bideford Shipyard Ltd, Bideford, UK for *A J G England* of Padstow as a dual-purpose passenger and fishing vessel. In 1975 sold to *M MacKenzie* of Ullapool, then to *Pentland Ferries*, *Wide Firth Ferry* in 1982, and *Orkney Islands Council* in 1986. Passenger-only vessel. Generally operates summer-only feeder service between Pierowall (Westray) and Papa Westray. In late 2020/early 2021 to be withdrawn and laid up.

GRAEMSAY Built by Ailsa Shipbuilding, Troon UK to operate between Stromness (Mainland), Moaness (Hoy) and Graemsay. Designed to offer an all-year-round service to these islands, primarily for passengers and cargo. Between October 2009 and January 2010 lengthened by 4.4 metres.

HOY HEAD Built by Appledore Shipbuilders Ltd, Appledore, UK to replace the THORSVOE on the 'South Isles service'. During winter 2012/13 extended by 14 metres at Cammell Laird Shiprepairers & Shipbuilders, Birkenhead, England.

NORDIC SEA Built by GS Marine Produktion AS, Haugsbygda, Norway for *Salten Cruise AS* of Bodø, Norway. Later operated for *Nordland County*. In April 2020 sold to *Orkney Ferries* to replace the GOLDEN MARIANA on the Westray - Papa Westray service.

SHAPINSAY Built by Yorkshire Drydock Ltd, Hull, UK for the service from Kirkwall (Mainland) to Shapinsay. In April 2011 lengthened by 6 metres at the Macduff Shipyards, Macduff, Scotland to increase car capacity from 12 to 16 and re-engined.

THORSVOE Built by Campbeltown Shipyard, Campbeltown, UK for the 'South Isles service'. In 1994 replaced by the new HOY HEAD and became the main reserve vessel for the fleet.

VARAGEN Built by Cochrane Shipbuilders, Selby, UK for *Orkney Ferries*, a private company established to start a new route between Gills Bay (Caithness, Scotland) and Burwick (South Ronaldsay, Orkney). However, due to problems with the terminals it was not possible to maintain regular services. In 1991, the company was taken over by *Orkney Islands Shipping Company* and the VARAGEN became part of their fleet, sharing the 'North Isles service' with the EARL SIGURD and the EARL THORFINN and replacing the freight vessel ISLANDER (494t, 1969).

P&O FERRIES

THE COMPANY *P&O Ferries Holdings Ltd* is a private sector company, a subsidiary of *Dubai World*, owned by the Government of Dubai. In Autumn 2002 *P&O North Sea Ferries*, P&O Irish Sea, *P&O Portsmouth* and *P&O Stena Line* (*Stena Line* involvement having ceased) were merged into a single operation.

MANAGEMENT Acting Chief Executive David Stretch, **Chief Financial Officer** Karl Howarth, **Managing Director Short Routes** Vacant, **Business Unit Director of Freight Services** Stijn Gheyl, **Business Unit Director Overnight Routes**, Peter Hebblethwaite.

ADDRESSES *Head Office and Dover Services* Channel House, Channel View Road, Dover, Kent CT17 9TJ, ***Hull*** King George Dock, Hedon Road, Hull HU9 5QA, ***Larne*** P&O Irish Sea, Larne

Harbour, Larne, Co Antrim BT40 1AW ***Rotterdam*** Beneluxhaven, Rotterdam (Europoort), Postbus 1123, 3180 Rozenburg, Netherlands, ***Zeebrugge*** Leopold II Dam 13, Havendam, 8380 Zeebrugge, Belgium.

TELEPHONE Administration *UK* +44 (0)1304 863000, **Passenger Reservations *UK*** 08716 64 64 64, ***France*** +33 (0)825 12 01 56, ***Belgium*** +32 (0)70 70 77 71, ***The Netherlands*** +31 (0)20 20 08333, ***Spain*** +34 (0)902 02 04 61, ***Luxembourg*** +34 (0)20 80 82 94. **Freight Reservations *UK*** 0870 6000 868, ***Republic of Ireland*** +353 (0)1 855 0522.

FAX Passenger Reservations *UK East and South Coast* +44 (0)1304 863464, ***West Coast*** 44 (0)02828 872195, ***The Netherlands*** +31 (0)118 1225 5215, ***Belgium*** +32 (0)50 54 71 12, **Freight Reservations *Cairnryan*** +44 (0)1581 200282, ***Larne*** +44 (0)28 2827 2477..

INTERNET Email customer.services@poferries.com **Website** www.poferries.com *(English, French, Dutch, German)* www.poirishsea.com *(English)* www.poferriesfreight.com *(English, French, German)*

ROUTES OPERATED Passenger Dover – Calais (1 hr 30 mins; ***PRIDE OF BURGUNDY, PRIDE OF CANTERBURY, PRIDE OF KENT, SPIRIT OF BRITAIN, SPIRIT OF FRANCE***; up to 25 per day), Hull – Zeebrugge (Belgium) (from 12 hrs 30 mins; ***PRIDE OF BRUGES, PRIDE OF YORK;*** 1 per day), Hull – Rotterdam (Beneluxhaven, Europoort) (The Netherlands) (from 10 hrs; ***PRIDE OF HULL, PRIDE OF ROTTERDAM***; 1 per day), Cairnryan – Larne (1 hr 45 min; ***EUROPEAN CAUSEWAY, EUROPEAN HIGHLANDER***; 7 per day), Liverpool – Dublin (8 hrs; ***NORBANK, NORBAY***; up to 2 per day. **Freight-only** Dover – Calais (1 hr 30 mins; ***EUROPEAN SEAWAY***; 2/3 per day (plus services on passenger ferries)), Tilbury – Zeebrugge (8 hrs; ***NORSKY, NORSTREAM***; 10 per week), Middlesbrough (Teesport) – Rotterdam (Beneluxhaven, Europoort) (16 hrs; ***WILHELMINE***; 3 per week), Middlesbrough (Teesport) – Zeebrugge (15 hrs 30 mins; ***BORE SONG, ESTRADEN***; 6 per week), Liverpool – Dublin (8 hrs; ***CLIPPER PENNANT***; 1 per day (plus services on passenger ferries)). **Container service** Hull – Zeebrugge (Belgium) (from 12 hrs 30 mins; ***ELISABETH***; 3 per week).

1F	BORE SONG	25586t	11	18.5k	195.0m	12P	-	210T	A2	NL	9443566
2F	CLIPPER PENNANT	14759t	09	22.0k	142.0m	12P	-	120T	A	CY	9372688
3F	ELISABETH	5067t	00	-	118.3m	0P		648teu	C	NL	9219862
4F	ESTRADEN	18205t	99	19.0k	162.7m	12P	130C	170T	A	FI	9181077
5	EUROPEAN CAUSEWAY	20646t	00	22.7k	159.5m	410P	315C	84T	BA2	BS	9208394
6	EUROPEAN HIGHLANDER	21128t	02	22.6k	162.7m	410P	315C	84T	BA2	BS	9244116
7F+	EUROPEAN SEAWAY	22986t	91	21.0k	179.7m	200P	-	120L	BA2	CY	9007283
8	NORBANK	17464t	93	22.5k	166.7m	114P	-	125T	A	NL	9056583
9	NORBAY	17464t	92	21.5k	166.7m	114P	-	125T	A	BM	9056595
10F	NORSKY	19992t	99	20.0k	180.0m	12P	-	194T	A	FI	9186182
11F	NORSTREAM	19992t	99	20.0k	180.0m	12P	-	194T	A	FI	9186194
12	PRIDE OF BRUGES	31598t	87	18.5k	179.0m	1050P	310C	185T	A	NL	8503797
13	PRIDE OF BURGUNDY	28138t	92	21.0k	179.7m	1420P	465C	120L	BA2	CY	9015254
14	PRIDE OF CANTERBURY	30635t	91	21.0k	179.7m	2000P	537C	120L	BA2	CY	9007295
15	PRIDE OF HULL	59925t	01	22.0k	215.4m	1360P	205C	263T	AS	BS	9208629
16	PRIDE OF KENT	30635t	92	21.0k	179.7m	2000P	537C	120L	BA2	CY	9015266
17	PRIDE OF ROTTERDAM	59925t	00	22.0k	215.4m	1360P	205C	263T	AS	NL	9208617
18	PRIDE OF YORK	31785t	87	18.5k	179.0m	1050P	310C	185T	A	BS	8501957
19	SPIRIT OF BRITAIN	47592t	11	22.0k-	212.0m	2000P	194C	180L	BA2	CY	9524231
20	SPIRIT OF FRANCE	47592t	12	22.0k-	212.0m	2000P	194C	180L	BA2	CY	9533816
21	WILHELMINE	21020t	12	15.8k	150.0m	12P	-	170T	A	MT	9539080

BORE SONG Built by Flensburger Schiffbau-Gesellschaft, Flensburg, Germany for *Bore Shipowners (Rettig Group Bore)* of Finland. In July 2011 chartered to *Mann Lines* to cover for the ESTRADEN'S refit. In September 2011 chartered to *P&O Ferries* and placed on the Middlesbrough – Zeebrugge route.

CLIPPER PENNANT Built by Astilleros Sevilla SA, Sevilla, Spain for *Seatruck Ferries*. In November 2018 chartered to *Canary Bridge Seaways,* a joint venture between *Fred. Olsen Express* and

European Causeway *(George Holland)*

Pride of York *(George Holland)*

Balearia to operate between the Spanish mainland and the Canary Islands. In December 2019 chartered to *P&O Ferries* to operate between Liverpool and Dublin.

ELISABETH Container ship built by J.J. Sietas KG Schiffswerft GmbH & Co for *Holwerda Shipmanagement BV* of The Netherlands. In May 2017 introduced onto the Hull - Zeebrugge route to relieve pressure on the two passenger ships.

ESTRADEN Built as the ESTRADEN by Aker Finnyards, Rauma, Finland for *Rederi Ab Engship* (later *Bore Shipowners*) of Finland and chartered to *ArgoMann*. Later in 1999 renamed the AMAZON. In 2001 the charter was taken over by *Mann Lines* and in August she resumed the name ESTRADEN. In 2006 *Rederi AB Engship* was taken over by *Rettig Group Bore* and she remained on charter to *Mann Lines*. In January 2015 chartered to *P&O Ferries* to replace the WILHELMINE of *Cobelfret Ferries* on the Rotterdam - Middlesbrough (Teesport) service. In June 2018 transferred to the Zeebrugge - Teesport service.

EUROPEAN CAUSEWAY Built by Mitsubishi Heavy Industries, Shimonoseki, Japan for *P&O Irish Sea* for the Cairnryan - Larne service.

EUROPEAN HIGHLANDER Built by Mitsubishi Heavy Industries, Shimonoseki, Japan for *P&O Irish Sea* for the Cairnryan - Larne service.

EUROPEAN SEAWAY Built by Schichau Seebeckwerft AG, Bremerhaven, Germany for *P&O European Ferries* for the Dover - Zeebrugge freight service. In 2000 a regular twice-daily freight-only Dover-Calais service was established, using this vessel which continued to operate to Zeebrugge at night. In 2001 car passengers (not foot or coach passengers) began to be conveyed on the Dover - Zeebrugge service. In 2003 the Zeebrugge service ended and she operated only between Dover and Calais in a freight-only mode. In 2004 withdrawn and laid up. In January 2005 returned to the Dover - Calais route. In July 2012 chartered to GLID, a joint venture between Centrica Renewable Energy Limited and EIG, for use by technicians working on the North Sea Lynn and Inner Dowsing wind farm array four miles off Skegness. In October 2012 returned to the Dover - Calais service. In April 2013 laid up at Tilbury. In August 2014 chartered as a wind farm accommodation and support vessel near the North German coast. In April 2015 returned to layup at Tilbury. In August 2015 returned to service on the Dover - Calais route.

NORBANK Built by Van der Giessen de Noord, Krimpen aan den IJssel, Rotterdam, The Netherlands for *North Sea Ferries* for the Hull - Rotterdam service. She was originally built for and chartered to *Nedlloyd* but the charter was taken over by *P&O* in 1996 and she was bought by *P&O* in 2003. She retains Dutch crew and registry. In May 2001 moved to the Felixstowe - Europoort route. In January 2002 transferred to *P&O Irish Sea* and operated on the Liverpool - Dublin route.

NORBAY Built by Van der Giessen de Noord, Krimpen aan den IJssel, Rotterdam, The Netherlands for *North Sea Ferries* for the Hull - Rotterdam service. Owned by *P&O*. In January 2002 transferred to *P&O Irish Sea* and operated on the Liverpool - Dublin route.

NORSKY, NORSTREAM Built by Aker Finnyards, Rauma, Finland for *Bore Line* of Finland and chartered to *P&O North Sea Ferries*. They generally operated on the Teesport - Zeebrugge service. In September 2011, the NORSTREAM was moved to the Tilbury - Zeebrugge route. In January 2013, the NORSKY was also moved to the Tilbury - Zeebrugge route.

PRIDE OF BRUGES Built as the NORSUN by NKK, Tsurumi, Japan for the Hull - Rotterdam service of *North Sea Ferries*. She was owned by *Nedlloyd* and was sold to *P&O* in 1996 but retains Dutch crew and registry. In May 2001 replaced by the PRIDE OF ROTTERDAM and in July 2001, after a major refurbishment, she was transferred to the Hull - Zeebrugge service, replacing the NORSTAR (26919t, 1974). In 2003 renamed the PRIDE OF BRUGES.

PRIDE OF BURGUNDY Built by Schichau Seebeckwerft AG, Bremerhaven, Germany for *P&O European Ferries* for the Dover - Calais service. When construction started she was due to be a sister vessel to the EUROPEAN SEAWAY (see Section 3) called the EUROPEAN CAUSEWAY and operate on the Zeebrugge freight route. However, it was decided that she should be completed as a passenger/freight vessel (the design allowed for conversion) and she was launched as the PRIDE OF BURGUNDY. In 1998, transferred to *P&O Stena Line* and renamed the P&OSL

Spirit of Britain *(George Holland)*

Pride of Kent *(Frank Lose)*

BURGUNDY. In 2002 renamed the PO BURGUNDY and in 2003 renamed the PRIDE OF BURGUNDY. In 2004 she operated mainly in freight-only mode. In 2005 returned to full passenger service.

PRIDE OF CANTERBURY Built as the EUROPEAN PATHWAY by Schichau Seebeckwerft AG, Bremerhaven, Germany for *P&O European Ferries* for the Dover - Zeebrugge freight service. In 1998 transferred to *P&O Stena Line*. In 2001 car/foot passengers were again conveyed on the route. In 2002/03 rebuilt as a full passenger vessel and renamed the PRIDE OF CANTERBURY; now operates between Dover and Calais.

PRIDE OF HULL Built by Fincantieri-Cantieri Navali Italiani SpA, Venezia, Italy for *P&O North Sea Ferries* to replace (with the PRIDE OF ROTTERDAM) the NORSEA and NORSUN plus the freight vessels NORBAY and NORBANK on the Hull - Rotterdam service.

PRIDE OF KENT Built as the EUROPEAN HIGHWAY by Schichau Seebeckwerft AG, Bremerhaven, Germany for *P&O European Ferries* for the Dover - Zeebrugge freight service. In 1998 transferred to *P&O Stena Line*. In Summer 1999 she operated full-time between Dover and Calais. She returned to the Dover - Zeebrugge route in the autumn when the P&OSL AQUITAINE was transferred to the Dover - Calais service. In 2001 car/foot passengers were again conveyed on the route. In 2002/03 rebuilt as a full passenger vessel and renamed the PRIDE OF KENT; now operates between Dover and Calais.

PRIDE OF ROTTERDAM Built by Fincantieri-Cantieri Navali Italiani SpA, Venezia, Italy. Keel laid as the PRIDE OF HULL but launched as the PRIDE OF ROTTERDAM. Owned by Dutch interests until 2006 when she was sold to *P&O Ferries*. Further details as the PRIDE OF HULL.

PRIDE OF YORK Built as the NORSEA by Govan Shipbuilders Ltd, Glasgow, UK for the Hull - Rotterdam service of *North Sea Ferries* (jointly owned by *P&O* and *The Royal Nedlloyd Group* of The Netherlands until 1996). In December 2001 she was replaced by the new PRIDE OF HULL and, after a two-month refurbishment, in 2002 transferred to the Hull - Zeebrugge service, replacing the NORLAND (26290t, 1974). In 2003 renamed the PRIDE OF YORK.

SPIRIT OF BRITAIN, SPIRIT OF FRANCE Built by STX Europe, Rauma, Finland for the Dover - Calais service. Car capacity relates to dedicated car deck only; additional cars can be accommodated on the freight decks as necessary.

WILHELMINE Built by the Kyokuyo Shipyard, Shimonoseki, Japan for *CLdN*. After completion, a additional deck and sponsons were retro-fitted at the Chengxi Shipyard, Jiangyin, China. Initially used on the Zeebrugge - Purfleet service. In January 2013 chartered to *P&O Ferries* to operate between Tilbury and Zeebrugge. After three weeks moved to the Middlesbrough - Rotterdam service. In November 2014 the charter ended and she was placed on the Zeebrugge - Purfleet service. She returned to *P&O Ferries* for five weeks during the refit period in January and February 2015 and again operated Middlesbrough - Rotterdam. In March 2019 chartered to *P&O Ferries* and placed on the Middlesbrough - Rotterdam route on a long-term basis.

Under Construction

22	NEWBUILDING 1	44600t	23	22.0k-	230.0m	1500P	200C	170L	BA2	CY	9895161
23	NEWBUILDING 2	44600t	23	22.0k-	230.0m	1500P	200C	170L	BA2	CY	9895173

NEWBUILDING 1, NEWBUILDING 2 Under construction by Guangzhou Shipyard International, Guangzhou, China for the Dover - Calais service. Double ended. The car capacity quoted is on the dedicated upper car deck only.

At the time of going to press, the MISIDA is on short term charter to *P&O Ferries*. In October she is to be chartered to *Sea-Cargo* and has been listed under that operator.

Norbay *(Miles Cowsill)*

Alfred *(Pentland Ferries)*

Red Kestral *(Andrew Cooke)*

Red Osprey *(Andrew Cooke)*

PENTLAND FERRIES

THE COMPANY *Pentland Ferries* is a UK private sector company.

MANAGEMENT Managing Director Andrew Banks, **Designated Person Ashore** Kathryn Scollie.

ADDRESS Pier Road, St Margaret's Hope, South Ronaldsay, Orkney KW17 2SW.

TELEPHONE Administration +44 (0)1856 831226, **Reservations** +44 (0)800 688 8998.

FAX Administration & Reservations +44 (0)1856 831697.

INTERNET Email sales@pentlandferries.co.uk **Website** www.pentlandferries.co.uk *(English)*

ROUTE OPERATED Gills Bay (Caithness) - St Margaret's Hope (South Ronaldsay, Orkney) (1 hour; ***ALFRED***; up to 4 per day).

1	ALFRED	2963t	19	16.0k	84.5m	430P	98C	12L	A	UK	9823467
2	ORCADIA	899t	78	13.0k	69.5m	-	40C	-	AS	UK	7615490
3•	PENTALINA	2382t	08	17.1k	59.0m	345P	70C	9L	A	UK	9437969

ALFRED Built by Strategic Marine Shipyard, Vũng Tàu, Vietnam.

ORCADIA Built as the SATURN by Ailsa Shipbuilding, Troon for *Caledonian MacBrayne* and initially used on the Wemyss Bay - Rothesay services. Between 1986 and 2005 she usually rotated on this service and services from Gourock; until 2000 this, in summer, included Clyde cruising but this was not repeated in 2001. In the summers 2005 - 2010, she operated additional peak summer sailings between Ardrossan and Brodick with a maximum capacity of 250 passengers. In October 2010 she took over the Gourock - Dunoon service. In June 2011 replaced by *Argyll Ferries* passenger ferries. During Summer 2011 she operated additional sailings between Ardrossan and Brodick. In September returned to the Gourock - Dunoon route to provide additional capacity for the Cowal Games. She was then laid up. In February 2015 sold to *Pentland Ferries* and renamed the ORCADIA.

PENTALINA Catamaran built by FBMA Marine, Cebu, Philippines for *Pentland Ferries.*

RED FUNNEL FERRIES

THE COMPANY *Red Funnel Ferries* is the trading name of the *Southampton, Isle of Wight and South of England Royal Mail Steam Packet Company Limited*, a British private sector company owned by a consortium of British and Canadian pension funds led by the West Midland Pensions Fund of the UK and the Workplace Safety and Insurance Board of the Province of Ontario, Canada.

MANAGEMENT CEO Fran Collins, **Commercial Director** Colin Hetherington.

ADDRESS 12 Bugle Street, Southampton SO14 2JY.

TELEPHONE Administration +44 (0)23 8001 9192 , **Reservations *UK*** 0844 844 9988, ***Elsewhere*** +44 (0)23 8001 9192.

FAX Administration & Reservations +44 (0)23 8024 8501.

INTERNET Email post@redfunnel.co.uk **Website** www.redfunnel.co.uk *(English),*

ROUTES OPERATED Conventional Ferries Southampton - East Cowes (55 mins; ***RED EAGLE, RED FALCON, RED OSPREY***; hourly). **Fast Passenger Ferries** Southampton - Cowes (22 mins; ***RED JET 4, RED JET 6, RED JET 7***; every hour or half hour). **Freight Ferry** (1 hour, 10 mins; ***RED KESTREL***; every 3 hours).

1	RED EAGLE	3953t	96	13.0k	93.2m	895P	200C	18L	BA	UK	9117337
2	RED FALCON	3953t	94	13.0k	93.2m	895P	200C	18L	BA	UK	9064047
3»p	RED JET 4	342t	03	35.0k	39.8m	277P	0C	0L	-	UK	9295854
4»p	RED JET 6	363t	16	35.0k	41.1m	275P	0C	0L	-	UK	9788083
5»p	RED JET 7	363t	18	35.0k	41.1m	275P	0C	0L	-	UK	9847645

Red Jet 6 *(Andrew Cooke)*

Eynhallow *(Miles Cowsill)*

6F	RED KESTREL	1070t	19	12.5k	74.3m	12P	-	12L	BA	UK	9847645
7	RED OSPREY	3953t	94	13.0k	93.2m	895P	200C	18L	BA	UK	9064059

RED EAGLE Built by Ferguson Shipbuilders, Port Glasgow, UK for the Southampton - East Cowes service. During Winter 2004/05 stretched by 10 metres and height raised by 3 metres at Gdansk, Poland. In spring 2018 she received an upgrade (as RED FALCON in 2014).

RED FALCON Built by Ferguson Shipbuilders, Port Glasgow, UK for the Southampton - East Cowes service. In 2004 stretched by 10 metres and height raised by 3 metres at Gdansk, Poland. In spring 2014 she received a £2m upgrade.

RED JET 4 Catamaran built North West Bay Ships Pty Ltd Hobart, Tasmania, Australia.

RED JET 6, RED JET 7 Catamaran built by Wight Shipyard, Cowes, Isle of Wight, UK.

RED KESTREL Built by Cammell Laird, Birkenhead. She is designed to provide additional year-round freight capacity for the Southampton - East Cowes route.

RED OSPREY Built by Ferguson Shipbuilders, Port Glasgow, UK for the Southampton - East Cowes service. In 2003 stretched by 10 metres and height raised by 3 metres at Gdansk, Poland. In spring 2015 she received an upgrade (as RED FALCON in 2014).

SHETLAND ISLANDS COUNCIL

THE COMPANY *Shetland Islands Council* is a British local government authority.

MANAGEMENT Ferry Operations Manager Kevin Main, **Marine Superintendent** Ian Pearson.

ADDRESS Port Administration Building, Sella Ness, Mossbank, Shetland ZE2 9QR.

TELEPHONE Administration +44 (0)1806 244200 **Reservations *Yell Sound, Bluemull*, Whalsay**, ***Skerries*** & ***Papa Stour***. ***Fair Isle*** +44 (0)1595 760363

FAX +44 (0)1806 244220.

INTERNET Email ferries@shetland.gov.uk **Website:** www.shetland.gov.uk/ferries *(English)*

ROUTES OPERATED Yell Sound Service Toft (Mainland) - Ulsta (Yell) (20 mins; ***DAGALIEN, DAGGRI***; up to 26 per day), **Bluemull Sound Service** (Gutcher (Yell) - Belmont (Unst) (10 mins; ***BIGGA, GEIRA***; up to 28 per day), Gutcher - Hamars Ness (Fetlar) (25 mins; ***BIGGA, GEIRA***; up to 8 per day), **Bressay** Lerwick (Mainland) - Maryfield (Bressay) (5 mins; ***LEIRNA***; up to 23 per day), **Whalsay** Laxo/Vidlin (Mainland) - Symbister (Whalsay) (30-45 mins; ***HENDRA, LINGA***; up to 18 per day), **Skerries** Vidlin (Mainland) - Out Skerries (1 hr 30 mins; ***FILLA***; up to 10 per week), Out Skerries - Lerwick (3 hours; ***FILLA***; 2 per week), **Fair Isle** (Grutness (Mainland) - Fair Isle (3 hrs; ***GOOD SHEPHERD IV***; 2 per week), **Papa Stour** West Burrafirth (Mainland) - Papa Stour (40 mins; ***SNOLDA***; up to 7 per week). ***FIVLA*** is used to cover while vessels other than ***GOOD SHEPHERD IV*** are at annual re-fit.

1	BIGGA	274t	91	11.0k	33.5m	96P	21C	2L	BA	UK	9000821
2	DAGALIEN	1861t	04	12.0k	65.4m	144P	30C	4L	BA	UK	9291626
3	DAGGRI	1861t	04	12.0k	65.4m	144P	30C	4L	BA	UK	9291614
4	FILLA	356t	03	12.0k	35.5m	30P	10C	2L	A	UK	9269192
5	FIVLA	230t	85	11.0k	29.9m	95P	10C	2L	BA	UK	8410237
6	GEIRA	226t	88	10.8k	29.9m	95P	10C	2L	BA	UK	8712489
7	GOOD SHEPHERD IV	76t	86	10.0k	18.3m	12P	2C	0L	C	UK	
8	HENDRA	248	82	11.0k	30.2m	95P	12C	2L	BA	UK	8200254
9	LEIRNA	420t	92	9.0k	35.1m	124P	20C	2L	BA	UK	9050199
10	LINGA	658t	01	11.0k	36.2m	100P	16C	2L	BA	UK	9242170
11	SNOLDA	130t	83	9.0k	24.4m	12P	6C	1L	A	UK	8302090

BIGGA Built by JW Miller & Sons Ltd, St Monans, Fife, UK. Used on the Toft - Ulsta service. In 2005 moved to the Bluemull Sound service.

DAGALIEN, DAGGRI Built by Stocznia Polnócna, Gdansk, Poland to replace the BIGGA and HENDRA on Toft - Ulsta service.

FILLA Built by Stocznia Polnócna, Gdansk, Poland for the Lerwick /Vidlin - Out Skerries service. She looks like an oil rig supply vessel and is capable of transporting fresh water for replenishing the tanks on the Skerries in case of drought. Additional to deck space vessel has 2 holds with capacity for 90 tons.

FIVLA Built by Ailsa Shipbuilding, Troon, UK. Now a spare vessel, though often used on the Bluemull service.

GEIRA Built by Richard Dunston (Hessle), Hessle, UK. Formerly used on the Laxo - Symbister route. Replaced by the HENDRA in 2005 and moved to the Bluemull Sound service.

GOOD SHEPHERD IV Built by JW Miller & Sons Ltd, St Monans, Fife, UK. Used on the service between Grutness (Mainland) and Fair Isle. This vessel is not roll-on roll-off; vehicles are conveyed by Lift on Lift off with a weight restriction of 1.5 tons. She is pulled up on the marine slip on Fair Isle at the conclusion of each voyage.

HENDRA Built by McTay Marine, Bromborough, Wirral, UK for the Laxo - Symbister service. In 2002 transferred to the Toft - Ulsta service. In 2004 replaced by new vessels DAGGRI and DAGALIEN and moved to the Bluemull Sound service. In May 2005 returned to the Laxo - Symbister service as second vessel.

LEIRNA Built by Ferguson Shipbuilders, Port Glasgow, UK. Used on the Lerwick - Maryfield (Bressay) service.

LINGA Built by Stocznia Polnócna, Gdansk, Poland. Used on the Laxo - Symbister service.

SNOLDA Built as the FILLA by Sigbjorn Iversen, Flekkefjord, Norway. Used on the Lerwick (Mainland) - Out Skerries and Vidlin (Mainland) - Out Skerries services. At other times she operated freight and charter services around the Shetland Archipelago. Passenger capacity was originally 20 from 1st April to 31st October inclusive but is now 12 all year. In 2003 renamed the SNOLDA; replaced by the new FILLA and, in 2004, transferred to the West Burrafirth - Papa Stour route which is now Roll on Roll off with hold space available.

STENA LINE

MANAGEMENT Chief Executive Niclas Mårtensson, **Trade Director North Sea** Annika Hult, **Trade Director Irish Sea** Paul Grant.

ADDRESS *UK* Stena House, Station Approach, Holyhead, Anglesey LL65 1DQ, ***The Netherlands*** PO Box 2, 3150 AA, Hoek van Holland, The Netherlands.

TELEPHONE Administration *UK* +44 (0)1407) 606631, ***The Netherlands*** +31 (0)174 389333, **Reservations *UK*** 0344 7707070 (from UK only), ***The Netherlands*** +31 (0)174 315811. **Freight – Commercial Vehicles over 6.0m** 08450 704 000 / 08708 503 535.

FAX Administration & Reservations *UK* +44 (0)1407 606811, ***The Netherlands*** +31 (0)174 387045, **Telex** 31272.

INTERNET Email info@stenaline.com **Website** www.stenaline.co.uk *(English)*,

ROUTES OPERATED Conventional Ferries Cairnryan - Belfast (2 hrs 15 mins; ***STENA SUPERFAST VII, STENA SUPERFAST VIII***; up to 6 per day, Port of Liverpool (Twelve Quays River Terminal, Birkenhead) - Belfast (8 hrs; ***STENA EDDA***, ***STENA MERSEY***; up to 2 per day), Holyhead - Dublin (3 hrs 15 mins; ***STENA ADVENTURER, STENA ESTRID***; 4 per day), Fishguard - Rosslare (3 hrs 15 mins on day sailings ***STENA EUROPE***; 2 per day), Rosslare - Cherbourg (17 - 20 hrs; ***STENA HORIZON***; 3 per week), Harwich - Hoek van Holland (The Netherlands) (7 hrs 30 mins; ***STENA BRITANNICA, STENA HOLLANDICA***; 2 per day). **Freight Ferries** Heysham - Belfast (7 hrs; ***STENA HIBERNIA, STENA SCOTIA***; 2 per day), Harwich - Rotterdam (8 hrs; ***SOMERSET, STENA FORERUNNER***; 11 per week), Killingholme - Hoek van Holland (11 hrs; ***STENA TRANSIT, STENA TRANSPORTER***; 1 per day), Killingholme - Rotterdam (13 hrs; ***HATCHE***, ***QEZBAN***; 6 per week).

1F	HATCHE	29004t	09	21.5k	193.0m	12P	-	249T	A	TR	9457165
2F	QEZBAN	29004t	10	21.5k	193.0m	12P	-	249T	A	TR	9457189

Stena Hibernia *(George Holland)*

Stena Estrid *(Gordon Hislip)*

Stena Mersey *(George Holland)*

Stena Hollandica *(Rob de Visser)*

3F	SOMERSET	21005t	00	18.0k	183.4m	12P	-	180T	A	NL	9188221
4	STENA ADVENTURER	43532t	03	22.0k	210.8m	1500P	-	210L	BA2	UK	9235529
5	STENA BRITANNICA	63600t	10	22.0k	240.0m	1200P	-	300T	BA2	UK	9419175
6	STENA EDDA	41671t	20	22k	214.5m	927P	300C	180L	BA2	CY	9807308
7	STENA ESTRID	41671t	19	22k	214.5m	927P	300C	180L	BA2	CY	9807293
8	STENA EUROPE	24828t	81	20.5k	149.0m	2076P	456C	60T	BA	UK	7901760
9F	STENA FORERUNNER	24688t	02	22.0k	195.3m	12P	-	210T	A2	NL	9227259
10F	STENA HIBERNIA	13017t	96	18.6k	142.5m	12P	-	114T	A	UK	9121637
11	STENA HOLLANDICA	63600t	10	22.5k	240.0m	1200P	-	300T	BA2	NL	9419163
12	STENA HORIZON	26500t	06	23.5k	186.5m	720P	160C	135L	A	IT	9332559
13•	STENA LAGAN	27510t	05	23.5k	186.5m	720P	160C	135T	A	BS	9329849
14	STENA MERSEY	27510t	05	23.5k	186.5m	720P	160C	135T	A	UK	9329851
15F	STENA SCOTIA	13017t	96	18.6k	142.5m	12P	-	114T	A	UK	9121625
16	STENA SUPERFAST VII	30285t	01	22.0k	203.3m	1200P	660C	110L	BA2	UK	9198941
17	STENA SUPERFAST VIII	30285t	01	22.0k	203.3m	1200P	660C	110L	BA2	UK	9198953
18F+	STENA TRANSIT	34700t	11	22.2k	212.0m	300P	-	290T	A2	NL	9469388
19F+	STENA TRANSPORTER	34700t	11	22.2k	212.0m	300P	-	290T	A2	NL	9469376

HATCHE Built as the MAAS VIKING by Odense Staalskibsværft A/S, Odense, Denmark for *Epic Shipping* of the UK and chartered to *Norfolkline*. Charter taken over by *DFDS Seaways*. Operated between Vlaardingen and Killingholme. In September 2012 sold to *CLdN* of Luxembourg and renamed the KENT. Operated from Rotterdam to Purfleet and Killingholme. In January 2013 renamed the HATCHE and chartered to *Ekol Lojistik (Alternative Transport)* of Turkey to operate between Trieste in Italy and Haydarpasa (Istanbul) in Turkey. In January 2014 sold to them. In January 2020 chartered to *Stena Line* and placed on the Killingholme - Rotterdam service.

QEZBAN Built as the WESSEX by Odense Staalskibsværft A/S, Odense, Denmark for *Epic Shipping* of the UK and chartered to *UN RoRo* of Turkey. Operated between Istanbul (Turkey) and Toulon (France). In February 2011 chartered to *LD Lines* to operate between Marseilles and Tunis. In March 2011 returned to *UN RoRo*. In March 2012 laid up in Greece. In September 2012 sold to *CLdN* of Luxembourg. In January 2013 renamed the QEZBAN and chartered to *Ekol Lojistik (Alternative Transport)* of Turkey to operate between Trieste in Italy and Haydarpasa (Istanbul) in Turkey. In January 2014 sold to them. In March 2020 chartered to *Stena Line* and placed on the Killingholme - Rotterdam service.

SOMERSET Built as the SPAARNEBORG by Flender Werft AG, Lübeck, Germany for *Wagenborg* of The Netherlands and time-chartered to *Stora-Enso* to operate between Zeebrugge and Göteborg in conjunction with *Cobelfret Ferries*. She also operated between Tilbury and Göteborg during 2010. In August 2011 chartered to the *Canadian MoD* to operate between Montreal and Cyprus in connection with the Libyan 'no fly zone'. On return in November she was laid up in Zeebrugge and in January 2012 moved to Göteborg. In August 2012 chartered to *LD Lines* to operate between Marseilles and Tunis. In March 2013 returned to the *Stora Enso/Cobelfret Ferries* Zeebrugge - Göteborg service. In November 2014 the arrangement between *Stora Enso* and *Cobelfret Ferries* ended and she was chartered to *SOL Continent Line* who took over the operation of the service, operating between Finland, Germany, Belgium and the UK. In January 2015 sold to *CNdL* and renamed the SOMERSET. Generally operated between Zeebrugge and Göteborg. In August 2018 chartered to *Stena Line* to operate between Rotterdam and Harwich.

STENA ADVENTURER Ro-pax vessel built by Hyundai Heavy Industries, Ulsan, South Korea, for *Stena RoRo* and chartered to *Stena Line* to operate between Holyhead and Dublin.

STENA BRITANNICA Built by Waden Yards in Wismar and Warnemünde, Germany, for *Stena Rederi* (bow sections constructed at Warnemünde and stern and final assembly at Wismar). Replaced the 2003 built STENA BRITANNICA on the Harwich - Hoek van Holland service.

STENA ESTRID, STENA EDDA Built by CMI Jinling Weihai Shipyard. They are known as 'E-Flexers' being of flexible construction so that their internal layout can be tailored to the needs of the routes they will operate on. They are designed to run traditional fuel but are under the class notation "gas ready" and can be converted to run on natural gas.

STENA EUROPE Built as the KRONPRINSESSAN VICTORIA by Götaverken Arendal AB, Göteborg, Sweden for *Göteborg-Frederikshavn Linjen* of Sweden (trading as *Sessan Linjen*) for their Göteborg – Frederikshavn service. Shortly after delivery, the company was taken over by *Stena Line* and services were marketed as *Stena-Sessan Line* for a period. In 1982 she was converted to an overnight ferry by changing one vehicle deck into two additional decks of cabins and she was switched to the Göteborg – Kiel route (with, during the summer, daytime runs from Göteborg to Frederikshavn and Kiel to Korsør (Denmark)). In 1989 she was transferred to the Oslo – Frederikshavn route and renamed the STENA SAGA. In 1994, transferred to *Stena Line BV*, renamed the STENA EUROPE and operated between Hoek van Holland and Harwich. She was withdrawn in June 1997, transferred to the *Lion Ferry* (a *Stena Line* subsidiary) Karlskrona – Gdynia service and renamed the LION EUROPE. In 1998 she was transferred back to *Stena Line* (remaining on the same route) and renamed the STENA EUROPE. In early 2002 the cabins installed in 1982 were removed and other modifications made and she was transferred to the Fishguard – Rosslare route.

STENA FORERUNNER Built by Dalian Shipyard Co Ltd, Dalian, China for *Stena RoRo* and chartered to *Transfennica*. In January 2018 chartered to *Stena Line* and placed on the Rotterdam – Harwich service. In August 2018 transferred to the Birkenhead – Belfast service. In February 2019 transferred to the Rotterdam – Killingholme service. In March 2020 transferred to the Rotterdam – Harwich route.

STENA HIBERNIA Built as the MAERSK IMPORTER by Miho Shipyard, Shimizu, Japan for *Norfolkline*. Used on the Scheveningen (from 2007 Vlaardingen) – Felixstowe service. In October 2009 moved to the Heysham-Belfast service. In July 2010 renamed the HIBERNIA SEAWAYS. In July 2011 renamed the STENA HIBERNIA. In September 2012 transferred to *Stena RoRo*. In November chartered to *Stena Line* and placed on the Birkenhead – Belfast service. In September 2015 moved to the Heysham – Belfast route.

STENA HOLLANDICA Built by Nordic Yards in Wismar and Warnemünde, Germany, for *Stena Rederi* (bow sections constructed at Warnemünde and stern and final assembly at Wismar) to replace the previous STENA HOLLANDICA on the Harwich – Hoek van Holland service. Entered service May 2010.

STENA HORIZON Built as the CARTOUR BETA by CN Visentini, Porto Viro, Italy for Levantina Trasporti of Italy. Chartered to *Caronte & Tourist* of Italy and operated between Messina and Salerno (Sicily). In October 2011 chartered to *Celtic Link Ferries*, renamed the CELTIC HORIZON and placed on the Rosslare – Cherbourg route. In March 2014 service and charter taken over by *Stena Line*. Renamed the STENA HORIZON.

STENA LAGAN Built as the LAGAN VIKING by CN Visentini, Donada, Italy for *Levantina Trasporti* of Italy. Chartered to *NorseMerchant Ferries* and placed on the Birkenhead – Belfast route. In 2008 sold to *Norfolkline*, then resold to *Epic Shipping* and chartered back. In August 2010, following *Norfolkline's* purchase by *DFDS Seaways*, she was renamed the LAGAN SEAWAYS. Between January and July 2011 she was operated by *Stena Line Irish Sea Ferries*, a 'stand-alone' company pending consideration of a take-over by *Stena Line* by the UK and Irish competition authorities. In July 2011 the take-over was confirmed and in August 2011 she was renamed the STENA LAGAN. In April 2012 she was sold to *Stena RoRo* and chartered back by *Stena Line*. In March 2020 replaced by the STENA ESTRID and sent to the Sedef Shipyard in Tuzla, Turkey for lengthening. This was delayed by about six months on account of the Covid-19 pandemic. It is unknown where she will operate when the work is completed in 2021.

STENA MERSEY Built as the MERSEY VIKING by CN Visentini, Donada, Italy for *Levantina Trasporti* of Italy. Chartered to *NorseMerchant Ferries* and placed on the Birkenhead – Belfast route. In 2008 sold to *Norfolkline*, then resold to *Epic Shipping* and chartered back. In August 2010, following *Norfolkline's* purchase by *DFDS Seaways*, she was renamed the MERSEY SEAWAYS. Between January and July 2011 she was operated by *Stena Line Irish Sea Ferries*, a 'stand-alone' company pending consideration of a take-over by *Stena Line* by the UK and Irish competition authorities. In July 2011 the take-over was confirmed and in August 2011 she was renamed the STENA MERSEY. In April 2012 she sold to *Stena RoRo* and chartered back by *Stena*

Stena Forerunner *(Rob de Visser)*

Stena Europe *(Gordon Hislip)*

Line. Due to be replaced by the STENA ESTRID in early 2021. She will then be lengthened and redeployed.

STENA SCOTIA Built as the MAERSK EXPORTER by Miho Shipyard, Shimizu, Japan for *Norfolkline*. Used on the Scheveningen (from 2007 Vlaardingen) - Felixstowe service until March 2009 when she was moved to the Heysham - Belfast route. In July 2010 renamed the SCOTIA SEAWAYS. In July 2011 renamed the STENA SCOTIA. In September 2013 transferred to *Stena RoRo* and placed on the charter market. In September 2014 chartered to *Stena Line* and inaugurated a new service between Rotterdam and Killingholme. In January 2018 transferred to Rotterdam - Harwich service. In August 2018 transferred to the Heysham - Belfast service.

STENA SUPERFAST VII, STENA SUPERFAST VIII Built as the SUPERFAST VII and SUPERFAST VIII by Howaldtswerke Deutsche Werft AG, Kiel, Germany for *Attica Enterprises* (now *Attica Group*) for use by *Superfast Ferries* between Rostock and Hanko. In 2006 sold to *Tallink*. The Finnish terminal was transferred to Helsinki and daily return trips between Helsinki and Tallinn were introduced. These ceased in September 2008. The operation was ceased for the winter season in December 2009 and 2010. Service resumed at the end of April 2010 and 2011. In August 2011 chartered to *Stena Line* and renamed the STENA SUPERFAST VII, STENA SUPERFAST VIII. In November 2011, after a major refit, they were placed on a service between Cairnryan and Belfast (replacing the Stranraer - Belfast service). In December 2017 purchased by *Stena Ropax*.

STENA TRANSIT, STENA TRANSPORTER Built by Samsung Heavy Industries, Koje, South Korea. Used on the Hoek van Holland - Killingholme service.

Under Construction

20	STENA EMBLA	41671t	21	22k	214.5m	927P	300C	180L	BA2	UK	9807322

STENA EMBLA Under construction for *Stena Line* by CMI Jinling Weihai Shipyard, Weihai, China. Due to be introduced on the Liverpool - Belfast route in early 2021.

WESTERN FERRIES

THE COMPANY *Western Ferries (Clyde) Ltd* is a British private sector company.

MANAGEMENT Managing Director Gordon Ross.

ADDRESS Hunter's Quay, Dunoon, Argyll PA23 8HJ.

TELEPHONE Administration +44 (0)1369 704452, **Reservations** Not applicable.

INTERNET Email enquiries@western-ferries.co.uk **Website** www.western-ferries.co.uk *(English)*

ROUTE OPERATED McInroy's Point (Gourock) - Hunter's Quay (Dunoon) (20 mins; ***SOUND OF SCARBA, SOUND OF SEIL, SOUND OF SHUNA, SOUND OF SOAY***; every 20 mins (15 mins in peaks)).

1	SOUND OF SCARBA	489t	01	11.0k	49.95m	220P	40C	4/5L	BA	UK	9237424
2	SOUND OF SEIL	497t	13	11.0k	49.95m	220P	40C	4/5L	BA	UK	9665217
3	SOUND OF SHUNA	489t	03	11.0k	49.95m	220P	40C	4/5L	BA	UK	9289441
4	SOUND OF SOAY	497t	13	11.0k	49.95m	220P	40C	4/5L	BA	UK	9665229

SOUND OF SCARBA, SOUND OF SHUNA Built by Ferguson Shipbuilders, Port Glasgow, UK for *Western Ferries*.

SOUND OF SEIL, SOUND OF SOAY Built by Cammell Laird Shiprepairers & Shipbuilders, Birkenhead, UK for *Western Ferries*.

Leirna *(Miles Cowsill)*

Sound of Soay *(Miles Cowsill)*

WIGHTLINK

THE COMPANY *Wightlink* is a British private sector company, 50% owned by *Basalt Infrastructure Partners LLP of the UK* (formerly known as *Balfour Beatty Infrastructure Partners (BBIP)*) and 50% by *Fiera Infrastructure Inc* of Canada.

MANAGEMENT Chief Executive Keith Greenfield, **Finance Director** Jonathan Pascoe **Operations Director** John Burrows, **Marketing and Innovation Director** Stuart James, **Business Development Director** Clive Tilley, **Human Resources Director** Karen Wellman.

ADDRESS Gunwharf Road, Portsmouth PO1 2LA.

TELEPHONE Administration and Reservations +44 (0)333 999 7333.

INTERNET Email bookings@wightlink.co.uk **Website** www.wightlink.co.uk *(English, Dutch, French, German)*

ROUTES OPERATED Conventional Ferries Lymington - Yarmouth (Isle of Wight) (approx 40 mins; ***WIGHT LIGHT, WIGHT SKY***; ***WIGHT SUN***; hourly), Portsmouth - Fishbourne (Isle of Wight) (approx 45 mins; ***ST. CLARE, ST. FAITH, VICTORIA OF WIGHT***; hourly with extras during morning peak). **Fast Cats** Portsmouth - Ryde (Isle of Wight) (passenger-only) (under 22 mins; ***WIGHT RYDER I, WIGHT RYDER II***; 2 per hour).

1	ST. CLARE	5359t	01	13.0k	86.0m	878P	186C	-	BA2	UK	9236949
2	ST. FAITH	3009t	89	12.5k	77.0m	771P	142C	12L	BA	UK	8907228
3	VICTORIA OF WIGHT	8200t	18	13.0k	89.7m	1208P	178C	-	BA2	UK	9791028
4	WIGHT LIGHT	2546t	08	11.0k	62.4m	360P	65C	-	BA	UK	9446972
5»p	WIGHT RYDER I	520t	09	20.0k	40.9m	260P	0C	-	-	UK	9512537
6»p	WIGHT RYDER II	520t	09	20.0k	40.9m	260P	0C	-	-	UK	9512549
7	WIGHT SKY	2546t	08	11.0k	62.4m	360P	65C	-	BA	UK	9446984
8	WIGHT SUN	2546t	09	11.0k	62.4m	360P	65C	-	BA	UK	9490416

ST. CLARE Built by Stocznia Remontowa, Gdansk, Poland for the Portsmouth - Fishbourne service. She is a double-ended ferry with a central bridge. During winter 2015/16 modified for double deck loading.

ST. FAITH Built by Cochrane Shipbuilders, Selby, UK for *Sealink British Ferries* for the Portsmouth - Fishbourne service.

VICTORIA OF WIGHT Built by the Cemre Shipyard, Yalova, Turkey for the Portsmouth - Fishbourne service. She is a hybrid diesel/battery electric vessel.

WIGHT LIGHT, WIGHT SKY, WIGHT SUN Built by Brodogradilište Kraljevica, Croatia for the Lymington - Yarmouth route.

WIGHT RYDER I, WIGHT RYDER II Catamarans built by FBMA Marine, Balamban, Cebu, Philippines. Operate on the Portsmouth - Ryde service.

Victoria of Wight *(Andrew Cooke)*

St Clare *(Andrew Cooke)*

Queen Mary
CUNARD
RED FUNNEL

Queen Mary 2 and **Red Falcon** *(Andrew Cooke)*

SECTION 2 – MINOR FERRY OPERATORS

ARGYLL AND BUTE COUNCIL

THE COMPANY *Argyll and Bute Council* is a British local government authority.

MANAGEMENT Head of Roads and Amenity Services Jim Smith.

Marine Operations Manager Stewart Clark.

ADDRESS 1A Manse Brae, Lochgilphead, Argyll PA31 8RD.

TELEPHONE Administration +44 (0)1546 604673.

FAX Administration +44 (0)1546 604738.

INTERNET Email stewart.clark@argyll-bute.gov.uk **Website** www.argyll-bute.gov.uk/transport-and-streets/ferry-travel

ROUTES OPERATED Vehicle ferries Seil – Luing (5 mins; ***BELNAHUA***; approx half-hourly), Port Askaig (Islay) – Feolin (Jura) (5 mins; ***EILEAN DHIURA***; approx half-hourly). **Passenger-only ferries** Port Appin – Lismore (10 mins; ***THE LISMORE***; approx hourly), Ellenabeich – Easdale (5 mins; ***EASDALE***; approx quarter-hourly).

1	BELNAHUA	35t	72	8.0k	17.1m	40P	5C	1L	BA	UK
2p	EASDALE	-	93	6.5k	6.4m	10P	0C	0L	-	UK
3	EILEAN DHIURA	86t	98	9.0k	25.6m	50P	13C	1L	BA	UK
4p	THE LISMORE	12t	88	8.0k	9.7m	20P	0C	0L	-	UK

BELNAHUA Built by Campbeltown Shipyard, Campbeltown, UK for *Argyll County Council* for the Seil – Luing service. In 1975, following local government reorganisation, transferred to *Strathclyde Regional Council*. In 1996, transferred to *Argyll and Bute Council*.

EASDALE Built for *Strathclyde Regional Council* for the Ellenabeich – Easdale passenger-only service. In 1996, following local government reorganisation, transferred to *Argyll and Bute Council*.

EILEAN DHIURA Built by McTay Marine, Bromborough, Wirral, UK for *Argyll and Bute Council* to replace the *Western Ferries (Argyll)* SOUND OF GIGHA on the Islay – Jura route. Now operated by the council.

THE LISMORE Built for *Strathclyde Regional Council* for the Port Appin – Lismore passenger-only service. In 1996, following local government reorganisation, transferred to *Argyll and Bute Council*.

ARRANMORE FAST FERRIES

THE COMPANY *Arranmore Fast Ferries*, trading as *Arranmore Blue Ferry* and *Tory Ferry*, is a Republic of Ireland private sector company.

MANAGEMENT Managing Director Seamus Boyle.

ADDRESS Blue Ferry Office, Burtonport, Letterkenny, Co. Donegal, Republic of Ireland.

TELEPHONE Administration & Reservations +353 (0)87 3171810**.**

INTERNET Email: info.fastferry@gmail.com **Website** arranmorefastferry.com *(English)*.

ROUTES OPERATED Arranmore Blue Ferry Burtonport (County Donegal) – Leabgarrow (Arranmore Island) (20 mins; ***CANNA, MORVERN***; up to 8 per day), **Tory Ferry** Magheroarty (County Donegal) – Tory Island (45 mins; ***QUEEN OF ARAN***; up to 4 per day).

1	CANNA	69t	76	8.0k	24.3m	140P	6C	1L	B	IR	7340423
2	MISNEACH	30t	78	7.0k	18.9m	80P	4C	-	B	IR	
3	MORVERN	83t	73	8.0k	26.6m	96P	10C	1L	B	IR	7235501
4p	OCEAN WARRIOR	18t	89	18.0k	14.3m	12P	0C	-	-	IR	
5p	QUEEN OF ARAN	113t	76	-	20.1m	96P	0C	-	-	IR	7527928

Eilean Dhiura *(Brian Maxted)*

Belnahua *(Brian Maxted)*

CANNA Built by James Lamont & Co Ltd, Port Glasgow, UK for *Caledonian MacBrayne*. She was the regular vessel on the Lochaline – Fishnish (Mull) service. In 1986 she was replaced by the ISLE OF CUMBRAE and until 1990 she served in a relief capacity in the north, often assisting on the Iona service. In 1990 she was placed on the Kyles Scalpay (Harris) – Scalpay service (replaced by a bridge in Autumn 1997). In Spring 1997 *Caledonian MacBrayne* was contracted to operate the Ballycastle – Rathlin Island route and she was transferred to this service. In June 2008 she was chartered by *Caledonian Maritime Assets Limited* to *Rathlin Island Ferry Ltd* who took over the operation of the service. In June 2017 replaced by the SPIRIT OF RATHLIN and withdrawn. In autumn 2017 sold to *Humphrey O'Leary,* Clare Island and, in 2020, chartered to *Arranmore Fast Ferries*.

MISNEACH Built at New Ross, Irish Republic for *Arranmore Island Ferry Services* of the Irish Republic and used on the Burtonport – Arranmore service. In 1992 sold to *Bere Island Ferries*. In 1993 inaugurated a car ferry service between Castletownbere and Bere Island. In 2004 disposed of and since then has been used as a work boat until purchased by *Arranmore Fast Ferries*, refurbished and became a reserve vessel.

MORVERN Built by James Lamont & Co Ltd, Port Glasgow, UK for *Caledonian MacBrayne*. After service on a number of routes she was, after 1979, the main vessel on the Fionnphort (Mull) – Iona service. In 1992 she was replaced by the LOCH BUIE and became a spare vessel. In 1995 sold to *Arranmore Island Ferry Services*. In 2001 sold to *Bere Island Ferries*. In February 2010 refurbished by Bere Island Boatyard and sold to *Arranmore Charters* (now *Arranmore Fast Ferries*). Extended in June 2012.

OCEAN WARRIOR Built by FBM Marine, Cowes, Isle of Wight as an RNLI Tyne class lifeboat ALEXANDER COUTANACHE (No1157) and operated at St Helier, Channel Islands until June 2009 when she became a relief vessel. Bought by *Arranmore Fast Ferries* in December 2014 and renamed the OCEAN WARRIOR.

QUEEN OF ARAN built in 1976 as the SHONAG OF KISHORN to work at the oil rig construction site in Loch Kishorn in Scotland. Moved to Ireland in 1985 and eventually became the QUEEN OF ARAN. In 2017 sold to *Arranmore Fast Ferries* and, after a major refit, placed on the Tory Island service.

ARRANMORE ISLAND FERRY SERVICES

THE COMPANY *Arranmore Island Ferry Services (Bád Farrantoireacht Arainn Mhór)*, trading as *Arranmore Red Ferry*, is a Republic of Ireland company, supported by *Roinn na Gaeltachta (The Gaeltacht Authority)*, a semi-state-owned body responsible for tourism and development in the Irish-speaking areas of The Republic of Ireland. They also operate the summer only Lough Swilly service.

MANAGEMENT Managing Director Dominic Sweeney.

ADDRESS Cara na nOilean, Burtonport Pier, Letterkenny, Co. Donegal, Republic of Ireland.

TELEPHONE Administration & Reservations *Arranmore Island Service* +353 (0)7495 42233, ***Lough Swilly Service*** +353 (0)87 211 2331.

INTERNET Email info@arranmoreferry.com loughswillyferry@gmail.com **Websites** arranmoreferry.com swillyferry.com *(English)*

ROUTES OPERATED *Arranmore Island Service* Burtonport (County Donegal) – Leabgarrow (Arranmore Island) (15 mins; ***RHUM***; up to 8 per day (Summer), 6 per day (Winter)), ***Lough Swilly Service (summer only)*** Buncrana (County Donegal) – Rathmullan (County Donegal) (20 mins; ***SPIRIT OF LOUGH SWILLY***; up to 8 per day).

1	COLL	69t	74	8.0k	25.3m	96P	6C	-	B	IR	7327990
2	RHUM	69t	73	8.0k	25.3m	96P	6C	-	B	IR	7319589
3	SPIRIT OF LOUGH SWILLY	110t	59	-	32.0m	130P	80C	-	BA	IR	

COLL Built by James Lamont & Co Ltd, Port Glasgow, UK for *Caledonian MacBrayne*. For several years she was employed mainly in a relief capacity. In 1986 she took over the Tobermory (Mull)

- Kilchoan service from a passenger-only vessel; the conveyance of vehicles was not inaugurated until 1991. In 1996 she was transferred to the Oban - Lismore route. In 1998 she was sold to *Arranmore Island Ferry Services*. Operates as spare vessel and also conveys cargo to Tory Island and is available for charter.

RHUM Built by James Lamont & Co Ltd, Port Glasgow, UK for *Caledonian MacBrayne*. Until 1987, she was used primarily on the Claonaig - Lochranza (Arran) service. After that time she served on various routes. In 1994 she inaugurated a new service between Tarbert (Loch Fyne) and Portavadie. In 1997 she operated between Kyles Scalpay and Scalpay until the opening of the new bridge on 16th December 1997. In 1998 she was sold to *Arranmore Island Ferry Services*.

SPIRIT OF LOUGH SWILLY Built as the LORELEY V by Ruthof, Mainz, Germany to operate between St Goarshausen and St Goar on the River Rhine. In 2004 replaced by a new vessel (the LORELEY VI) and became a reserve vessel. In 2007, sold to the *Waterford Castle Hotel* and renamed the LORELEY and, in 2008, replaced the previous ferry. She was modified for cable guidance. In August 2014 replaced by the MARY FITZGERALD and laid up. In July 2017 sold to sold to *Arranmore Island Ferry Services*, changed back to self steering and renamed the SPIRIT OF LOUGH SWILLY. Placed on the Lough Swilly service.

BERE ISLAND FERRIES

THE COMPANY *Bere Island Ferries Ltd* is a Republic of Ireland private sector company.

MANAGEMENT Operator Colum Harrington.

ADDRESS Ferry Lodge, West End, Bere Island, Beara, County Cork, Republic of Ireland.

TELEPHONE Administration +353 (0)27 75009, **Reservations** Not applicable, **Mobile** +353 (0)86 2423140.

INTERNET Email biferry@eircom.net **Website** bereislandferries.com *(English)*

1	HOUTON LASS	58t	60	9.0k	22.9m	12P	10C	1L	B	IR
2	OILEAN NA H-OIGE	69t	80	7.0k	18.6m	75P	4C	-	B	IR
3	SANCTA MARIA	67t	83	7.0k	18.6m	75P	4C	-	B	IR

HOUTON LASS Built by Magnaport Marine Ltd, Poole, UK for Flotta Oil Terminals, Stromness, Orkney Islands. Later sold for use as an antipollution vessel on the Black Isle, near Inverness. In November 2013 delivered to *Bere Island Ferries Ltd*. During 2014-2016 refurbished and lengthened in Galway. Mainly in use for transporting lorries but is also used for taking (up to) 10 cars during busy times.

OILEAN NA H-OIGE Built as the EILEAN NA H-OIGE by Lewis Offshore Ltd, Stornoway, UK for *Western Isles Islands Council* (from 1st April 1996 the *Western Isles Council* and from 1st January 1998 *Comhairle Nan Eilean Siar*) for their Ludaig (South Uist) - Eriskay service. From 2000 operated from a temporary slipway at the Eriskay causeway. This route ceased in July 2001 following the full opening of the causeway and she was laid up. In 2002 she was moved to the Eriskay - Barra service. In 2003 replaced by the LOCH BHRUSDA of *Caledonian MacBrayne* and laid up. Later sold to *Bere Island Ferries* and renamed the OILEAN NA H-OIGE (same name - "The Island of Youth" - in Irish rather than Scots Gaelic).

SANCTA MARIA Built as the EILEAN BHEARNARAIGH by George Brown & Company, Greenock, UK for *Western Isles Islands Council* for their Otternish (North Uist) - Berneray service. From 1996 until 1999 she was operated by *Caledonian MacBrayne* in conjunction with the LOCH BHRUSDA on the service between Otternish and Berneray and during the winter she was laid up. Following the opening of a causeway between North Uist and Berneray in early 1999, the ferry service ceased and she became reserve vessel for the Eriskay route. This route ceased in July 2001 following the opening of a causeway and she was laid up. In 2002 operated between Eriskay and Barra as reserve vessel. In 2003 sold to *Transalpine Redemptorists Inc*, a community of monks who live on Papa Stronsay, Orkney. Used for conveying supplies to the island - not a public service. In 2008 sold to *Bere Island Ferries*. Entered service in May 2009.

BK MARINE

THE COMPANY *BK Marine* is a UK company.

MANAGEMENT Managing Director Donald Gordon Fraser Ross.

ADDRESS Herrislea House Hotel, Veensgarth, Tingwall, Shetland ZE2 9SB.

TELEPHONE Administration & Reservations +44 (0)1595 840208.

INTERNET Email boats@bkmarine.co.uk **Website** bkmarine.co.uk *(English)*

ROUTE OPERATED ***All year*** Foula - Walls (Mainland) (2 hours; ***NEW ADVANCE***; 2 per week (Winter), 3 per week (Summer)), ***Summer only*** Foula - Scalloway (3 hrs 30 mins; ***NEW ADVANCE***; alternate Thursdays).

1	NEW ADVANCE	25t	96	8.7k	9.8m	12P	1C	0L	C	UK

NEW ADVANCE Built by Richardson's, Stromness, Orkney, UK for *Shetland Islands Council* for the Foula service. Although built at Penryn, Cornwall, she was completed at Stromness. She has a Cygnus Marine GM38 hull and is based on the island where she can be lifted out of the water. Vehicle capacity is to take residents' vehicles to the island - not for tourist vehicles. In 2004 it was announced that the vessel and service would be transferred to the *Foula Community*. However, it was then found that under EU rules the route needed to be offered for competitive tender. In July 2006 the contract was awarded to *Atlantic Ferries Ltd* which began operations in October 2006. In August 2011 replaced by *BK Marine*.

CLARE ISLAND FERRY COMPANY

THE COMPANY *Clare Island Ferry Company* is owned and operated by the O'Grady family, natives of Clare Island, Republic of Ireland, who have been operating the Clare Island Mail Boat Ferry service since 1880.

MANAGEMENT Managing Director Chris O'Grady.

ADDRESS Clare Island Ferry Co Ltd, Clare Island, Co Mayo, F28 AT04, Republic Of Ireland.

TELEPHONE +353 (0)98 23737, +353 (0)98 25212, +353 (0)87 9004115.

INTERNET Email bookings@clareislandferry.com **Website** www.clareislandferry.com *(English)*

ROUTE OPERATED Roonagh (Co Mayo) - Clare Island (15 mins; ***CLEW BAY QUEEN, EIGG, PIRATE QUEEN, SEA SPRINTER***; ***Winter*** 1 to 2 trips per day, ***Summer*** up to 5 per day, Roonagh - Inishturk (50 mins; ***CLEW BAY QUEEN, EIGG, SEA SPRINTER***; ***Winter*** 1 per day ***Summer*** up to 2 per day. Tourist vehicles are not normally carried.

1	CLEW BAY QUEEN	64t	72	10.0k	21.9m	96P	6C	-	B	IR	7217872
2	EIGG	91t	75	8.0k	24.2m	75P	6C	-	B	IR	7340411
3p•	PIRATE QUEEN	73t	96	10.5k	19.8m	96P	0C	-	-	IR	
4p	SEA SPRINTER	16t	93	22.0k	11.6m	35P	0C		-	IR	

CLEW BAY QUEEN Built as the KILBRANNAN by James Lamont & Co Ltd, Port Glasgow, UK for *Caledonian Steam Packet* (later *Caledonian MacBrayne*). Used on a variety of routes until 1977, she was then transferred to the Scalpay (Harris) - Kyles Scalpay service. In 1990 she was replaced by the CANNA and, in turn, replaced the CANNA in her reserve/relief role. In 1992 sold to *Arranmore Island Ferry Services* and renamed the ÁRAINN MHÓR. She was subsequently sold to *Údarás na Gaeltachta* and leased back to *Arranmore Island Ferry Services*. In 2008 she was sold to *Clare Island Ferry Company* and renamed the CLEW BAY QUEEN. She operates a passenger and heavy freight service to both Clare Island and Inishturk all year round. In winter passenger capacity is reduced to 47 with 3 crew. Fitted with crane for loading and unloading cargo. Number is Lloyd's Number, not IMO.

EIGG Built by James Lamont & Co, Port Glasgow, UK for *Caledonia MacBrayne*. Since 1976 she was employed mainly on the Oban - Lismore service. In 1996 she was transferred to the Tobermory (Mull) - Kilchoan route, very occasionally making sailings to the Small Isles (Canna,

Eigg, Muck and Rum) for special cargoes. In 1999 her wheelhouse was raised to make it easier to see over taller lorries and she returned to the Oban - Lismore route. In June 2018 sold to *Clare Island Ferry Company*. She is a reserve ferry and also available for charter as a workboat. Number is Lloyd's Number, not IMO.

PIRATE QUEEN Built by Arklow Marine Services in 1996 for *Clare Island Ferry Company*. She operated a daily passenger and light cargo service to Clare Island and Inishturk all year round. In winter passenger capacity was reduced to 47 with 3 crew. Fitted with crane for loading and unloading cargo. Currently laid up for sale or charter.

SEA SPRINTER Built by Lochin Marine, East Sussex, UK for *Island Ferries* (now *Aran Island Ferries*) of the Irish Republic. In June 2015 sold to *Clare Island Ferries*.

CROSS RIVER FERRIES

THE COMPANY *Cross River Ferries Ltd* is a Republic of Ireland company, part of the *Doyle Shipping Group*.

MANAGEMENT Operations Manager Eoin O'Sullivan.

ADDRESS Westlands House, Rushbrooke, Cobh, County Cork, P24 H940, Republic of Ireland.

TELEPHONE Administration +353 (0)21 481 1485 **Reservations** Not applicable.

INTERNET Email cork@dsg.ie **Website** crossriverferries.ie *(English)*

ROUTE OPERATED Carrigaloe (near Cobh, on Great Island) - Glenbrook (Co Cork) (4 mins; ***CARRIGALOE, GLENBROOK***; frequent service 07.00 - 00.15 (one or two vessels used according to demand)).

1	CARRIGALOE	225t	70	8.0k	49.1m	200P	27C	-	BA	IR	7028386
2	GLENBROOK	225t	71	8.0k	49.1m	200P	27C	-	BA	IR	7101607

CARRIGALOE Built as the KYLEAKIN by Newport Shipbuilding and Engineering Company, Newport (Gwent), UK for the *Caledonian Steam Packet Company* (later *Caledonian MacBrayne*) for the Kyle of Lochalsh - Kyleakin service. In 1991 sold to *Marine Transport Services Ltd* and renamed the CARRIGALOE. She entered service in March 1993. In Summer 2002 chartered to the *Lough Foyle Ferry Company*, returning in Spring 2003.

GLENBROOK Built as the LOCHALSH by Newport Shipbuilding and Engineering Company, Newport (Gwent), UK for the *Caledonian Steam Packet Company* (later *Caledonian MacBrayne*) for the Kyle of Lochalsh - Kyleakin service. In 1991 sold to *Marine Transport Services Ltd* and renamed the GLENBROOK. She entered service in March 1993.

FRAZER FERRIES

THE COMPANY *Frazer Ferries Ltd*, is a Republic of Ireland company. In June 2016 it took over *Passage East Ferries* and *Lough Foyle Ferry Service*. The *Carlingford Ferry* started in June 2017.

MANAGEMENT Director John Driscol, **Chief Executive** Paul O'Sullivan **Manager, Passage East Ferry** Peter Hayes.

ADDRESSES Head Office 23 Howley's Quay, Limerick, V94 WTK7, Republic of Ireland, **Lough Foyle Ferry** The Pier, Greencastle, Co Donegal, Republic of Ireland, **Carlingford Ferry** Greenore Port, The Harbour, Greenore, Co. Louth, A91 A0V1, Republic of Ireland. **Passage East Ferry** Barrack Street, Passage East, Co Waterford, X91 C52E, Republic of Ireland.

TELEPHONE Head Office +353 (0)61 316390 **Passage East Ferry** +353 (0)51 382480.

INTERNET Carlingford Lough Ferry Website carlingfordferry.com *(English)*, **Lough Foyle Ferry** www.loughfoyleferry.com *(English)*, **Passage East Ferry Email** passageferry@eircom.net **Website** www.passageferry.ie *(English)*

ROUTES OPERATED Carlingford Lough Ferry Greenore, Co Louth, Republic of Ireland - Greencastle, Co Down, Northern Ireland (20 minutes; ***FRAZER AISLING GABRIELLE***; hourly), **Passage East Ferry** Passage East (County Waterford) - Ballyhack (County Wexford) (7 mins;

Frazer Tintern *(Nick Widdows)*

Spirit of Lough Swilly *(Nick Widdows)*

FRAZER TINTERN; frequent service), ***Summer Service* Lough Foyle Ferry *July – September*** Greencastle (Inishowen, Co Donegal, Republic of Ireland) – Magilligan (Co Londonderry, Northern Ireland) (15 mins; ***FRAZER MARINER***; frequent service).

1	FRAZER AISLING GABRIELLE	324t	78	10.0k	47.9m	300P	44C	-	BA	IR	7800033
2	FRAZER MARINER	-	83	7.2k	43.0m	100P	20C	-	BA	IR	
3	FRAZER STRANGFORD	186t	69	10.0k	32.9m	263P	20C	-	BA	IR	6926311
4	FRAZER TINTERN	236t	71	9.0k	54.8m	130P	30C	-	BA	IR	

FRAZER AISLING GABRIELLE Built as the SHANNON WILLOW by Scott & Sons (Bowling) Ltd, Bowling, Glasgow, UK for *Shannon Ferry Ltd*. In 2000 replaced by the SHANNON BREEZE and laid up for sale. In 2003 sold to the *Lough Foyle Ferry Company Ltd* and renamed the FOYLE VENTURE. In November 2015 sold to *Frazer Ferries*. In July 2016 re-opened the *Lough Foyle Ferry;* this ceased in October. In February 2017 renamed the FRAZER AISLING GABRIELLE. In July 2017 inaugurated a new Carlingford Lough service.

FRAZER MARINER Built as the BERNE-FARGE for *Schnellastfähre Berne-Farge GmbH* (from 1993 *Fähren Bremen-Stedingen GmbH*) to operate across the River Weser (Vegesack – Lemwerder and Berne – Farge). In January 2017 sold to *Frazer Ferries*. In July 2017 renamed the FRAZER MARINER and began operating between Greencastle and Magilligan.

FRAZER TINTERN Built as the STADT LINZ by Schiffswerft Oberwinter, Oberwinter, Rhein, Germany for *Rheinfähre Linz – Remagen GmbH* of Germany and operated on the Rhine between Linz and Remagen. In 1990 renamed the ST JOHANNES. In 1997 sold to *Fähren Bremen-Stedingen GmbH*, renamed the VEGESACK and operated across the Weser between Lemwerder and Vegesack. In 2003 she became a reserve vessel and in 2004 was renamed the STEDINGEN. Later sold to *Schraven BV* of The Netherlands and refurbished. In Autumn 2005 sold to *Passage East Ferry* and renamed the FBD TINTERN. During 2017 renamed the FRAZER TINTERN

FRAZER STRANGFORD Built as the STRANGFORD FERRY by Verolme Dockyard Ltd, Cork, Republic of Ireland for *Down County Council*. Subsequently transferred to the *DOE (Northern Ireland)* and then the *DRD (Northern Ireland)*. Following entry into service of the STRANGFORD II in February 2016, she was withdrawn. In December 2017 sold to *Arranmore Island Ferry Services* (Red Boats) and renamed the STRANGFORD 1. In June 2018 sold to *Frazer Ferries*. In March 2019 renamed the FRAZER STRANGFORD. Used as a reserve vessel.

THE HIGHLAND COUNCIL

THE COMPANY *The Highland Council* is a Scottish local authority.

MANAGEMENT Area Roads Operations Manager Richard Porteous, **Ferry Foremen** Allan McCowan and Donald Dixon.

ADDRESS *Area Office* Lochybridge Depot, Carr's Corner Industrial Estate, Fort William PH33 6TQ, ***Ferry Office*** Ferry Cottage, Ardgour, Fort William PH33 7AA.

TELEPHONE Administration *Area Office* +44 (0)1349 781083, ***Corran*** +44 (0)1855 841243.

INTERNET Email communityservices@highland.gov.uk

Website www.highland.gov.uk/info/1526/public_and_community_transport/812/

corran_ferry_timetable_and_fares *(English)*

ROUTES OPERATED Vehicle Ferries Corran – Ardgour (5 mins; ***CORRAN, MAID OF GLENCOUL***; half-hourly).

1	CORRAN	351t	01	10.0k	42.0m	150P	30C	2L	BA	UK	9225990
2	MAID OF GLENCOUL	166t	75	8.0k	32.0m	116P	16C	1L	BA	UK	7521613

CORRAN Built by George Prior Engineering Ltd, Hull, UK for *The Highland Council* to replace the MAID OF GLENCOUL as main vessel.

MAID OF GLENCOUL Built by William McCrindle Ltd, Shipbuilders, Ardrossan, UK for *Highland Regional Council* for the service between Kylesku and Kylestrome. In 1984 the ferry service was replaced by a bridge and she was transferred to the Corran - Ardgour service. In April 1996, ownership transferred to *The Highland Council*. In 2001 she became the reserve vessel.

The *Highland Council* also supports both services operated by *Highland Ferries*.

HIGHLAND FERRIES

THE COMPANY *Highland Ferries* is a UK private sector operation. Services are operated under contract to *The Highland Council*.

MANAGEMENT Operator Dougie Robertson.

TELEPHONE Administration +44(0)7468 417137 **Reservations** Not applicable.

INTERNET Email southuist24@hotmail.co.uk **Website** highlandferries.co.uk *(English)*

1p	BHOY TAYLOR	15T	80	7.5k	9.8m	12P	0C	0L	-	UK
2	RENFREW ROSE	65t	84	7.6k	17.5m	12P	3C	0L	B	UK

ROUTES OPERATED Vehicle Ferry *1st June – 30th September* Cromarty - Nigg (Ross-shire) (10 mins; ***RENFREW ROSE***; half-hourly), **Passenger-only Ferry** Fort William - Camusnagaul (10 mins; ***BHOY TAYLOR***; up to 5 per day).

BHOY TAYLOR Built as the CAILIN AN AISEAG by Buckie Shipbuilders Ltd, Buckie, UK for *Highland Regional Council* and used on the Fort William - Camusnagaul passenger-only service. In 2006 the service transferred to *Geoff Ward* under contract with a different vessel. In 2013 the CAILIN AN AISEAG resumed service with *Highland Ferries* as contractor. In April 2013 she as renamed the BHOY TAYLOR.

RENFREW ROSE Built by MacCrindle Shipbuilding Ltd, Ardrossan for *Strathclyde PTE* (later *Strathclyde Partnership for Transport*). Built as a small car ferry but operated passenger only between Renfrew and Yoker (apart from occasionally carrying ambulances in earlier days before they became too heavy). In March 2010 laid up. In June 2012 sold to *Arranmore Fast Ferries* for use as a passenger/car ferry. In June 2016 sold to *Highland Ferries* to reopen the Cromarty - Nigg service.

INISHBOFIN ISLAND DISCOVERY

THE COMPANY *Inishbofin Island Discovery Ltd* is an Irish Republic private sector Company.

MANAGEMENT Managing Director Pat Concannon.ETS Merré

ADDRESS Cloonamore, Inishbofin Island, Co Galway, Republic of Ireland.

TELEPHONE Administration and Reservations +353 (0)95 45819, Mobile +353 (0)86 1718829 and +353 (0)87 3667185

FAX +353 (0)95 45984.

INTERNET Email info@inishbofinferry.ie **Website** inishbofinislanddiscovery.com *(English)*

ROUTE OPERATED *Passenger Service* Cleggan, Co Galway - Inishbofin Island (30 mins, ***ISLAND ADVENTURE, ISLAND DISCOVERY***, ***ISLAND EXPLORER***; up to 3 per day. **Cargo Service** Cleggan, Co Galway - Inishbofin Island (30 mins, ***RAASAY***, 2 per week).

1p	ISLAND ADVENTURE	130t	94	10.9k	27.1m	250P	0C	0L	-	IR	8346553
2p	ISLAND DISCOVERY	107t	91	10.9k	25.0m	99P	0C	0L	-	IR	8650851
3p	ISLAND EXPLORER	-	99	10.9k	15.0m	72P	0C	0L	-	IR	
4	RAASAY	69t	76	8.0k	24.3m	12P	6C	1L -	B	IR	7340435

ISLAND ADVENTURE Built by Société des Ets Merré (SEEM.), Nort-sur-Erdr, France. Previously the JOLIE FRANCE II of Vedettes Jolie France, France. Acquired by Inishbofin Island Discovery Ltd in 2018 and renamed the ISLAND ADVENTURE.

ISLAND DISCOVERY Built by Arklow Marine Service, Arklow, Republic of Ireland.

ISLAND EXPLORER Built by Kingfisher Boats Previously the DINGLE BAY Acquired by *Inishbofin Island Discovery Ltd* in and renamed the ISLAND EXPLORER.

RAASAY Built by James Lamont & Co Ltd, Port Glasgow, UK for and used primarily on the Sconser (Skye) - Raasay service. In 1997 she was replaced by the LOCH STRIVEN, became a spare/relief vessel and inaugurated in October 2003 the winter service between Tobermory (Mull) and Kilchoan (Ardnamurchan). From summer 2016 operated as second vessel on Oban - Lismore route. In March 2018 withdrawn and sold to *Humphrey O'Leary* of Clare Island, Co Mayo. In August sold to *Inishbofin Island Discovery* to operate the cargo service. Number is Lloyds Number, not IMO.

ISLES OF SCILLY STEAMSHIP COMPANY

THE COMPANY *Isles of Scilly Steamship Company* is a British private sector company.

MANAGEMENT Chief Executive Officer Stuart Reid, **Marketing & Communications Manager** Sharon Sandercock.

ADDRESS *Scilly* PO Box 10, Hugh Town, St Mary's, Isles of Scilly TR21 0LJ, ***Penzance*** Steamship House, Quay Street, Penzance, Cornwall, TR18 4BZ.

TELEPHONE Administration & Reservations +44 (0) 1736 334220.

INTERNET Email sales@islesofscilly-travel.co.uk **Website** www.islesofscilly-travel.co.uk *(English)*,

ROUTES OPERATED *Passenger services:* Penzance - St Mary's (Isles of Scilly) (2 hrs 50 mins; ***SCILLONIAN III***; 1 per day), St Mary's - Tresco/St Martin's/St Agnes/Bryher; ***LYONESSE LADY, SWIFT LADY (inter-island boats)***; irregular), ***Freight service***: ***GRY MARITHA***; Freight from Penzance Monday, Wednesday and Fridays (weather dependant, all year round).

1F	GRY MARITHA	590t	81	10.5k	40.3m	6P	5C	1L	C	UK	8008462
2	LYONESSE LADY	40t	91	9.0k	15.5m	4P	1C	0L	AC	UK	
3	SCILLONIAN III	1346t	77	15.5k	67.7m	485P	5C	1L	C	UK	7527796
4F	SWIFT LADY	-	04	30.0k	8.4m	0P	0C	0L	-	UK	

GRY MARITHA Built by Moen Slip AS, Kolvereid, Norway for *Gjofor* of Norway. In design she is a coaster rather than a ferry. In 1990 she was sold to the *Isles of Scilly Steamship Company*. She operates a freight and passenger service all year (conveying most goods to and from the Islands). During the winter she provides the only sea service to the islands, the SCILLONIAN III being laid up.

LYONESSE LADY Built Lochaber Marine Ltd of Corpach, Fort William, Scotland, for inter-island ferry work.

SCILLONIAN III Built by Appledore Shipbuilders Ltd, Appledore, UK for the Penzance - St Mary's service. She operates from late March to November and is laid up in the winter. She is the last major conventional passenger/cargo ferry built for UK waters and probably Western Europe. Extensively refurbished during Winter 1998/99 and 2012/13. She can carry cars in her hold and on deck, as well as general cargo/perishables, boats, trailer tents and passenger luggage.

SWIFT LADY Stormforce 8.4 RIB (Rigid Inflatable Boat) built by Redbay Boats of Cushendall, Co Antrim, Northern Ireland for inter-island ferry work conveying mail and as back-up to the LYONESSE LADY.

MURPHY'S FERRY SERVICE

THE COMPANY *Murphy's Ferry Service* is privately operated.

MANAGEMENT Operator Brendan Murphy.

ADDRESS Lawrence Cove, Bere Island, Co Cork, Republic of Ireland.

TELEPHONE Landline + 353 (0)27 75988, **Mobile** +353 (0)87 2386095.

INTERNET Email info@murphysferry.com **Website** www.murphysferry.com *(English)*,

ROUTE OPERATED Castletownbere (Pontoon – 3 miles to east of town centre) – Bere Island (Lawrence Cove, near Rerrin) (20 mins; ***IKOM K***; up to 8 per day).

1	IKOM K	55t	99	10.0k	16.0m	60P	4C	1L	B	IR	

IKOM K Built by Arklow Marine Services, Arklow, Republic of Ireland for *Murphy's Ferry Service*.

RATHLIN ISLAND FERRY

THE COMPANY *Rathlin Island Ferry Ltd* is a UK private sector company owned by Ciarán and Mary O'Driscoll of County Cork, Republic of Ireland.

MANAGEMENT Managing Director Ciarán O'Driscoll.

ADDRESS Ballycastle Ferry Terminal, 18 Bayview Road, Ballycastle, County Antrim BT54 6BT.

TELEPHONE Administration & Reservations +44 (0)28 2076 9299.

INTERNET Email info@rathlinballycastleferry.com

Website www.rathlinballycastleferry.com *(English),*

ROUTE OPERATED Vehicle Ferry Ballycastle – Rathlin Island (45 min; ***SPIRIT OF RATHLIN***; up to 4 per day). **Passenger-only Fast Ferry** (20 min; ***RATHLIN EXPRESS***; up to 6 per day). The service is operated on behalf of the *Northern Ireland Department of Regional Development*.

1»p	RATHLIN EXPRESS	31t	09	18.0k	17.7m	98P	0C	0L	-	UK	
2	SPIRIT OF RATHLIN	105t	17	8.3k	25.0m	125P	5C	1L	B	UK	9780122

RATHLIN EXPRESS Built by Arklow Marine Services, Arklow, Republic of Ireland for *Rathlin Island Ferry Ltd*.

SPIRIT OF RATHLIN Built by Arklow Marine Services, Arklow, Irish Republic for *DRD (Northern Ireland)*, UK to replace the CANNA. Chartered to *Rathlin Island Ferry Ltd*.

SHANNON FERRY

THE COMPANY *Shannon Ferry Group Ltd* is a Republic of Ireland private company owned by eighteen shareholders on both sides of the Shannon Estuary.

MANAGEMENT Managing Director Eugene Maher.

ADDRESS Ferry Terminal, Killimer, County Clare, V15 FK09, Republic of Ireland.

TELEPHONE Administration +353 (0)65 9053124, **Reservations** Phone bookings not available; Online booking available at www.shannonferries.com

FAX Administration +353 (0)65 9053125, **Reservations** Fax bookings not available; Online booking available at www.shannonferries.com

INTERNET Email enquiries@shannonferries.com **Website** www.shannonferries.com *(English),*

ROUTE OPERATED Killimer (County Clare) – Tarbert (County Kerry) (20 mins; ***SHANNON BREEZE, SHANNON DOLPHIN***; hourly (half-hourly during June, July, August and September)).

1	SHANNON BREEZE	611t	00	10.0k	80.8m	350P	60C	-	BA	IR	9224910
2	SHANNON DOLPHIN	501t	95	10.0k	71.9m	350P	52C	-	BA	IR	9114933

SHANNON BREEZE, SHANNON DOLPHIN Built by Appledore Shipbuilders, Appledore, UK for *Shannon Ferry Group Ltd*.

SHERKIN ISLAND FERRY

THE COMPANY The *Sherkin Island Ferry* is privately operated in the Republic of Ireland.

MANAGEMENT Operator: Vincent O'Driscoll.

ADDRESS Sherkin Ferry, The Cove, Baltimore, Skibbereen, Co Cork, P81 RW71, Republic of Ireland.

Scillonian III *(Andrew Cooke)*

Strangford II *(Nick Widdows)*

TELEPHONE Administration +353 (0)87 244 7828. **Ferry Boat** +353 (0)87 911 7377.

INTERNET Email info@sherkinferry.com **Website** www.sherkinferry.com *(English)*

ROUTE OPERATED Passenger only Baltimore (Co Cork) – Sherkin Island (10 minutes; ***MYSTIC WATERS***; ***YOKER SWAN***; up to 10 per day). **Note:** No vehicle service advertised.

1p	MYSTIC WATERS	100t	72		19.8m	99P	0C	0L	-	IR	8943038
2	YOKER SWAN	65t	84		21.9m	50P	3C	0L	B	IR	

MYSTIC WATERS Built by Ryton Marine Ltd, Wallsend, UK as the FREDA CUNNINGHAM for *Tyne & Wear PTE* and operated between North Shields and South Shields. Withdrawn in 1993 and sold to *Tyne Towage Ltd*, Newcastle and renamed the ANYA DEV. Later sold and renamed the LADY LAURA. In 2006 sold to *Sherkin Island Ferry* and renamed the MYSTIC WATERS.

YOKER SWAN Built by MacCrindle Shipbuilding Ltd, Ardrossan for *Strathclyde PTE* (later *Strathclyde Partnership for Transport*). Built as a small car ferry but operated passenger only between Renfrew and Yoker (apart from carrying ambulances in earlier days before they became too heavy). In March 2010 laid up. Later sold to *Sherkin Island Ferry* for use as a passenger/car ferry. She is used as required to convey vehicles and freight to and from the island, and sometimes conveys passengers. No public vehicle service is advertised.

SKYE FERRY

THE COMPANY The *Skye Ferry* is owned by the *Isle of Skye Ferry Community Interest Company*, a company limited by guarantee.

MANAGEMENT Ferry Development Manager Jo Crawford.

ADDRESS 6 Coulindune, Glenelg, Kyle, Ross-shire IV40 8JU.

TELEPHONE Administration +44 (0)1599 522700. **Reservations** Not applicable.

INTERNET Email info@skyeferry.co.uk **Website** skyeferry.co.uk *(English),*

ROUTE OPERATED *Easter – October only* Glenelg – Kylerhea (Skye) (10 mins; ***GLENACHULISH***; frequent service).

1	GLENACHULISH	44t	69	9.0k	20.0m	12P	6C	-	BSt	UK

GLENACHULISH Built by Ailsa Shipbuilding Company, Troon, UK for the *Ballachulish Ferry Company* for the service between North Ballachulish and South Ballachulish, across the mouth of Loch Leven. In 1975 the ferry was replaced by a bridge and she was sold to *Highland Regional Council* and used on a relief basis on the North Kessock – South Kessock and Kylesku – Kylestrome routes. In 1983 she was sold to *Murdo MacKenzie*, who had operated the Glenelg – Skye route as ferryman since 1959. The vessel was eventually bought by *Roddy MacLeod* and the service resumed in September 1990. The *Isle of Skye Ferry Community Interest Company* reached agreement with *Mr MacLeod* that he would operate the ferry in 2006. In 2007 she was sold to the Company. During winter 2012 she was chartered to *The Highland Council* to operate between North and South Strome following a road closure due to a rock fall. She is the last turntable ferry in operation.

STRANGFORD LOUGH FERRY SERVICE

THE COMPANY The *Strangford Lough Ferry Service* is operated by the *DFI Transport NI*, a Northern Ireland Government Department (formerly operated by *Department of the Environment (Northern Ireland)*).

MANAGEMENT Ferry Manager Tim Tew.

ADDRESS Strangford Lough Ferry Service, The Slip, Strangford, Co Down BT30 7NE.

TELEPHONE Administration +44 0300 200 7898, **Reservations** Not applicable.

INTERNET Email Strangfordferry@infrastructure-ni.gov.uk

Website www.nidirect.gov.uk/strangford-ferry-timetable *(English),*

ROUTE OPERATED Strangford - Portaferry (County Down) (10 mins; ***PORTAFERRY II, STRANGFORD II***; half-hourly).

1	PORTAFERRY II	312t	01	12.0k	38.2m	260P	28C	-	BA	UK	9237436
2	STRANGFORD II	405t	16	12.0k	64.0m	260P	28C	-	BA	UK	9771561

PORTAFERRY II Built by McTay Marine, Bromborough, Wirral, UK for *DRD (Northern Ireland)*.

STRANGFORD II Built by Cammell Laird, Birkenhead for *DRD (Northern Ireland)*, UK to replace the STRANGFORD FERRY. Entered service February 2017.

C TOMS & SON LTD

THE COMPANY *C Toms & Son Ltd* is a British private sector company.

MANAGEMENT Managing Director Allen Toms.

ADDRESS East Street, Polruan, Fowey, Cornwall PL23 1PB.

TELEPHONE Administration +44 (0)1726 870232, **Reservations** Not applicable.

INTERNET Email enquiries@ctomsandson.co.uk **Website** www.ctomsandson.co.uk *(English)*

ROUTE OPERATED ***Car Ferry*** Fowey - Bodinnick (Cornwall) (5 mins; ***GELLAN, JENACK***; frequent), ***Passenger Ferry*** Fowey - Polruan (Cornwall) (5 mins; ***KALEY, LADY DIANA, LADY JEAN, THREE COUSINS***; frequent).

1	GELLAN	50t	03	4.5k	36.0m	50P	10C	-	BA	UK
2	JENACK	60t	00	4.5k	36.0m	50P	15C	-	BA	UK
3p	KALEY	7.6t	03	-	9.5m	48P	0C	-	-	UK
4p	LADY DIANA	-	81	-	8.2m	36P	0C	-	-	UK
5p	LADY JEAN	-	-	-	-	12P	0C	-	-	UK
6p	THREE COUSINS	-	14	-	-	12P	0C	-	-	UK

GELLAN, JENACK Built by C Toms & Sons Ltd, Fowey, UK.

KALEY, LADY DIANA, LADY JEAN, THREE COUSINS Built by C Toms & Sons Ltd, Fowey, UK.

VALENTIA ISLAND CAR FERRY

THE COMPANY *Valentia Island Car Ferry* is the trading name of *Valentia Island Ferries Ltd,* an Republic of Ireland private sector company.

MANAGEMENT Manager Richard Foran.

ADDRESS Valentia Island, County Kerry, Republic of Ireland.

TELEPHONE Administration +353 (0)87 168 3373, **Reservations** Not applicable.

FAX Administration +353 (0)66 76377, **Reservations** Not applicable.

INTERNET Email reforan@indigo.ie **Website** www.valentiaisland.ie/life-business/valentia-island-car-ferry/

ROUTE OPERATED Reenard (Co Kerry) - Knightstown (Valentia Island) (5 minutes; ***GOD MET ONS III***; frequent service, 1st April - 30th September).

1	GOD MET ONS III	95t	63	-	43.0m	95P	18C	-	BA	IR

GOD MET ONS III Built by BV Scheepswerven Vh HH Bodewes, Millingen, The Netherlands for *FMHE Res* of The Netherlands for a service across the River Maas between Cuijk and Middelaar. In 1987 a new bridge was opened and the service ceased. She was latterly used on contract work in the Elbe and then laid up. In 1996 acquired by *Valentia Island Ferries* and inaugurated a car ferry service to the island. **Note** This island never had a car ferry service before. A bridge was opened at the south end of the island in 1970; before that a passenger/cargo service operated between Reenard Point and Knightstown.

Ben Woollacott *(Nick Widdows)*

WOOLWICH FREE FERRY

THE COMPANY The *Woolwich Free Ferry* is operated by *Briggs Marine*, a British private sector company on behalf of *Transport for London*.

ADDRESS New Ferry Approach, Woolwich, London SE18 6DX.

TELEPHONE Administration +44 (0)20 8853 9400, **Reservations** Not applicable.

FAX Administration +44 (0)20 8316 6096, **Reservations** Not applicable.

INTERNET Website www.tfl.gov.uk/modes/river/woolwich-ferry *(English)*,

ROUTE OPERATED Woolwich - North Woolwich (free ferry) (5 mins; ***BEN WOOLLACOTT***, ***DAME VERA LYNN***; every 10 mins (weekdays - two ferries in operation), every 15 mins (weekends - one ferry in operation)).

1	BEN WOOLLACOTT	1538t	18	8.0k	62.2m	150P	42C	12L	BA	UK	9822011
2	DAME VERA LYNN	1539t	18	8.0k	62.2m	150P	42C	12L	BA	UK	9822023

BEN WOOLLACOTT, DAME VERA LYNN Built by Remontowa Shipbuilding, Gdansk, Poland. They are diesel electric battery hybrid vessels.

P&O
DFDS

SECTION 3 – GB & IRELAND – FREIGHT ONLY FERRIES

CLDN/COBELFRET FERRIES

THE COMPANIES *CLdN Cobelfret SA* is a Luxembourg private sector company. There are a number of subsidiary companies. *CLdN* stands for *Compagnie Luxembourgouise de Navigation*.

MANAGEMENT CLdN Ro-Ro SA (Luxembourg) Caroline Dubois, **CLdN ro-ro Agencies Ltd (UK)** Karla Fairway.

ADDRESSES ***Luxembourg*** **CLdN Cobelfret SA & CLdN ro-ro SA**, 3-7 rue Schiller, 2519 Luxembourg, ***UK*** CLdN ro-ro UK Ltd, Long Reach House, London Road, Purfleet, Essex RM19 1RP. ***Irish Republic*** CLdN ro-ro SA, Port Centre, 2nd Floor, Alexandra Road, Dublin Port, Dublin 1, D01 H4C6, Republic of Ireland.

TELEPHONE ***Luxembourg*** **CLdN Cobelfret SA** +352 (0)26 44 631, **CLdN ro-ro SA** +352 (0)26 44 661 ***UK*** +44 (0)1708 865522, ***Irish Republic*** +353 (0)1 856 1608.

FAX ***Luxembourg*** **CLdN Cobelfret SA** +352 (0)26 44 63 298, **CLdN ro-ro SA** +352 (0)26 44 66 299 ***UK*** +44 (0)1708 866419, ***Irish Republic*** +353 (0)1 704 0164.

INTERNET Email admin.roro@cldn.com **Website** www.cldn.com *(English)*

ROUTES OPERATED Cobelfret Ferries Services Zeebrugge - Purfleet (9 hrs; 2/3 per day), Zeebrugge - Killingholme (13 hrs; 6 per week), **CLdN Services** Rotterdam - Purfleet (14 hrs 30 mins); 6 per week), Rotterdam - Killingholme (14 hrs; 6 per week), Zeebrugge - Esbjerg (24hrs; 2 per week*), Zeebrugge - Dublin (35-41 hrs; 3 per week), Rotterdam - Dublin (41-47 hrs; 3 per week), Zeebrugge - Cork (35 hrs; 1 per week*), Rotterdam - Leixoes (Portugal) (64-69 hrs; 3 per week), Zeebrugge - Santander (50 hrs; 3 per week, Zeebrugge - Göteborg (32-33 hrs; 2 per week (joint service with *DFDS Seaways* providing four services per week; commercially they operate independently and buy capacity on each others ships), Dublin - Liverpool - Santander (Dublin -Santander 65 hrs, Liverpool - Santander 47 hrs). NOTE: Because vessels are so often moved between routes it is impossible to say which ro-ro vessels will be on which routes. *Note: One Zeebrugge - Esbjerg service per week operates to/from Cork. ***CLdN Container service*** Rotterdam - Dublin (43/47 hrs; ***ARX*** ; 1 per week).

Contract Services for Ford Motor Company Vlissingen - Dagenham (11 hrs; ***ADELINE, CELESTINE, UNDINE***; 2 per day).

1	ADELINE	21020t	12	15.8k	150.0m	12P	-	170T	A	MT	9539092
2	AMANDINE	33960t	11	18.5k	195.4m	12P	-	270T	A	MT	9424871
3	ARX	6901t	05	13.8k	139.8m	0P		707 TEU	C	MT	9328625
4	CAPUCINE	16342t	11	16.0k	150.0m	12P	-	140T	A	MT	9539066
5	CATHERINE	21287t	02	18.0k	182.2m	12P	-	200T	A2	MT	9209453
6	CELANDINE	23987t	00	17.9k	162.5m	12P	630C	157T	A	MT	9183984
7	CELESTINE	23986t	96	17.8k	162.5m	12P	630C	157T	A	MT	9125372
8	CELINE	74273t	17	17.9k	235.0m	12P	1600C	580T	A2	MT	9789233
9	CLEMENTINE	23986t	97	17.8k	162.5m	12P	630C	157T	A	BE	9125384
10	DELPHINE	74273t	18	17.9k	235.0m	12P	1600C	580T	A2	MT	9789245
11	HERMINE	50443t	19	17.6k	211.6m	12P	-	400T	A2	MT	9831177
12	LAURELINE	50443t	19	18.0k	212.0m	12P	-	400T	A	MT	9823352
13	MAZARINE	31340t	09	18.5k	195.4m	12P	-	250T	A	MT	9376696
14	MELEQ	32770t	17	21.0k	209.6m	12P	-	262T	A2	MT	9809112
15	MELUSINE	23987t	99	17.8k	162.5m	12P	630C	157T	A	BE	9166637
16	OPALINE	33960t	10	18.5k	195.4m	12P	-	270T	A	MT	9424869
17	PALATINE	31340t	09	18.5k	195.4m	12P	-	250T	A	MT	9376701
18	PAULINE	49166t	06	21.7k	200.0m	12P	656C	258T	A	MT	9324473
19	PEREGRINE	25593t	10	18.5k	195.4m	12P	-	180T	A	MT	9376725
20	SEVERINE	16342t	12	16.0k	150.0m	12P	-	140T	A	MT	9539078
21	SIXTINE	50443t	19	17.6k	211.6m	12P	-	400T	A2	MT	9831165
22	UNDINE	11854t	91	15.0k	147.4m	8P	350C	100T	A2	MT	9006112

Victorine *(Gordon Hislip)*

Mazarine *(Rob de Visser)*

23	VALENTINE	23987t	99	18.0k	162.5m	12P	630C	157T	A	BE	9166625
24	VESPERTINE	31340t	10	18.5k	195.4m	12P	-	250T	A	MT	9376713
25	VICTORINE	23987t	00	17.8k	162.5m	12P	630C	157T	A	BE	9184029
26	YASMINE	49166t	07	21.7k	200.0m	12P	656C	258T	A	MT	9337353
27	YSALINE	50443t	19	18.0k	212.0m	12P	-	400T	A	MT	9823364

ADELINE Built by the Kyokuyo Shipyard, Shimonoseki, Japan. After competition, an additional deck and sponsons were retro-fitted at the Chengxi Shipyard, Jiangyin, China.

AMANDINE Built by Flensburger Schiffbau-Gesellschaft, Flensburg, Germany. Operates mainly between Rotterdam and Killingholme and Rotterdam/Zeebrugge and Dublin.

ARX Container ship built as the LUPUS 1 by Detlef Hegemann Rolandwerft, Berne, Germany. In June 2005 chartered to *C2C Line* operating between Zeebrugge and Dublin and renamed the C2C LUPUS. In July 2007 renamed the C2C AUSTRALIS. In June 2010 purchased by an associated company of *CLdN* and renamed the ARX.

CAPUCINE, SEVERINE Built by the Kyokuyo Shipyard, Shimonoseki, Japan for *CLdN*. Initially operated on their Ipswich - Rotterdam service. This service was suspended in August 2012. In September, they were chartered to *Stena Line* and placed on the Harwich - Rotterdam service. Charter ended in January 2018. In February 2018 the CAPUCINE was chartered to the *Italian Ministry of Defence* and in June 2018 the SEVERINE was chartered to *GNV* of Italy. The SEVERINE returned in September 2018 and operated on *CLdN* services; in February 2020 she was chartered to *Grendi Trasporti Marittimi* of Italy to operate between Marina di Carrara, Porto Torres and Cagliari.

CATHERINE Built as the ROMIRA by Zhonghua Shipyard, Zhonghua, China for *Dag Engström Rederi* of Sweden. For six months engaged on a number of short-term charters, including *Cobelfret Ferries* who used her on both the Rotterdam - Immingham and Zeebrugge - Purfleet routes. In September 2002 purchased by *Cobelfret Ferries* and, in November 2002, renamed the CATHERINE and placed on the Rotterdam - Immingham service. In Spring 2003 chartered to the *US Defense Department* to convey materials to the Persian Gulf. Returned in late summer and operated thereafter on the Rotterdam - Immingham service. In January 2009 chartered to *CoTuNav* of Tunisia. In February 2010 returned to *Cobelfret* service and operated on the Rotterdam - Purfleet service. In March 2010 again chartered to *CoTuNav*. In March 2011 chartered to *RMR Shipping* to operate between Western Europe and Antwerpen, Eemshaven, Harwich and Dublin to Lagos (Nigeria). In May 2011 returned to *Cobelfret Ferries*. Now operates mainly on the Zeebrugge - Göteborg route.

CELANDINE, VALENTINE, VICTORINE Built by Kawasaki Heavy Industries, Sakaide, Japan for *Cobelfret*. The CELANDINE was originally to be called the CATHERINE and the VICTORINE the CELANDINE. The names were changed before delivery. In May 2011 the CELANDINE was chartered to *RMR Shipping*. Returned in November 2013.

CELESTINE Built by Kawasaki Heavy Industries, Sakaide, Japan as the CELESTINE. In 1996 chartered to the *British MoD* and renamed the SEA CRUSADER. She was originally expected to return to *Cobelfret Ferries* in early 2003 and resume the name CELESTINE; however, the charter was extended because of the Iraq war. Returned in September 2003 and placed on the Zeebrugge - Immingham service. In November 2006 moved to the Zeebrugge - Purfleet route. In November 2008 moved to the Oostende - Dartford service. In April 2009 the route became Oostende - Purfleet. In April 2010 chartered to *RMR Shipping*. In May 2014 returned to *Cobelfret Ferries* and in May 2016 transferred to the Dagenham - Vlissingen service.

CELINE, DELPHINE Built by Hyundai Mipo Dockyard, Ulsan, South Korea. They are convertible to LPG propulsion and designed to be useable on deep sea ro-ro services as well as *CLdN's* current short sea routes. They mainly operate between Zeebrugge and Killingholme and Zeebrugge and Dublin.

CLEMENTINE Built by Kawasaki Heavy Industries, Sakaide, Japan for *Cobelfret Ferries*. Mainly used on the Zeebrugge - Immingham service. In 2007 moved to the Zeebrugge - Purfleet route. In March 2013 chartered to *RMR Shipping*. In July 2013 chartered to *DFDS Seaways* and placed on the Immingham - Cuxhaven service. In November 2014 returned to *Cobelfret Ferries*. In January 2015 she retuned to charter with *DFDS Seaways* for four weeks.

HERMINE, LAURELINE, SIXTINE, YSALINE Built by Hyundai Mipo Dockyard, Ulsan, South Korea. Used on a variety of routes.

MAZARINE, PALATINE, PEREGRINE, VESPERTINE Built by Flensburger Schiffbau-Gesellschaft, Flensburg, Germany. Between Autumn 2019 and Spring 2019 an extra deck was added to the MAZARINE, PALATINE and VESPERTINE at Stocznia Remontowa, Gdansk, Poland, giving them the similar capacity to the AMANDINE and OPALINE. The extension of the PEREGRINE was deferred.

MELEQ Built by Flensburger Schiffbau-Gesellschaft, Flensburg, Germany for *Alternative Transport (Ekol)* of Turkey. In January 2019 chartered to *CLdN*. In January 2019 purchased by *CLdN* and re-flagged to Malta. May be renamed.

MELUSINE Built by Kawasaki Heavy Industries, Sakaide, Japan for *Cobelfret*. Similar to the CLEMENTINE.

OPALINE Built by Flensburger Schiffbau-Gesellschaft, Flensburg, Germany. Operates mainly between Rotterdam and Killingholme and Rotterdam and Dublin.

PAULINE, YASMINE Built by Flensburger Schiffbau-Gesellschaft, Flensburg, Germany to operate on the Zeebrugge - Killingholme route. They now operate mainly on the Rotterdam - Killingholme service.

UNDINE Built by Dalian Shipyard, Dalian, China for *Cobelfret Ferries*. Currently mainly used on the Dagenham - Vlissingen route. She was occasionally used on a weekend Southampton - Vlissingen service but this ceased in 2012 following the closure of the Southampton Ford Transit factory. Occasional weekend trips are made to Middlesbrough (Teesport).

CLdN also own the SOMERSET on charter to *Stena Line* and the WILHELMINE on charter to *P&O Ferries*.

Under Construction

28	NEWBUILDING 1	50443t	22	18.0k	212.0m	12P	-	400T	A	MT	9889708
29	NEWBUILDING 2	50443t	22	18.0k	212.0m	12P	-	400T	A	MT	9889710

NEWBUILDING 1, NEWBUILDING 2 Under construction by Hyundai Mipo Dockyard, Ulsan, South Korea. To be LNG powered.

FINNLINES

THE COMPANY *Finnlines PLC* is a Finnish private sector company owned by Grimaldi of Italy. Services to the UK are marketed by *Finnlines UK Ltd*, a British private sector company.

MANAGEMENT President & CEO Emanuele Grimaldi, **Head of Group Marketing, Sales and Customer Service, Line Manager Germany and North Sea ro-ro** Staffan Herlin.

ADDRESS *Finland* PO Box 197, 00181 Helsinki, Finland, ***UK*** Finnlines UK Ltd, Finhumber House, Queen Elizabeth Dock, Hedon Road, HULL HU9 5PB.

TELEPHONE Administration & Reservations *Finland* +358 (0)10 343 50, ***UK*** +44 (0)1482 377 655.

INTERNET *Email Finland* info.fi@finnlines.com ***UK*** info.uk@finnlines.com ***Website*** www.finnlines.com *(English, Finnish, German, Swedish, Russian)*

ROUTES OPERATED Irregular service from St Petersburg, Helsinki, Rauma and Kotka to Hull, Immingham, Amsterdam, Antwerpen and Bilbao. For details see website. In view of the fact that ships are liable to be transferred between routes, the following is a list of all Finnlines Cargo Service ro-ro vessels, including those which currently do not serve the UK. Ro-pax vessels on Baltic services are listed in Section 6.

1	FINNBREEZE	33816t	12	21.0k	217.8m	12P	600C	320T	A	FI	9468889
2	FINNHAWK	11530t	01	20.0k	162.2m	12P	-	140T	A	FI	9207895
3	FINNKRAFT	11530t	00	20.0k	162.2m	12P	-	140T	A	FI	9207883

4	FINNMASTER	12251t	98	20.0k	154.5m	12P	-	124T	A2	FI	9132014
5	FINNMERCHANT	23235t	03	21.0k	193.0m	12P	-	180T	A	FI	9234082
6	FINNMILL	25732t	02	20.0k	187.6m	12P	-	190T	A	FI	9212656
7	FINNPULP	25732t	02	20.0k	187.6m	12P	-	190T	A	FI	9212644
8	FINNSEA	33816t	12	21.0k	217.8m	12P	600C	320T	A	FI	9468891
9	FINNSKY	33816t	12	21.0k	217.8m	12P	600C	320T	A	FI	9468906
10	FINNSUN	33816t	12	21.0k	217.8m	12P	600C	320T	A	FI	9468918
11	FINNTIDE	33816t	12	21.0k	217.8m	12P	600C	320T	A	FI	9468920
12	FINNWAVE	33816t	12	21.0k	217.8m	12P	600C	320T	A	FI	9468932
13	FIONIA SEA	25609t	09	20.0k	184.8m	12P	-	250T	AS	UK	9395343

FINNBREEZE, FINNSEA, FINNSKY, FINNSUN, FINNTIDE, FINNWAVE Built by Jinling Shipyard, Nanjing, China for *Finnlines*. The vessels were lengthened by approximately 30 metres at Remontowa Shipyard, Gdansk, Poland between November 2017 and December 2018.

FINNHAWK Built by Jinling Shipyard, Nanjing, China for the *Macoma Shipping Group* and chartered to *Finnlines*. In April 2008 purchased by *Finnlines*. Currently operates used on service between Finland and The Netherlands, Belgium, the UK and Spain.

FINNKRAFT Built by Jinling Shipyard, Nanjing, China for the *Macoma Shipping Group* and chartered to *Finncarriers*. In April 2008 purchased by *Finnlines*. Currently operates on services between Finland and Germany.

FINNMASTER Built as the UNITED TRADER by Fosen Mekaniske Verksteder A/S, Rissa, Norway for *United Shipping* (a subsidiary of *Birka Shipping*) of Finland and chartered to *Transfennica*. During 2000 used on their Kemi - Oulu - Antwerpen - Felixstowe service. In 2001 the route was transferred to *Finnlines* and the vessels used sub-chartered to them (charter later transferred to *Finnlines*). In 2002 *United Shipping* was renamed *Birka Cargo* and she was renamed the BIRKA TRADER. In 2006 the service ceased and she was transferred to other *Finnlines* routes. In 2008 the charter was extended a further four years. In January 2013 chartered to *Transfennica*. In July 2013 renamed the TRADER. In January 2015 sold to *Finnlines* but not delivered until the end of the year, when the charter ended. In January 2016 renamed the FINNMASTER. In November 2016 chartered to *DFDS Seaways*. Operated mainly between Immingham and Rotterdam. In July 2017 charter ended and she returned to *Finnlines*, operating on a new service between Oxelösund (Sweden) and Naantali (Finland). Now used on all *Finnlines* services.

FINNMERCHANT Built as the LONGSTONE by Flensburger Schiffbau-Gesellschaft, Flensburg, Germany for *AWSR Shipping* (later Foreland Shipping). Chartered to *Transfennica* and operated between Hanko (Finland) and Lübeck (Germany). In January 2009 chartered to *Finnlines* and placed on the Helsinki - Aarhus route. In January 2012 chartered to *North Sea RoRo*. In March 2013 the operation ceased and the charter was taken over by *DFDS Seaways* and she was placed on the Immingham - Cuxhaven route. In May took over the Zeebrugge - Rosyth route. In October 2013 sold to *C Bulk NV* of Belgium, an associated company of *CLdN/Cobelfret Ferries*. In April 2014 charter to *DFDS* ended and she was chartered to an Australian operator. In November 2014 renamed the DORSET. In December 2014 the charter ended and she returned to *CLdN*. In early January 2015 placed on the Zeebrugge - Purfleet service. Later in the month sold to *Finnlines* and renamed the FINNMERCHANT.

FINNMILL, FINNPULP Built by Jinling Shipyard, Nanjing, China for the *Macoma Shipping Group* and chartered to *Finnlines*. In 2008 purchased by *Finnlines*. During Winter 2008/09 extra ramps were added at STX Europe Helsinki shipyard to enable ro-ro traffic to be conveyed on the weather deck.

FIONIA SEA Built as the TOR FIONIA by Jinling Shipyard, Nanjing, China for *Macoma Shipping Ltd* of the UK. Launched as the JINGLING 3. She was time-chartered to *DFDS Tor Line* for ten years (with an option on a further three). Delivered in May 2009 and initially replaced the TOR BEGONIA, TOR FICARIA and TOR FREESIA while they were being lengthened. In October 2011 renamed the FIONIA SEAWAYS. Charter ended at the end of January 2020. In February 2020 renamed the FIONIA SEA and chartered to *Finnlines*.

Under construction

14	FINNECO I	64000t	21	-	238.0m	12P	-	410T	A	FI	-
15	FINNECO II	64000t	22	-	238.0m	12P	-	410T	A	FI	-
16	FINNECO III	64000t	22	-	238.0m	12P	-	410T	A	FI	-

FINNECO I, FINNECO II, FINNECO III Grimaldi Green 5th Generation (GG5G) Class hybrid vessels under construction by Jinling Shipyard, Nanjing, China. As well as the trailer deck capacity, there will be 5,600 square metres of car decks and space for 300 TEU of containers on the weather deck.

MANN LINES

THE COMPANY *Mann Lines* are owned by *Mann & Son (London) Ltd* of Great Britain.

MANAGEMENT CEO Bill Binks, **General Manager (UK)** David Brooks.

ADDRESS Mann & Son (London) Ltd, The Naval House, Kings Quay Street, Harwich CO12 3JJ.

TELEPHONE Administration & Reservations *UK* +44 (0)1255 245200, ***Germany*** +49 (0)421 1638 50, ***Finland*** +358 (0)2 275 0000, ***Estonia*** +372 (0)679 1450.

FAX Administration & Reservations *UK* +44 (0)1255 245219, ***Germany*** + 49 (0)421 1638 520, ***Finland*** +358 (0)2 253 5905, ***Estonia*** +372 (0)679 1455.

INTERNET Email enquiry@manngroup.co.uk **Website** www.mannlines.com *(English, Finnish, Estonian, German, Russian)*

ROUTES OPERATED Harwich (Navyard) - Rotterdam - Cuxhaven (Germany) - Paldiski (Estonia) - Turku (Finland) - Bremerhaven (Germany) - Harwich (***ML FREYJA***; weekly).

1	ML FREYJA	23000t	17	19.0k	190.8m	12P	-	180T	A	IT	9799977

ML FREYJA Built by CN Visentini, Donada, Italy and chartered to *Mann Lines*. In June 2017 sub-chartered to *SOL Continent Line* for six months. In December 2017 entered service with *Mann Lines*.

NEPTUNE LINES

THE COMPANY *Neptune Lines Shipping & Managing Enterprises SA* is Greek company operating throughout Europe.

ADDRESS 5-9 Iassonos Street, GR - 18537 Piraeus, Greece.

TELEPHONE +30 210 45 57 700.

FAX +30 210 42 83 858.

INTERNET Website www.neptunelines.com *(English)*

ROUTES OPERATED (Northern Europe only) *Circuit 1* Santander - Rosslare - Portbury - Zeebrugge - Le Havre - Southampton, ***Circuit 2*** Santander - Portbury - Zeebrugge - Le Havre - Southampton.

1	NEPTUNE AEGLI	21611t	02	20.0k	158.0m	12P	1500C	104T	AQ	MT	9240964
2	NEPTUNE DYNAMIS	21611t	02	20.0k	158.0m	12P	1500C	104T	AQ	MT	9240976
3	NEPTUNE GALENE	37692t	14	19.3k	169.6m	0P	3800C	56T	AQ	GR	9668491
4	NEPTUNE ILIAD	36825t	10	19.3k	169.6m	0P	3800C	56T	AQ	MT	9440100
5	NEPTUNE ITHAKI	36902t	10	19.3k	169.6m	0P	3800C	56T	AQ	MT	9440083
6	NEPTUNE KEFALONIA	36902t	09	19.3k	169.6m	0P	3800C	56T	AQ	MT	9438717
7	NEPTUNE ODYSSEY	36902t	10	19.3k	169.6m	0P	3800C	56T	AQ	MT	9440095
8	NEPTUNE THALASSA	37692t	14	19.3K	169.6m	0P	3800C	56T	AQ	MT	9668506

NEPTUNE AEGLI Built by Barreras Shipyard, Vigo, Spain. Retractable mezzanine decks mean she can operate as a car carrier or a ro-ro freight ferry winter 2017 she operated for *P&O Ferries* during the refit period between Hull and Zeebrugge in order to maintain a daily freight service.

Misida *(Gordon Hislip)*

Neptune Aegli *(John Bryant)*

NEPTUNE DYNAMIS As NEPTUNE AEGLI. In winters 2018, 2019 and 2020 she operated for *P&O Ferries* during the refit period between Hull and Zeebrugge in order to maintain a daily freight service.

NEPTUNE GALENE NEPTUNE ILIAD, NEPTUNE ITHAKI, NEPTUNE KEFALONIA, NEPTUNE ODYSSEY, NEPTUNE THALASSA Built by Built by Hyundai Mipo Dockyard, Ulsan, South Korea.

SEA-CARGO

THE COMPANY *Sea-Cargo AS* of Norway is a subsidiary of *Seatrans AS* of Norway.

MANAGEMENT Managing Director Ole Saevild, **Director Business Development** Erik A Paulsen, **General Manager (Immingham)** Mark Brighton, **General Manager (Aberdeen)** Ian Shewan.

ADDRESS *Norway* Wernersholmvegen 5, 5232 Paradis, Norway, ***Immingham*** Sea-Cargo UK, West Riverside Road, Immingham Dock, Immingham DN40 2NT, ***Aberdeen*** Sea-Cargo Aberdeen Ltd, Matthews Quay, Aberdeen Harbour, Aberdeen, AB11 5PG.

TELEPHONE Administration & Bookings *Bergen* +47 55 10 84 84, ***Immingham*** +44 (0)1469 577119, ***Aberdeen*** +44 (0)1224 596481.

FAX Administration & Reservations *Bergen* +47 85 02 82 16, ***Immingham*** 44 (0)1469 577708, ***Aberdeen*** +44 (0)1224 582360.

INTERNET Email mail@sea-cargo.no **Website** www.sea-cargo.no *(English)*

ROUTES OPERATED *Sea-Cargo* operate a network of services from West Norway to Amsterdam, Aberdeen, Immingham and Esbjerg. The schedule varies from week to week and is shown on the company website. The ***SC AHTELA*** is generally used on the twice-weekly Immingham - Tanager, Haugesund, Bergen and Odda service and the ***SEA-CARGO EXPRESS*** on the weekly Aberdeen - Tanager, Haugesund, Bergen, Florø, Ålesund, Kristiansund, Trondheim and Molde service.

1	BORE BAY	10572t	96	20.0k	138.8m	12P	-	105T	A2	FI	9122007
2	MISANA	14100t	07	20.0k	163.9m	12P	-	150T	A	FI	9348936
3	MISIDA	14100t	07	20.0k	163.9m	12P	-	150T	A	FI	9348948
4	SC AHTELA	8610t	91	14.8k	139.5m	12P	-	92T	AS	MT	8911736
5	SC ASTREA	9528t	91	13.5k	129.1m	0p	-	58T	A	BS	8917895
6	SC CONNECTOR	12251t	97	15.0k	154.5m	12P	-	124T	AS	MT	9131993
7	SEA-CARGO EXPRESS	6693t	12	16.0k	117.4m	0P	-	35T	A	MT	9358060
8	TRANS CARRIER	9953t	94	14.5k	144.5m	0P	-	94T	AS	BS	9007879

BORE BAY Built as the HERALDEN by Umoe Sterkoder AS, Kristiansund, Norway for *Rederi AB Engship* of Finland and chartered to *Transfennica*. In 2006 *Rederi AB Engship* was taken over by *Rettig Group Bore*. In 2007 converted at COSCO Shipyard, Nantong, China to add a garage on top of the weather deck, renamed AUTO BAY and placed on long-term charter to *UECC*. Generally used on the Baltic or Iberian services. In 2017 converted back to conventional ro-ro format by Fayard, Odense, Denmark and renamed the BORE BAY. Chartered to *Grandi Navi Veloci (GNV)* of Italy. In February 2018 chartered to *Transfennica*. From April to August 2018 chartered to *Stena Line* to operate between, Gdynia and Nynäshamn. From August 2019 until December 2019 chartered to *Brittany Ferries* to replace the MN PELICAN which was undergoing a major refit. In January 2020 chartered to *Sea-Cargo*.

MISANA Built by J J Sietas, Hamburg, Germany for *Godby Shipping AB* of Finland and time-chartered to *UPM-Kymmene* of Finland to operate between Finland, Spain and Portugal. In July 2013 charter taken over by *Finnlines*. In January 2016 long-term chartered to *Stena RoRo*, who then sub-chartered them to *Transfennica*. In January 2018 sub-chartered to *Stena Line* and placed on the Harwich - Rotterdam service. In March 2020 charter ended. Laid up. In August 2020 chartered to *Sea-Cargo*.

MISIDA Until January 2020 as MISANA. In January 2020 charter ended. Chartered to *DFDS Seaways* for two weeks operating on the Vlaardingen - Immingham and Esbjerg - Immingham routes. In February chartered to *CoTuNav* of Tunisia to operate between Rades and Marseille. Charter terminated in April and laid -up. In July 2020 chartered to *P&O Ferries* to operate between Liverpool and Dublin. In October 2020 to be chartered to *Sea-Cargo*.

SC AHTELA Built as the AHTELA by Brodogradiliste "Sava", Macvanska Mitrovica, Yugoslavia, completed by Fosen Mekaniske Verksteder, Rissa, Norway for *Rederi AB Gustav Erikson* of Finland. Chartered to *Transfennica*. In 1995 chartered to *DFDS Tor Line*. In 1996 chartered to *Finncarriers Oy* of Finland and in 1997 renamed the FINNOAK. In 1998, extended in Klaipėda, Lithuania by 17 metres. In 2007 sold to *Hollming Oy* of Finland and in 2008 the charter ended and she was renamed the AHTELA. Chartered to *Navirail* of Estonia to operate between Helsinki and Muuga (Estonia). Between February and May 2011 chartered to *Sea-Cargo* to operate between Esbjerg (Denmark) and Egersund (Norway). In October 2012 purchased by *Sea-Cargo* and renamed the SC AHTELA.

SC ASTREA Built as the ASTREA by Tangen Verft Kragerø A/S, Kragerø, Norway for *Finncarriers* of Finland. Operated between Finland and Spain - Portugal via Antwerpen. In 2006 chartered to *Danish MoD*. In 2007 chartered to *Sea-Cargo*. In August 2011 purchased by *Sea-Cargo* and renamed the SC ASTREA. Until early 2016 used primarily for moving windfarm equipment. In February placed on the Norway - Immingham service.

SC CONNECTOR Built as the UNITED EXPRESS by Fosen Mekaniske Verksteder A/S, Rissa, Norway for *United Shipping* (a subsidiary of *Birka Shipping*) of Finland and chartered to *Transfennica*. During 2000 used on their Kemi - Oulu - Antwerpen - Felixstowe service. In 2001 the route was transferred to *Finnlines* and the vessel used sub-chartered to them (charter later transferred to *Finnlines*). In 2002 *United Shipping* was renamed *Birka Cargo* and she was renamed the BIRKA EXPRESS. In 2008 the charter was extended a further four years. In June 2013 renamed the EXPRESS. In November 2013 chartered to *Transfennica*. In April 2014 sold to *Sea-Cargo* but initially continued to operate for *Transfennica*. During winter 2015 re-engined and modified to allow to side loading. In February 2015 renamed the SC CONNECTOR. Entered service in late April.

SEA-CARGO EXPRESS One of two vessels ordered in 2005 from Bharati Ratnagiri Ltd, Mumbai, India for *Sea-Cargo*. The order for the second ship was cancelled. Trailers are carried on the main deck only. Containers are carried on the weather deck and pallets on the lower decks. A crane is provided for the containers and a side door for pallets. She operates on the Aberdeen - Norway service.

TRANS CARRIER Built as the KORSNÄS LINK by Brodogradiliste Kraljevica, Kraljevica, Croatia for *SeaLink AB* of Sweden and due to be time-chartered to *Korsnäs AB*, a Swedish forest products company. However, due to the war in Croatia, delivery was seriously delayed and she was offered for sale. In 1994 sold to the *Swan Group* and renamed the SWAN HUNTER. She was placed on the charter market. In 1997 she was chartered to *Euroseabridge* and renamed the PARCHIM. In 1999 the charter ended and she resumed the name SWAN HUNTER. In 1999 she was sold to *SeaTrans* and renamed the TRANS CARRIER. She operated for *Sea-Cargo*. In 2005 chartered to *Finnlines* and used on the Finland to Spain/Portugal service. In 2006 returned to *Sea-Cargo*. In January and February 2009 lengthened by 18.9 metres in Poland.

SEATRUCK FERRIES

THE COMPANY *Seatruck Ferries Ltd* is a British private sector company. It is part of the *Clipper Group*.

MANAGEMENT Chairman Peter Lybecker, **CEO** Alistair Eagles.

ADDRESSES *Heysham (HQ)* North Quay, Heysham Port, Heysham, Morecambe, Lancs LA3 2UH, ***Warrenpoint*** Seatruck House, The Ferry Terminal, Warrenpoint, County Down BT34 3JR, ***Liverpool:*** Seatruck Ferry Terminal, Brocklebank Dock, Port of Liverpool, L20 1DB, ***Dublin***: Seatruck Dublin, Terminal 5, Alexandra Road, Dublin 1 Irish Republic.

TELEPHONE Administration +44 (0)1524 855377, **Reservations *Heysham*** +44 (0)1524 853512. ***Warrenpoint*** +44 (0)28 754400, ***Liverpool*** + (0)151 9333660, ***Dublin*** + (0) 353 18230492.

FAX Administration +44 (0)28 4175 4545, **Reservations *Warrenpoint*** +44 (0)28 4177 3737, ***Heysham*** +44 (0)1524 853549.

INTERNET Email aje@seatruckgroup.co.uk **Website** www.seatruckferries.com *(English)*

ROUTES OPERATED Heysham - Warrenpoint (9 hrs; ***SEATRUCK PERFORMANCE, SEATRUCK PRECISION***; 2 per day), Heysham - Dublin (9 hrs; ***CLIPPER POINT***; 1 per day), Liverpool - Dublin (9 hrs;, ***SEATRUCK PACE, SEATRUCK PANORAMA, SEATRUCK POWER, SEATRUCK PROGRESS***; up to 4 per day).

1	CLIPPER POINT	14759t	08	22.0k	142.0m	12P	-	120T	A	CY	9350666
2	SEATRUCK PACE	14759t	09	22.0k	142.0m	12P	-	120T	A	CY	9350678
3	SEATRUCK PANORAMA	14759t	09	22.0k	142.0m	12P	-	120T	A	CY	9372676
4	SEATRUCK PERFORMANCE	19722t	12	21.0k	142.0m	12P	-	151T	A	IM	9506227
5	SEATRUCK POWER	19722t	11	21.0k	142.0m	12P	-	151T	A	IM	9506215
6	SEATRUCK PRECISION	19722t	12	21.0k	142.0m	12P	-	151T	A	IM	9506239
7	SEATRUCK PROGRESS	19722t	11	21.0k	142.0m	12P	-	151T	A	IM	9506203

CLIPPER POINT Built by Astilleros de Huelva SA, Huelva, Spain for *Seatruck Ferries*. In May 2012 chartered to *DFDS Seaways* and placed on the Immingham-Cuxhaven route. In April 2013 chartered to the organisers of the 'SATA Rally Azores 2013' car rally to take cars from Portugal to the Azores. In May began operating for *DFDS Seaways* in the Baltic. In October transferred to the Immingham - Cuxhaven route. In June 2015 the charter ended. In July she was chartered to *InterShipping*, of Morocco to operate between Algeciras and Tangiers. In September 2016 the charter ended and she returned to *Seatruck Ferries*.

SEATRUCK PACE Built as the CLIPPER PACE by Astilleros Sevilla SA, Sevilla, Spain for *Seatruck Ferries*. In March 2012 renamed the SEATRUCK PACE. In January 2013 chartered to *Blue Water Shipping* of Denmark to carry wind turbine parts between Mostyn (Wales) and Esbjerg. Now operates on the Liverpool - Dublin route.

SEATRUCK PANORAMA Built by Astilleros de Huelva SA, Huelva Spain for *Seatruck Ferries*. Launched as the CLIPPER PENNANT and renamed the CLIPPER PANORAMA before delivery. In December 2011 renamed the SEATRUCK PANORAMA.

SEATRUCK PERFORMANCE Built as the SEATRUCK PERFORMANCE by Flensburger Schiffbau-Gesellschaft, Flensburg, Germany for *Seatruck Ferries*. In September 2012 chartered to *Stena Line* and renamed the STENA PERFORMER. She operated on both the Heysham - Belfast and Birkenhead - Belfast services. In August 2018 returned to *Seatruck Ferries*, renamed the SEATRUCK PERFORMANCE and placed on the Heysham - Warrenpoint service.

SEATRUCK POWER, SEATRUCK PROGRESS Built by Flensburger Schiffbau-Gesellschaft, Flensburg, Germany for *Seatruck Ferries*.

SEATRUCK PRECISION Built as the SEATRUCK PRECISION by Flensburger Schiffbau-Gesellschaft, Flensburg, Germany for *Seatruck Ferries*. In September 2012 chartered to *Stena Line* and renamed the STENA PRECISION. She operated on the Heysham - Belfast service. In September 2015 moved to the Birkenhead - Belfast route. In August 2018 returned to *Seatruck Ferries*, renamed the SEATRUCK PRECISION and placed on the Heysham - Warrenpoint service.

Seatruck Ferries also own the ARROW, currently on charter to *Isle of Man Steam Packet Company* and the CLIPPER PENNANT, currently on charter to *P&O Ferries*.

FLOTA SUARDIAZ

THE COMPANY *Flota Suardiaz SL* is owned by *Grupo Suardiaz,* a Spanish private sector logistics company which operates divisions in ports, bunkering, warehousing, haulage, freight forwarding and shipping.

MANAGEMENT Presidente Don Juan Riva, **Director General** Alfredo Menendez Garcia.

ADDRESSES Spain Calle Ayala, 6 28001 Madrid, Spain, **UK** Suardiaz Shipping Ltd, Suardiaz House, 193 Shirley Road, Southampton SO15 3FG.

TELEPHONE Spain +34 914 31 66 40, **UK** +44 (0) 2380 211 981.

FAX Spain + 34 914 36 46 74, **UK** +44 (0) 2380 335309.

INTERNET Email infoweb@suardiaz.com, **Website** www.suardiaz.com *(English, Spanish).*

ROUTES OPERATED Northern Europe/Spain/Canaries/Med Lines Emden - Sheerness - Zeebrugge - Santander - Vigo - Las Palmas - Tenerife - Casablanca - Mostaganem - Barcelona (weekly with up to two sailings per week on some sections including Emden - Sheerness and Las Palmas - Tenerife - Barcelona). **Atlantic Line** Zeebrugge - St Nazaire - Vigo - Tanger Med (twice weekly with St Nazaire - Vigo four sailings per week). **Algeria Line** Barcelona - Marseille - Alger - Mostagenem (weekly).

Services listed carry unaccompanied ro-ro cargo together with large volumes of trade cars for vehicle manufacturers and distributors and interwork between routes. Occasional irregular calls are made at North Shields, Vlissingen, Le Havre and Southampton and sailings can sometimes omit scheduled ports. The Atlantic Line is operated with European Union funding from the TEN-T Programme and supported by a GEFCO car carrying contract between St Nazaire and Vigo. Vessels are regularly transferred between routes and are often chartered out for short periods to other operators and vehicle manufacturers. In view of this, the following is a list of all vessels in the *Flota Suardiaz* fleet including those not currently serving the UK.

1	BOUZAS	15224t	02	18.5k	149.4m	12P	1265C	105T	A	ES	9249996
2	GALICIA	16361t	03	15.0k	149.4m	12P	1390C	110T	A	PT	9268409
3	GRAN CANARIA CAR	9600t	01	18.0k	132.5m	0P	1150C	42T	AS	PT	9218014
4	IVAN	8191t	96	14.6k	102.5m	0P	853C	73T	A	PT	9112040
5	L'AUDACE	15222t	99	18.5k	149.4m	12P	1233C	105T	A	ES	9187318
6	LA SURPRISE	15222t	00	18.5k	149.4m	12P	1233C	105T	A	PT	9198719
7	SUAR VIGO	16361t	03	18.5k	149.4m	12P	1356C	110T	A	ES	9250000
8	TENERIFE CAR	13122t	02	20.0k	149.4m	12P	1354C	54T	AS	PT	9249984
9	VIKING CONSTANZA	20216t	09	18.0k	139.9m	0P	2000C	65T	AQR	SG	9407689

BOUZAS, GALICIA, L'AUDACE, LA SURPRISE, SUAR VIGO Built by Hijos de J. Barreras SA, Vigo, Portugal for *Flota Suardiaz* of Spain for use on services in the Mediterranean and to the Canaries, U.K. and Benelux. The vessels are highly flexible with a 12-driver capacity and three full height freight decks, each fitted with a mezzanine deck for cars, together with a further dedicated car deck. In addition to operating for *Flota Suardiaz* a number of vessels have spent periods on charter to *UECC*. The L'AUDACE was chartered to *P&O Ferries* to operate between Hull and Zeebrugge in early 2015. Since early 2017 she has been on charter to *Priority Ro-Ro Services* in the Caribbean sailing between Santo Domingo, Dominican Republic and San Juan, Puerto Rico.

GRAN CANARIA CAR Built as HARALD FLICK by Hijos de J. Barreras SA, Vigo, Portugal for *Naviera del Odiel*, one of the shareholders in Barreras and placed on 10 year charter to *Flota Suardiaz* of Spain for use on services in the Mediterranean and to the Canaries, U.K. and Benelux. Renamed GRAN CANARIA CAR before entering service. In 2008 ownership passed to *Navicar SA* a subsidiary of *Flota Suardiaz*. In addition to operating for *Flota Suardiaz* has been chartered to *UECC* on several occasions.

IVAN Built by Astilleros De Murueta, Vizcaya, Spain for *Adamastor - Sociedade de Navegação, Lda* a subsidiary of *Flota Suardiaz* for use on short sea services. For many years she operated a now ceased service from Sheerness and Grimsby to Calais.

TENERIFE CAR Built by Hijos de J. Barreras SA, Vigo, Portugal for *Navicar SA* a subsidiary of *Flota Suardiaz* for use on services in the Mediterranean and to the Canaries, UK and Benelux.

VIKING CONSTANZA Built by Kyokuyo Shipyard Corporation, Japan for *Gram Car Carriers*, Norway for operation on the charter market as part of a series of four vessels. Of short sea PTCC design the vessels have both stern and quarter ramps. In 2015 chartered by *UECC*. In 2017 chartered by *Suardiaz*.

Finnsky *(John Bryant)*

Seatruck Power *(Andrew Cooke)*

TRANSFENNICA

THE COMPANY *Transfennica Ltd* is a Finnish private sector company wholly owned by *Spliethoff Bevrachtingskantoor* of The Netherlands.

MANAGEMENT Managing Director Dirk P. Witteveen, **Sales Director (UK)** Andrew Clarke.

ADDRESSES *Finland* Eteläranta 12, 00130 Helsinki, Finland, ***UK*** Finland House, 47 Berth, Tilbury Port, Tilbury, Essex RM18 7EH.

TELEPHONE Administration & Reservations *Finland* +358 (0)9 13262, ***UK*** +44 (0)1375 363 900.

FAX Administration & Reservations *Finland* +358 (0)9 652377, ***UK*** +44 (0)1375 840 888.

INTERNET Email *Finland* info@transfennica.com ***UK*** info.uk@transfennica.com

Website www.transfennica.com *(English, Finnish, Russian)*

ROUTES OPERATED Tilbury (weekly) to various destinations in Finland and Russia. Please see the website. All *Transfennica* ships are listed below as ships are sometimes moved between routes.

1	BORE SEA	25586t	11	18.5k	195.0m	12P	-	210T	A2	NL	9443554
2	CORONA SEA	25609t	08	20.0k	184.8m	12P	-	250T	AS	UK	9357597
3	GENCA	28301t	07	22.0k	205.0m	12P	-	200T	A2	NL	9307372
4	HAFNIA SEA	25609t	08	20.0k	184.8m	12P	-	250T	AS	UK	9357602
5	KRAFTCA	28301t	06	22.0k	205.0m	12P	-	200T	A2	NL	9307360
6	PLYCA	28301t	09	22.0k	205.0m	12P	-	200T	A2	NL	9345398
7	PULPCA	28301t	08	22.0k	205.0m	12P	-	200T	A2	NL	9345386
8	SEAGARD	10488t	99	21.0k	153.5m	12P	-	134T	A2	FI	9198977
9	TIMCA	28301t	06	22.0k	205.0m	12P	-	200T	A2	NL	9307358
10	TRICA	28301t	07	22.0k	205.0m	12P	-	200T	A2	NL	9307384

BORE SEA Built by Flensburger Schiffbau-Gesellschaft, Flensburg, Germany for *Bore Shipowners (Rettig Group Bore)* of Finland. In May 2011 chartered to *Transfennica* and operated between Zeebrugge and Bilbao. In January 2013 chartered for three years to *Fret Cetam* of France and used for the conveyance of parts for Airbus aircraft. In September 2016 chartered to *CLdN/Cobelfret Ferries*. Initially used mainly on the Zeebrugge – Purfleet service but later also used on the Iberian routes. In January 2018 chartered to *Transfennica*.

CORONA SEA Built as the TOR CORONA by Jinling Shipyard, Nanjing, China for *Macoma Shipping Ltd* of the UK and time-chartered to *DFDS Tor Line* for ten years. Used on the Fredericia – København – Klaipėda service. In April 2012 renamed the CORONA SEAWAYS. In January 2018 chartered to *Transfennica* and, in February, renamed the CORONA SEA.

GENCA, KRAFTCA, PLYCA, PULPCA, TIMCA, TRICA Built by New Szczecin Shipyard (SSN), Szczecin, Poland for *Spliethoff Bevrachtingskantoor*, owners of *Transfennica*.

HAFNIA SEA Built as the TOR HAFNIA by Jinling Shipyard, Nanjing, China for *Macoma Shipping Ltd* of the UK and time-chartered to *DFDS Tor Line* for ten years. Until 2013, mainly operated on the Immingham – Esbjerg route. In March 2011 renamed the HAFNIA SEAWAYS. In January 2015 chartered to *Cobelfret Ferries* for four weeks. In January 2018 chartered to *Transfennica* and in March 2018 renamed the HAFNIA SEA.

SEAGARD Built by J J Sietas KG, Hamburg, Germany for *Bror Husell Chartering* of Finland (later acquired by *Bore Shipowning* of Finland) and chartered to *Transfennica*.

UECC

THE COMPANY *United European Car Carriers AS* is a Norwegian private sector company jointly owned in equal shares by *Nippon Yusen Kabushiki Kaisha (NYK)* of Japan and *Wallenius Lines* of Sweden. *UECC* consists of companies in Norway, Germany, Spain, France, Portugal and the UK. The fleet technical and ship management department is based in Grimsby (UK).

MANAGEMENT Chief Executive Officer Glenn Edvardsen.

ADDRESSES Norway Karenlyst Allè 57, 0277 Oslo, **UK** Units 5B & 5C Appian Way, Europa Park, Grimsby, DN31 2UT.

TELEPHONE Norway +47 21 00 98 00, **UK** +44 (0)1472 269429.

FAX Norway +47 21 00 98 01, **UK** +44 (0)207 628 2858.

INTERNET Email marketing@uecc.com, **Website** www.uecc.com *(English)*.

ROUTES OPERATED

Atlantic Service Vigo - Le Havre - Zeebrugge - Sheerness - Portbury - Vigo (***HOEGH PUSAN***; weekly), Vigo - Zeebrugge - Bremerhaven - Drammen - Cuxhaven - Southampton - Vigo (***SPICA LEADER, PROMETHEUS LEADER***; weekly), **Baltic Service** Southampton - Zeebrugge - Bremerhaven - Malmo - Hanko - St Petersburg - Gdynia - Southampton (***AUTO ECO, AUTO ENERGY***; weekly), **Bristol Service** Portbury - Pasajes (***AUTOSUN***; weekly), **Biscay Services** Santander - Pasajes - Zeebrugge - Southampton - Santander (***AUTOSKY***; weekly), Santander - Pasajes - Rotterdam - Zeebrugge - Santander (***AUTOSTAR,*** weekly), Pasajes - Zeebrugge - Southampton - Le Havre - Pasajes (***P-CLASS,*** weekly), **Norway Service** Bremerhaven - Oslo - Wallhamn - Bremerhaven (***AUTOPREMIER***; twice weekly), **North – South Service** Bremerhaven - Zeebrugge - Portbury - Vigo - Sagunto - Tarragona - Savona - Livorno - Pireaus - Autoport - Yenikoy - Bremerhaven (***CORAL LEADER, EMERALD LEADER, OPAL LEADER, VEGA LEADER,*** weekly).

Services listed carry unaccompanied ro-ro cargo together with large volumes of trade cars and often call at additional ports for an inducement. In addition, short-sea contract sailings for vehicle manufacturers and distributors are operated throughout Northern Europe and a Grimsby - Zeebrugge shuttle service is operated. Vessels regularly transfer between routes and contracts and the following is a list of vessels currently in the *UECC* owned fleet including those not presently serving the UK. The fleet is supplemented by chartered deep sea ocean-going PCTC vessels with side and quarter ramps many of which are owned by parent companies *NYK Line* and *Wallenius Lines* and Eukor (which is 40% owned by Wallenius). Such vessels at the time of preparation and considered out of the scope of this book were the SPICA LEADER, CORAL LEADER, EMERALD LEADER, OPAL LEADER, VEGA LEADER and PROMETHEUS LEADER which belong to parent *NYK Line,* the PASSERO chartered from German ship owning Group F. Laeisz and the HOEGH PUSAN chartered from Höegh Autoliners.

1	AUTO ECO	43424t	16	18.6k	181.0m	OP	3800C	-	QRS	PT	9736365
2	AUTO ENERGY	43424t	16	18.6k	181.0m	OP	3800C	-	QRS	PT	9736377
3	AUTOPREMIER	11591t	97	20.0k	128.8m	OP	1220C	-	AS	PT	9131943
4	AUTOPRESTIGE	11596t	99	20.0k	128.8m	OP	1220C	-	AS	PT	9190157
5	AUTOPRIDE	11591t	97	20.0k	128.8m	OP	1220C	-	AS	PT	9131955
6	AUTOPROGRESS	11591t	98	20.0k	128.8m	OP	1220C	-	AS	PT	9131967
7	AUTOSKY	21010t	00	20.9k	140.0m	OP	2080C	-	AS	PT	9206774
8	AUTOSTAR	21010t	00	20.9k	140.0m	OP	2080C	-	AS	PT	9206786
9	AUTOSUN	21094t	00	20.9k	140.0m	OP	1220C	-	AS	PT	9227053

AUTO ECO, AUTO ENERGY Designated as E-Class both are Dual fuel LNG Ice Class 1A pure car and truck carriers with side and quarter ramps built by Kawasaki Heavy Industries at NACKS shipyard, Nantong, China for *UECC*. Used on Baltic services, the vessels are refuelled by a specialist barge in Zeebrugge. Both vessels are used on the Baltic service. Due to the Covid-19 crisis the AUTOECO has temporarily been deployed to the Biscay service in place of laid up P-class vessels.

AUTOPREMIER, AUTOPRESTIGE, AUTOPROGRESS, AUTOPRIDE Built by Frisian Shipyard, Harlingen, the Netherlands for *UECC*. Designated P-class, they are an enlarged version of the now scrapped R-class and built to a 'Grimsby-Max' specification with greater capacity for ro-ro cargo. Generally used on scheduled sailings between Iberia and the Benelux and UK or between Germany and Norway. In April 2020 the AUTOPRIDE and AUTOPROGRESS were laid up in the UK on the River Fal due to the Covid-19 crisis.

AUTOSKY, AUTOSTAR, AUTOSUN Built by Tsuneishi Zosen, Tadotsu, Japan for *UECC* Designated S-class, they are a further enlargement of the P-class and R-class designs and are normally used on Biscay services.

Under Construction

11	NEWBUILDING 1	35660	21	-	169.0m OP	3600C	-	QRS	NO	9881299	-
12	NEWBUILDING 2	35660	21	-	169.0m OP	3600C	-	QRS	NO	9881304	-
13	NEWBUILDING 3	35660	21	-	169.0m OP	3600C	-	QRS	NO	9895812	-

NEWBUILDING 1, NEWBUILDING 2, NEWBUILDING 3 Dual fuel LNG Battery Hybrid Ice Class 1A pure car and truck carriers with side and quarter ramps being built by China Ship Building Trading Co Ltd and Jiangnan Shipyard Group Co. Ltd. The vessels will be smaller than the E-Class and there is an option for a further vessel.

WAGENBORG-HOLMEN PAPER SHIPPING

THE COMPANY *Wagenborg-Holmen Paper Shipping* is a joint venture between *Wagenborg Shipping* of The Netherlands and *Holmen Paper AB*, an international company based in Sweden.

ADDRESS Wagenborg Shipping Sweden AB, Box 207, 201 22 Malmö, Sweden.

TELEPHONE +46 40 93 71 00.

INTERNET Email info.sweden@wagenborg.se **Website** www.wagenborg.com/shipping/roro-liner-service-baltic-europe *(English)*

ROUTES OPERATED *Circuit 1* – Harraholmen (Sweden) – Bremen (Germany) – Sheerness (UK) – Terneuzen (Netherlands) – Cuxhaven (Germany) – Södertalje (Sweden) – Harraholmen (12 days; ***BALTICBORG, BOTHNIABORG***; 1 per week), ***Circuit 2*** Hallstavik (Sweden) – Norrköping (Sweden) – Terneuzen – Sheerness – Södertalje (Sweden) – Norrköping (2 weeks; ***EXPORTER***, ***SHIPPER***; 1 per week).

1	BALTICBORG	12460t	04	16.5 k	153.1m	OP	-	104T	A	NL	9267716
2	BOTHNIABORG	12460t	04	16.5 k	153.1m	OP	-	104T	A	NL	9267728
3	EXPORTER	6620t	91	16.5k	122.0m	OP	-	90T	A	FI	8820860
4	SHIPPER	6620t	91	16.5k	122.0m	OP	-	90T	A	FI	8911748

BALTICBORG, BOTHNIABORG Built by Bodewes Volharding, Volharding, The Netherlands (hull built by Daewoo Mangalia Heavy Industries SA, Mangalia, Romania) for *Wagenborg Shipping* of The Netherlands. Time-chartered to *Kappa Packaging* (now *Smurfit Kappa Group)*. Placed on service between Piteå and Northern Europe. Northbound journeys (Terneuzen – Piteå) marketed as *RORO2 Stockholm*, with a call at Södertälje (Sweden (near Stockholm)) and, from 2005, the section Bremen – Sheerness – Terneuzen marketed as *RORO2 London*. In 2007 these arrangements ceased and *Mann Lines* took over the marketing of northbound traffic, a northbound call at Harwich (Navyard) being introduced and the Södertälje call being replaced by a call at Paldiski in Estonia. This arrangement ceased in 2013 and they reverted to their previous schedules.

EXPORTER Built as the GRANÖ by Brodogradiliste "Sava", Macvanska Mitrovica, Yugoslavia (fitted out by Fosen Mekaniske Verksteder of Rissa, Norway) for *Rederi AB Gustav Erikson* of Finland and chartered to *Transfennica* for service between Finland and Germany. In 1995 the owning company became *United Shipping* and in 2002 *Birka Cargo AB*. In 2000 she was chartered to the *Korsnäs Paper Group* to carry their traffic from Gävle (Sweden) to Chatham and Terneuzen (The Netherlands). In 2002 she was renamed the BIRKA EXPORTER. In 2005 the charter and operation of the services were taken over by *DFDS Tor Line*. The northbound Terneuzen – Gävle section became a ferry route marketed as part of the *DFDS Tor Line* network. This arrangement ceased in 2006. In 2008 chartered to *Finnlines*. In January 2010 chartered to *Holmen Paper AB*. In June 2013 renamed the EXPORTER.

SHIPPER Built as the STYRSÖ and renamed the BIRKA SHIPPER in 2002 and the SHIPPER in June 2013. Otherwise all details as the EXPORTER.

WALLENIUS SOL

THE COMPANY *Wallenius SOL* is a joint venture *Wallenius Lines* and *Swedish Orient Line*, both Swedish private sector companies.

MANAGEMENT Managing Director Ragnar Johansson, **Head of Communications** Richard Jeppsson.

ADDRESSES Klippan 1A, 414 51 Gothenburg, Sweden.

TELEPHONE +46 31 354 40 50.

FAX +46 (0)31-354 40 01.

INTERNET Email info@wallenius-sol.com **Website** wallenius-sol.com *(English)*

ROUTES OPERATED Oulu - Kemi - Pietarsaari - Lübeck - Antwerpen - Zeebrugge - Tilbury - Zeebrugge - Vaasa - Oulu (***THULELAND***, ***TUNDRALAND***; 1 per week), Kemi - Oulu - Terneuzen - Antwerpen - Zeebrugge - Vaasa - Kemi (1 per week - Service currently suspended)

1	TAVASTLAND	23128t	06	16.0k	190.7m	12P	-	200T	A	SE	9334959
2	THULELAND	23128t	06	16.0k	190.7m	12P	-	200T	A	SE	9343261
3	TUNDRALAND	23128t	07	16.0k	190.7m	12P	-	200T	A	SE	9343273
4	VASALAND	20203t	84	19.5k	155.0m	12P	-	150T	A	UK	8222111

TAVASTLAND Built as the TRANSPAPER by Aker Finnyards, Rauma, Finland for *Baltic Container Shipping* of the UK and chartered to *Rederi AB Transatlantic* of Sweden. Operated on services operated for Stora Enso Paper Group, mainly in the Baltic. In December 2016 chartered to *SOL Continent Line* and used on their Baltic service; she was renamed the TAVASTLAND. Usually operates on the Kemi - Oulu - Lübeck route but could be moved to a North Sea service.

THULELAND Built as the TRANSPULP by Aker Finnyards, Rauma, Finland for *Baltic Container Shipping* of the UK and chartered to *Rederi AB Transatlantic* of Sweden. Operated on service operated for Stora Enso Paper Group, mainly in the Baltic. In early 2011 transferred to the Göteborg - Tilbury (once weekly) and Göteborg - Zeebrugge (*CLdN* service) (once weekly) services. In January 2013 began operating twice weekly to Tilbury, replacing the SELANDIA SEAWAYS of *DFDS Seaways*. In January 2015 chartered to *SOL Continent Line*. In December 2016 renamed the THULELAND.

TUNDRALAND Built as the TRANSTIMBER by Aker Finnyards, Rauma, Finland for *Baltic Container Shipping* of the UK and chartered to *Rederi AB Transatlantic* of Sweden. Operated on service operated for Stora Enso Paper Group, mainly in the Baltic. In January 2015 chartered to *SOL Continent Line*. In August 2017 she was renamed the TUNDRALAND.

VASALAND Built as the OIHONNA by Rauma-Repola OY, Rauma, Finland for *Effoa-Finska Ångfartygs Ab*, of Finland. In December 1986 sold to *Fincarriers Ab* of Finland. In November 2003 sold to *Stena RoRo* of Sweden and renamed the VASALAND. Over the ensuing years, chartered to a number of companies including *Finnlines* and *Transfennica*. In September 2009 chartered to *SOL Continent Line*, initially operating purely in the Baltic but since 2016 used on their North Sea service.

Under construction

5	NEWBUILDING 1	59761t	21	20.0k	242.0m	12P	-	420T	A	SE	9884693
6	NEWBUILDING 2	59761t	21	20.0k	242.0m	12P	-	420T	A	SE	9884708
7	NEWBUILDING 3	59761t	21	20.0k	242.0m	12P	-	420T	A	SE	9884679
8	NEWBUILDING 4	59761t	21	20.0k	242.0m	12P	-	420T	A	SE	9884681

NEWBUILDING 1, NEWBUILDING 2, NEWBUILDING 3, NEWBUILDING 4 Under construction by Yantai CIMC Raffles Shipyard, Yantai, China. To run on LNG.

NO SMOKING
TRANSFENNICA
TIMCA

02338093
Aqua Crystal
DE WATERBUS

Timca *(Andrew Cooke)*

SECTION 4 –
RO-RO OPERATORS CONVEYING PRIVATE TRAFFIC

The following operators employ ro-ro freight ships for the conveyance of their own traffic or traffic for a limited number of customers and do not normally solicit general traffic from hauliers or shippers.

FORELAND SHIPPING

THE COMPANY *Foreland Shipping Limited* (formerly *AWSR Shipping Limited*) is a UK private sector company. The principal shareholder in *Foreland Shipping* is *Hadley Shipping Group.*

MANAGEMENT Chairman Peter Morton, **Managing Director** Paul Trudgeon, **Operations Director** Stuart Williams.

ADDRESS 117-119 Houndsditch, London EC3A 7BT.

TELEPHONE +44 (0)20 7480 4140.

FAX +44 (0)20 7280 8790.

INTERNET Email enquiries@foreland-shipping.co.uk **Website** www.foreland-shipping.co.uk *(English)*

ROUTES OPERATED No public routes are operated. Ships are for charter to the *UK Ministry of Defence* for their 'Strategic Sealift Capability'.

1	ANVIL POINT	23235t	03	17.1k	193.0m	12P	-	180T	A	UK	9248540
2	EDDYSTONE	23235t	02	17.1k	193.0m	12P	-	180T	A	UK	9234070
3	HARTLAND POINT	23235t	03	17.1k	193.0m	12P	-	180T	A	UK	9248538
4	HURST POINT	23235t	02	17.1k	193.0m	12P	-	180T	A	UK	9234068

ANVIL POINT, HARTLAND POINT Built by Harland & Wolff, Belfast, UK for *AWSR Shipping*. To FSG design.

EDDYSTONE, HURST POINT Built by Flensburger Schiffbau-Gesellschaft, Flensburg, Germany for *AWSR Shipping*.

LD SEAPLANE

THE COMPANY *LD Seaplane* (formerly *Fret-CETAM*) is a French private sector company, 100% owned by *Louis Dreyfus Armateurs SAS*.

MANAGEMENT General Manager Jean-Louis Cadoret.

ADDRESS LD Seaplane, 21 Quai Gallieni – 92158, Suresnes Cedex, France.

TELEPHONE +33 (0)5 3459 1339.

INTERNET Email contact@lda.fr **Website** www.lda.fr/ld-seaplane-145 *(English, French)*

ROUTES OPERATED Mostyn (Wales) – Bordeaux (France) ***CIUDAD DE CADIZ***, Tunis – Tangiers Med – Cadiz (Spain) – Bordeaux ***VILLE DE BORDEAUX***, Hamburg – St Nazaire – Bordeaux ***CITY OF HAMBURG***. Vessels are used for conveying Airbus materials under contract. Spare capacity and light ship sailings are regularly used for conveying trailers, heavy rolling cargo and trade cars and calls are often made at other ports for such cargos and regularly include Pasajes, Santander, Portbury, Sheerness and Zeebrugge. In addition vessels are regularly chartered out for short periods when idle.

1	CITY OF HAMBURG	15643t	08	180k	126.5m	4P	853C	31T	A	FR	9383558
2	CIUDAD DE CADIZ	15643t	09	180k	126.5m	4P	853C	31T	A	FR	9383560
3	VILLE DE BORDEAUX	21528t	04	210k	154.3m	12P	658C	123T	A	FR	9270842

CITY OF HAMBURG, CIUDAD DE CADIZ Built by Singapore Technologies Marine Ltd, Singapore for *Louis Dreyfus Armateurs* of France. Able to operate as a conventional ro-ro or as a car carrier using portable mezzanine decks and a dedicated car deck.

VILLE DE BORDEAUX Built by JinLing Shipyard, Nanjing, China for *Louis Dreyfus Armateurs* of France. Able to operate as a conventional ro-ro or as a car carrier using portable mezzanine decks. Short periods have been previously been spent on charter to *Trasmediterranea*, *UECC*, *Cobelfret*, *LD Lines* and *P&O North Sea Ferries*. In 2009 laid up for a year in St Nazaire when Airbus production was temporarily reduced.

SCA

THE COMPANY *SCA* is a Swedish company.

MANAGEMENT Managing Director (UK) Steve Harley.

ADDRESS *Sweden* Box 805, 851 23, Sundsvall, Sweden**, *UK*** Interforest Terminal London Ltd, 44 Berth, Tilbury Dock, Essex RM18 7HP.

TELEPHONE Administration & Reservations *Sweden* +46 (0)60 19 30 00, ***UK*** +44 (0)300 003 7160.

FAX Administration & Reservations *Sweden* +46 (0)60-19 35 65, ***UK*** +44 (0)1375 488503.

INTERNET Email info@sca.com **Website** www.sca.com/en/logistics *(English)*

ROUTE OPERATED Umeå - Sundsvall - Sheerness - Rotterdam (Eemhaven) - Helsingborg - Oxelösund - Umeå (8/9 day round trip; ***SCA OBBOLA, SCA ORTVIKEN, SCA ÖSTRAND***; 1 per week).

1	SCA OBBOLA	20168t	96	16.0k	170.6m	OP	-	-	A	SE	9087350
2	SCA ORTVIKEN	20154t	97	16.0k	170.4m	OP	-	-	A	SE	9087374
3	SCA ÖSTRAND	20171t	96	16.0k	170.6m	OP	-	-	A	SE	9087362

SCA OBBOLA, SCA ORTVIKEN, SCA ÖSTRAND Built as the OBBOLA, ORTVIKEN and ÖSTRAND by Astilleros Españoles, Sevilla, Spain for *Gorthon Lines* and chartered to *SCA Transforest*. They are designed for the handling of forest products in non-wheeled 'cassettes' but can also accommodate trailers. The ORTVIKEN was lengthened during Autumn 2000 and the others during 2001. In June 2001 purchased by *SCA Transforest*. In spring 2016 renamed the SCA OBBOLA, SCA ORTVIKEN and SCA ÖSTRAND.

SECTION 5 – GB & IRELAND – CHAIN, CABLE ETC FERRIES

CUMBRIA COUNTY COUNCIL

Address Highways and Transport, Economy and Infrastructure Directorate, County Offices, Kendal, Cumbria LA9 4RQ **Tel** +44 (0)1539 713040, **Fax** +44 (0)1539 713035.

Internet Email george.sowerby@cumbria.gov.uk *(English* **Website** www.cumbria.gov.uk/roads-transport/highways-pavements/windermereferry.asp *(English)*

Route Bowness-on-Windermere – Far Sawrey.

1	MALLARD	-	90	-	25.9m	140P	18C	-	BA

MALLARD Chain ferry built by F L Steelcraft, Borth, Dyfed for *Cumbria County Council*.

DARTMOUTH – KINGSWEAR FLOATING BRIDGE CO LTD

Address DKFBC Ltd, Dart Marina, Sandquay Road, Dartmouth, Devon TQ6 9PH. **Tel** +44 (0)7866 531687.

Internet Website www.dartmouthhigherferry.com *(English)*

Route Dartmouth – Kingswear (Devon) across River Dart (higher route) (forms part of A379).

1	HIGHER FERRY	540t	09	-	52.7m	240P	32C	-	BA

HIGHER FERRY Built by Ravestein BV, Deest, The Netherlands under contract to Pendennis Shipyard, Falmouth, who fitted the vessel out between January and June 2009.

ISLE OF WIGHT COUNCIL (COWES FLOATING BRIDGE)

Address Cowes Floating Bridge, Medina Road, Cowes, Isle of Wight PO31 7BX. **Tel** +44 (0)1983 293041. **Internet Website** www.iwfloatingbridge.co.uk/timetable **Route** Cowes – East Cowes. ***Note*** the service is unable to operate at times of very low tide; a passenger service by launch is operated. Details are shown on the website.

1	FLOATING BRIDGE NO 6	-	17	-	38.0m	-	20C	-	BA
2•	NO 5	-	76	-	33.5m	-	15C	-	BA

FLOATING BRIDGE NO 6 Chain ferry built by Mainstay Marine Solutions Ltd, Pembroke Dock, UK.

NO 5 Chain ferry built by Fairey Marine, East Cowes, UK for *Isle of Wight County Council*, now *Isle of Wight Council*. In January 2017 withdrawn for sale. Laid up at Gosport.

KING HARRY FERRY AND CORNWALL FERRIES

Address 2 Ferry Cottages, Feock, Truro, Cornwall TR3 6QJ. **Tel** +44 (0)1326 741 194..

Internet Email info@falriver.co.uk **Website** www.falriver.co.uk *(English)*

Route Philliegh – Feock (Cornwall) (across River Fal).

1	KING HARRY FERRY	500t	06	-	55.2m	150P	34C	-	BA	UK	9364370

KING HARRY FERRY Chain ferry built by Pendennis Shipyard, Falmouth (hull constructed at Ravestein Shipyard, Deest, The Netherlands) to replace the previous King Harry ferry. Number is Lloyd's number, not IMO.

LUSTY BEG ISLAND FERRY

Address Lusty Beg, Boa Island, Kesh, County Fermanagh BT93 8AD.

Tel +44 (0)28 686 33300 **Fax** +44 (0)28 686 32033

Bramble Bush Bay *(Kevin Mitchell)*

Oldenburg *(Brian Maxted)*

Internet Email info@lustybegisland.com **Website** www.lustybegisland.com *(English)*

Route Boa Island, County Fermanagh – Lusty Beg Island (Lower Lough Erne).

1	CORLOUGHAROO	-	-	-	10.0m	30P	2C	-	BA	UK	

CORLOUGHAROO Cable ferry, built for *Lusty Beg Island*.

REEDHAM FERRY

Address Reedham Ferry, Ferry Inn, Reedham, Norwich NR13 3HA. **Tel** +44 (0)1493 700429.

Internet Email info@reedhamferry.co.uk **Website** www.reedhamferry.co.uk *(English)*

Route Acle – Reedham – Norton (across River Yare, Norfolk).

1	REEDHAM FERRY	-	84	-	11.3m	20P	3C	-	BA		

REEDHAM FERRY Chain ferry built by Newsons, Oulton Broad, Lowestoft, UK for *Reedham Ferry*. Maximum vehicle weight: 12 tons.

SANDBANKS FERRY

Address ***Company*** Bournemouth-Swanage Motor Road and Ferry Company, Shell Bay, Studland, Swanage, Dorset BH19 3BA. **Tel** +44 (0)1929 450203, ***Ferry*** Floating Bridge, Ferry Way, Sandbanks, Poole, Dorset BH13 7QN. **Tel** +44 (0)1929 450203.

Internet Email email@sandbanksferry.co.uk **Website** www.sandbanksferry.co.uk *(English)*

Route Sandbanks – Shell Bay (Dorset).

1	BRAMBLE BUSH BAY	625t	93	-	74.4m	400P	48C	-	BA	UK	9072070

BRAMBLE BUSH BAY Chain ferry, built by Richard Dunston (Hessle) Ltd, Hessle, UK for the *Bournemouth-Swanage Motor Road and Ferry Company*. Number is Lloyd's number, not IMO.

SOUTH HAMS DISTRICT COUNCIL

Address Lower Ferry Office, The Square, Kingswear, Dartmouth, Devon TQ6 0AA. **Tel** +44 (0)1803 861234.

Internet Website www.southhams.gov.uk/DartmouthLowerFerry *(English)*

Route Dartmouth – Kingswear (Devon) across River Dart (lower route).

1	THE TOM AVIS	-	94	-	33.5m	50P	8C	-	BA		
2	THE TOM CASEY	-	89	-	33.5m	50P	8C	-	BA		

THE TOM AVIS Float (propelled by tugs) built by C Toms & Sons, Fowey, UK for *South Hams District Council*.

THE TOM CASEY Float (propelled by tugs) built by Cosens, Portland, UK for *South Hams District Council*.

TORPOINT FERRY

Address 2 Ferry Street, Torpoint, Cornwall PL11 2AX. **Tel** +44 (0)1752 812233.

Internet Website www.tamarcrossings.org.uk *(English)*

Route Devonport (Plymouth) – Torpoint (Cornwall) across the Tamar. The three ferries operate in parallel, each on her own 'track'. Pre-booking is not possible and the above number cannot be used for that purpose.

1	LYNHER II	748t	06	-	73.0m	250P	73C	-	BA	-	9310941
2	PLYM II	748t	04	-	73.0m	250P	73C	-	BA	-	9310927
3	TAMAR II	748t	05	-	73.0m	250P	73C	-	BA	-	9310939

LYNHER II, PLYM II, TAMAR II Chain ferries built by Ferguson Shipbuilders Ltd, Port Glasgow, UK to replace 1960s-built ships. Number is Lloyds number, not IMO.

WATERFORD CASTLE RESORT

Address The Island, Waterford, X91 Y722, Irish Republic. **Tel** +353 (0)51 878203.

Internet Email info@waterfordcastleresort.com **Website** www.waterfordcastleresort.com *(English)*

Route Grantstown - Little Island (in River Suir, County Waterford).

1	MARY FITZGERALD	122t	72	10.0k	35.0m	100P	14C	-	BA	IR	8985531

MARY FITZGERALD Built as the STEDINGEN by Abeking & Rasmussen, Lemwerder, Germany for *Schnellastfähre Berne-Farge GmbH* (from 1993 *Fähren Bremen-Stedingen GmbH*) to operate across the River Weser (Vegesack - Lemwerder and Berne - Farge). In 2004 sold to the *Lough Foyle Ferry Company Ltd* and renamed the FOYLE RAMBLER. Generally used on the Buncrana - Rathmullan (Lough Swilly) service, which did not resume in summer 2014. In 2014 sold to *Waterford Castle Hotel* and renamed the MARY FITZGERALD. Modified to be cable guided. Number is Lloyds number, not IMO.

SECTION 6 –

GB & IRELAND – MAJOR PASSENGER-ONLY FERRIES

There are a surprisingly large number of passenger-only ferries operating in the British Isles, mainly operated by launches and small motor boats. There are, however, a few 'major' operators who operate only passenger vessels (of rather larger dimensions) and have not therefore been mentioned previously.

Appledore Instow Ferry LIZZIE M (2010, 6.7m, 12 passengers), SHEILA M (2019, 7.6m, 12 passengers). **Route operated** Appledore (Devon) - Instow (Devon) (across River Torridge). **Website** www.appledoreinstowferry.com *(English)*

Aran Island Ferries BANRÍON NA FARRAIGE (117t, 27.4m, 1984, 195 passengers, IMO 8407709) (ex ARAN EXPRESS 2007), CEOL NA FARRAIGE (234t, 2001, 37.4m, 294 passengers, IMO 9246750), DRAÍOCHT NA FARRAIGE (318t, 1999, 35.4m, 294 passengers, IMO 9200897), GLÓR NA FARRAIGE (170t, 1985, 33.5m, 244 passenger, IMO 8522391) (ex ARAN FLYER 2007). **Routes operated** Rossaveal (Co Galway) - Inishmor, Rossaveal - Inis Meáin, Rossaveal - Inisheer. **Tel** +353 (0)91 568903, **Fax** +353 (0)91 568538, **Email** info@aranislandferries.com **Website** www.aranislandferries.com *(English)*

Blue Funnel Cruises HYTHE SCENE (66t, 1992, 21.3m, 162 passengers - catamaran) (ex GREAT EXPECTATIONS 2017), JENNY BLUE (ex OSSIAN OF STAFFA 2017) (1993, 13.7m, 65 passengers), JENNY R* (12t, 1984, 13.7m, 75 passengers), OCEAN SCENE (279t, 1994, 29.0m, 350 passengers - catamaran, IMO 8633865), OLIVER B* (21t, 1988, 12.2m, 62 passengers) (ex SOLENT PRINCE 2001, JENNY ANN 1999, FINGAL OF STAFFA). Note: The HYTHE SCENE is the regular ferry. Other vessels in the fleet (which are used for charters and excursions) can cover as necessary. **Route Operated** Southampton - Hythe, **Tel** +44 (0)2380 239800 **Email** office@bluefunnel.co.uk **Website** www.bluefunnel.co.uk *(English)*. *The JENNY R is owned by *Blue Funnel* but operated by *Solent and Wightline Cruises Ltd*, the OLIVER B is owned by *Solent and Wightline Cruises Ltd* but operated by *Blue Funnel Cruises*.

Carmarthen Bay Ferries GLANSTEFFAN (2018, 8.0m, 10 passengers (amphibian)). **Route Operated** Ferryside - Llanstephan (Carmarthenshire, Wales). **Tel** +44 (0)1267 874000. **Email** info@carmarthenbayferries.co.uk **Website** www.carmarthenbayferries.co.uk *(English, Welsh)*

Clydelink ISLAND TRADER (12 passengers), SILVER SWAN (12 passengers) **Route operated** Renfrew - Yoker (operated on behalf of *Strathclyde Partnership for Transport*). **Tel** +44 (0)871 705 0888, **Website** www.clydelink.co.uk *(English)*.

Cremyll Ferry (Plymouth Boat Trips) EDGCUMBE BELLE (35t, 1957, 17.6m, 128 passengers) (ex HUMPHREY GILBERT 1978) **Route operated** Stonehouse, Plymouth, Devon - Cremyll, Cornwall. **Note:** River craft owned by this operator are also used for the ferry service on some occasions.

Star of Doolin *(Miles Cowsill)*

Spirit of Portsmouth and **Queen Mary 2** *(Andrew Cooke)*

Tel +44 (0)1752 253153 or +44 (0)7971 208381 **Email** info@plymouthboattrips.co.uk **Website** www.plymouthboattrips.co.uk/ferries/cremyll-ferry *(English)*

Dartmouth Steam Railway & Riverboat Company DARTMOUTH PRINCESS (ex DEVON BELLE II 2000) (22t, 1990, 18.3m, 156 passengers), KINGSWEAR PRINCESS (27t, 1978, 19.1m, 150 passengers) (ex TWIN STAR II 2010). **Route operated** Dartmouth – Kingswear. **Note:** River craft owned by this operator are also used for the ferry service on some occasions. **Tel** +44 (0)1803 555872, **Email** sales@dsrrb.co.uk **Website** www.dartmouthrailriver.co.uk/tours/dartmouth-to-kingswear-passenger-ferry *(English)*

Doolin2Aran Ferries DOOLIN DISCOVERY (2009, 15.2m, 72 passengers), HAPPY HOOKER (77t, 1989, 19.8m, 96 passengers), JACK B (2005, 15.2m, 67 passengers), ROSE OF ARAN (113t, 1976, 20.1m, 96 passengers. IMO 7527916), SPIRIT OF DOOLIN (115t, 2001, 24.0m, 200 passengers, IMO 8347935) (ex STAR RIVIERA 2020), STAR OF DOOLIN (121t, 2018, 24.0m, 200 passengers, IMO 8346565). **Routes operated** Doolin – Inisheer, Doolin – Inishmore, Doolin – Inishmaan. Also Cliffs of Moher Cruise. **Tel** +353 (0)65 707 5949, **Email** info@doolin2aranferries.com **Website** www.doolin2aranferries.com *(English)*.

Doolin Ferry (O'Brien Line) DOOLIN EXPRESS, (161t, 2010, 24.5m, 250 passengers, IMO 8791966), (ex BLANCHE HERMINE 2016, ex SAINT VINCENT DE PAUL 2014), ARAN ISLANDS EXPRESS (131t, 2013, 26.0m, 240 passengers, IMO 8346503) (ex DOUCE FRANCE 2020), GALWAY GIRL (99t, 1967, 24.1m, 200 passengers) (ex CORSAIRE D'EMERAUDE 2014, BELLE DU CAP 2009, LA BELLE DU CAP 1981, LES DEUX LEOPARDS 1978) (laid up), TRANQUILITY (62t, 1988, 21.9m, 100 passengers). **Routes operated** Doolin – Inisheer, Doolin – Inishmaan, Doolin – Inishmore. Also cruises to Cliffs of Mohr. **Tel** +353 (0)65 707 5555, +353 (0)65 707 5618, **Email** info@doolinferry.com **Website** www.doolinferry.com *(English)*

Exe2Sea Cruises MY QUEEN (1929, 37t, 18m, 127 passengers) (ex GONDOLIER QUEEN) (reserve), ORCOMBE (23t, 1954, 14.3m, 90 passengers), PRINCESS MARINA (1936, 15.8m, 60 passengers). **Route operated** Exmouth – Starcross. **Tel** +44 (0)7934 461672. **Email** starcrossferry@yahoo.co.uk **Website** www.facebook.com/StarcrossExmouthFerry *(English)*

Fleetwood – Knott End Ferry (operated by *Wyre Marine Services Ltd*) WYRE ROSE (2005, 10.0m length, 32 passengers). **Route operated** Fleetwood – Knott End. **Tel** +44 (0)1253 871113, **Ferry mobile** +44 (0) 7793 270934, **Email** info@wyremarine.co.uk **Website** www.wyre.gov.uk/info/200311/transport_and_parking/130/knott_end_to_fleetwood_ferry *(English)*

Gosport Ferry HARBOUR SPIRIT (293t, 2015, 32.8m, 297 passengers, IMO 9741669), SPIRIT OF GOSPORT (300t, 2001, 32.6m, 300 passengers, IMO 8972089), SPIRIT OF PORTSMOUTH (377t, 2005, 32.6m, 300 passengers, IMO 9319894). **Route operated** Gosport – Portsmouth. **Tel** +44 (0)23 9252 4551, **Fax:** +44(0)23 9252 4802, **Email** admin@gosportferry.co.uk **Website** www.gosportferry.co.uk *(English)*

Gravesend – Tilbury Ferry (operated by the *JetStream Tours*) THAMES SWIFT (25.6t, 1995, 18.3m, 50 passengers (tri-maran)), (ex MARTIN CHUZZLEWIT 2001), JACOB MARLEY (29t, 1985, 15.5m, 98 passengers) (ex SOUTHERN BAY ROSE 2016, ex SEAWAYS EXPRESS 2006, ex CONDOR KESTREL), URIAH HEEP (25.6t, 1999, 18.3m, 60 passengers, (tri-maran) – undergoing major restoration). **Note** the THAMES SWIFT is the regular ferry; the JACOB MARLEY may substitute on occasions and also the URIAH HEEP (possibly renamed) when restoration (following an accident when used on the Southampton – Hythe service in 2016) is complete. **Route operated** Gravesend (Kent) – Tilbury (Essex), **Tel** +44 (0)1634 525202, **Email** bookings@jetstreamtours.com **Website** www.jetstreamtours.com *(English)*

Hamble – Warsash Ferry CLAIRE (2.1t, 1985, 7.3m, 12 passengers), EMILY (3.7t, 1990, 8.5m, 12 passengers. **Route operated** Hamble – Warsash (across Hamble River). **Tel** +44 (0)23 8045 4512, **Mobile** +44 (0)7720 438402 Duty Ferryman +44 (0) 7827 157154. **Email** mike@hambleferry.co.uk, **Website** www.hambleferry.co.uk *(English)*

Harwich Harbour Foot & Bicycle Ferry HARBOUR FERRY (8t, 1969, 11.4m, 58 passengers) (ex lifeboat from the liner CANBERRA, ex TAURUS 2012, ex PUFFIN BILLI, 2016). **Routes operated** Harwich (Ha'penny Pier) – Shotley (Marina), Harwich – Felixstowe (Landguard Point) (Easter to end of September). **Tel** +44 (0)1728 666329, **Email** chris@harwichharbourferry.com **Website**

www.harwichharbourferry.com *(English)*

Hayling Ferry (operated by **Baker Trayte Marine Ltd**). PRIDE OF HAYLING 1989, 11.9m, 63 passengers), **Route operated** Eastney – Hayling Island. **Tel/Fax:** +44 (0)23 9229 4800, +44 (0)23 9266 2942, **Ferry Mobile** +44 (0)7500 194854, **Website** www.haylingferry.net *(English)*

Hovertravel ISLAND FLYER (161t, 2016, 22.4m, 80 passengers, IMO 9737797, Griffon Hovercraft 12000TD/AP), SOLENT FLYER (161t, 2016, 40.0k, 22.4m, 80 passengers, IMO 9737785, Griffon Hovercraft 12000TD/AP). **Route operated** Southsea – Ryde. **Tel** +44 1983 617400, +44 (0)1983 811000, **Email** info@hovertravel.com **Website** www.hovertravel.co.uk *(English)*

Isle of Sark Shipping Company BON MARIN DE SERK (118t, 1983, 20.7m, 131 passengers, IMO 8303056 (laid up)), CORSAIRE DES ILES II (2007, 23.0m, 157 passengers (ex ORAZUR II 2013).SARK BELLE (50t, 1979, 26.2m, 180 passengers) (ex BOURNEMOUTH BELLE 2011), SARK VENTURE (133t, 1986, 21.3m, 122 passengers, IMO 8891986) (laid up), SARK VIKING (Cargo Vessel) (104t, 2007, 21.2m, 12 passengers, IMO 8648858).

Route operated St Peter Port (Guernsey) – Sark. **Tel** +44 (0) 1481 724059, **Email** info@sarkshipping.gg **Website** www.sarkshippingcompany.com *(English)*

John O'Groats Ferries PENTLAND VENTURE (186t, 1987, 29.6m, 250 passengers, IMO 8834122). **Route operated** John O'Groats – Burwick (Orkney). **Tel** +44 (0)1955 611353, **Email** Office@jogferry.co.uk **Website** www.jogferry.co.uk *(English)*

Kintyre Express KINTYRE EXPRESS 5 (2012, 13.3m, 12 passengers), **Routes operated** Campbeltown – Ballycastle, Port Ellen (Islay) – Ballycastle. **Tel** +44 (0)1586 555895, **Email** info@kintyreexpress.com **Website** www.kintyreexpress.com *(English)*

The Little Ferry Company SPIKE ISLANDER (2009, 13.0m, 12 passengers), **Route Operated** St Peter Port (Guernsey) – Alderney. **Tel** +44 (0)1481 724810, **Website** www.thelittleferrycompany.com *(English)*

Travel Trident HERM TRIDENT V (79t, 1989, 25.9m, 250 passengers), TRIDENT VI (79t, 1992, 22.3m, 250 passengers). **Route operated** St Peter Port (Guernsey) – Herm. **Tel** +44 (0)1481 721379, **Fax** +44 (0)1481 700226, **Email** peterwilcox@cwgsy.net **Website** www.traveltrident.com *(English)*

Lundy Company OLDENBURG (294t, 1958, 43.6m, 267 passengers, IMO 5262146). **Routes operated** Bideford – Lundy Island, Ilfracombe – Lundy Island. Also North Devon coastal cruises and River Torridge cruises. **Tel** +44 (0)1237 470074, **Fax** +44 (0)1237 477779, **Email** info@lundyisland.co.uk **Website** www.lundyisland.co.uk *(English)*

Manche Iles Express (trading name of Société Morbihannaise de Navigation) GRANVILLE (325t, 2006, 41.0m, 245 passengers, IMO 9356476 – catamaran) (ex BORNHOLM EXPRESS 2014), VICTOR HUGO (387t, 1997, 35.0m, 195 passengers, IMO 9157806 – catamaran) (ex SALTEN 2003). **Routes operated** Jersey – Guernsey, Granville – Jersey – Sark – Guernsey, Portbail or Carteret – Jersey, Guernsey and Sark, Diélette – Alderney – Guernsey. **Tel *France*** +33 0825 131 050, **Guernsey** +44 (0)1481 701316, ***Jersey*** +44 (0)1534 880756, **Website** www.manche-iles-express.com *(French, English)*

Mersey Ferries ROYAL IRIS OF THE MERSEY (464t, 1960, 46.3m, 650 passengers, IMO 8633712) (ex MOUNTWOOD 2002), SNOWDROP (670t, 1960, 46.6m, 650 passengers, IMO 8633724) (ex WOODCHURCH 2004). **Routes operated** Liverpool (Pier Head) – Birkenhead (Woodside), Liverpool – Wallasey (Seacombe) with regular cruises from Liverpool and Seacombe to Salford along the Manchester Ship Canal. **Tel** +44 (0)151 330 1866, **Website** www.merseyferries.co.uk *(English)*

Mudeford Ferry (Derham Marine) FERRY DAME (4t, 1989, 9.1m, 48 passengers), JOSEPHINE (10.5t, 1997, 10.7m, 70 passengers – catamaran), JOSEPHINE II (10.5t, 2013, 11.0m, 86 passengers – catamaran). **Route operated** Mudeford Quay – Mudeford Sandbank. **Tel** +44 (0)7968 334441 **Email** information@mudefordferry.co.uk **Website** www.mudefordferry.co.uk *(English)*

Nexus (trading name of Tyne & Wear Integrated Transport Authority) PRIDE OF THE TYNE (222t, 1993, 24.0m, 240 passengers, IMO 9062166), SPIRIT OF THE TYNE (174t, 2006, 25.0m, 200 passengers). **Route operated** North Shields – South Shields. Also cruises South Shields – Newcastle. **Tel** +44 (0)191 2020747, **Website** www.nexus.org.uk/ferry *(English)*

Solent Flyer *(Darren Holdaway)*

Snowdrop *(Darren Holdaway)*

O'Malley Ferries, Clare Island NAOMH CIARAN II (35t, 1982, 17.7m, 97 passengers, TORMORE (67t, 1992, 17.7m, 75 passengers), TRUE LIGHT (19t, 2002, 12.8m, 38 passengers). **Routes Operated** Roonagh (Co Mayo) – Inishturk, (50 mins), Roonagh – Clare, Island. **Tel** +353(0) 98 25045, **Mobiles** +353(0)87 660 0409, +353(0)86 887 0814, **Email** enquiry@omalleyferries.com **Website** www.omalleyferries.com *(English)*

Uber Boat by Thames Clippers (trading name of Collins River Enterprises Ltd) AURORA CLIPPER (181t, 2007, 37.8m, 27.5k, 220 passengers, IMO 9451824), CYCLONE CLIPPER (181t, 2007, 37.8m, 27.5k, 220 passengers, IMO 9451880), GALAXY CLIPPER (155t, 2015, 34.0m, 155 passengers, IMO 9783784), HURRICANE CLIPPER (181t, 2002, 37.8m, 27.5k, 220 passengers, IMO 9249702), JUPITER CLIPPER (155t, 2017, 35.0 m, 28.0k, 170 passengers, IMO 9223796), MERCURY CLIPPER (155t, 2017, 35.0 m, 28.0k, 170 passengers, IMO 9223801), METEOR CLIPPER (181t, 2007, 37.8m, 27.5k, 220 passengers, IMO 9451812), MONSOON CLIPPER (181t, 2007, 37.8m, 27.5k, 220 passengers, IMO 9451795), MOON CLIPPER (98t, 2001, 32.0m, 25.0k, 138 passengers, IMO 9245586) (ex DOWN RUNNER 2005), NEPTUNE CLIPPER (155t, 2015, 34.0m, 155 passengers, IMO 9783796), SKY CLIPPER (60t, 1992, 25.0m, 62 passengers) (ex VERITATUM 1995, SD10 2000), STAR CLIPPER (60t, 1992, 25.0m, 62 passengers) (ex CONRAD CHELSEA HARBOUR 1995, SD9 2000), STORM CLIPPER (60t, 1992, 25.0m, 62 passengers) (ex DHL WORLDWIDE EXPRESS 1995, SD11 2000), SUN CLIPPER (98t, 2001, 32.0m, 25.0k, 138 passengers, IMO 9232292) (ex ANTRIM RUNNER 2005), TORNADO CLIPPER (181t, 2007, 37.8m, 27.5k, 220 passengers, IMO 9451783), TWIN STAR (45t, 1974, 19.2m, 120 passengers), TYPHOON CLIPPER (181t, 2007, 37.8m, 27.5k, 220 passengers, IMO 9451771, (2015, 34.0m, 154 seats), VENUS CLIPPER (172t, 2019, 38.0m, 25.0k, 220 passengers, IMO 9867736) The 'Typhoon', 'Tornado', 'Cyclone' and 'Monsoon', 'Aurora' and 'Meteor' Clippers were designed by AIMTEK and built by Brisbane Ship Constructions in Australia in 2007. 'Galaxy' and 'Neptune' were designed by One2three Naval Architects and built by Incat Tasmania, Hobart, Australia, 'Jupiter', 'Mercury' and 'Venus' were also designed by One2three Naval Architects but were built by Wight Shipyard, East Cowes, Isle of Wight. **Routes operated** Embankment – Waterloo – Blackfriars – Bankside – London Bridge – Tower – Canary Wharf – Greenland – Masthouse Terrace – Greenwich – North Greenwich – Woolwich, Bankside – Millbank – St George (Tate to Tate Service), Putney – Wandsworth – Chelsea Harbour – Cardogan – Embankment – Blackfriars, Canary Wharf – Rotherhithe DoubleTree by Hilton Docklands Hotel (TWIN STAR).**Tel** +44 (0)870 781 5049, **Fax** +44 (0)20 7001 2222, **Email** web@thamesclippers.com **Website** www.thamesclippers.com *(English)*

Waverley Excursions WAVERLEY (693t, 1946, 73.13m, 860 passengers, IMO 5386954). **Routes operated** Excursions all round British Isles. However, regular cruises in the Clyde, Bristol Channel, South Coast and Thames provide a service which can be used for transport purposes and therefore she is in a sense a ferry. She is the only seagoing paddle steamer in the world. NOTE: Due to the need to replace boilers the WAVERLEY did not operate in 2019. Resumed service on 22nd August 2020. **Tel** +44 (0)845 130 4647, **Fax** +44 (0)141 243 2224, **Email** info@waverleyexcursions.co.uk **Website** www.waverleyexcursions.co.uk *(English)*

Western Isles Cruises Ltd LARVEN (21t, 2017, 14.2m, 42 passengers (catamaran)), WESTERN ISLES (54t, 1960, 18.0m, 82 passengers). **Route Operated** Mallaig – Inverie (Knoydart) – Tarbet Loch Nevis – Inverie and Tarbet, **Tel** +44 (0)1687 462233, **Email** info@westernislescruises.co.uk, **Website** www.westernislescruises.co.uk *(English)*

Western Lady Ferry Service WESTERN LADY VI (ex TORBAY PRINCESS ex DEVON PRINCESS II) (50t, 1981, 19.2m, 145 passengers), WESTERN LADY VII (ex TORBAY PRINCESS II, ex BRIXHAM BELLE II, ex DEVON PRINCESS III) (46t, 1984, 19.8m, 150 passengers). **Route Operated** Torquay – Brixham. **Tel** +44 (0)1803 293797, **Website** www.westernladyferry.com *(English)* Note: The service is now part of *Dartmouth Steam Railway & Riverboat Company* but is marketed separately.

White Funnel BALMORAL (735t, 1949, 62.2m, 800 passengers, IMO 5034927) Excursions in Bristol Channel, North West, South Coast, Thames and Clyde. However, no services operated in 2018, 2019 or 2020. Services may resume in 2021. **Email** balmoral@whitefunnel.co.uk **Website** www.whitefunnel.co.uk *(English)*

Sky Clipper *(Andrew Cooke)*

Hurricane Clipper *(Andrew Cooke)*

DESTINATION
VISBORG
Välkommen till

Visborg *(John Bryant)*

SCANDINAVIA & NORTH EUROPEAN REVIEW

The following geographical review again takes the form of a voyage along the coast of the Netherlands and Germany, round the Southern tip of Norway, down the Kattegat, through the Great Belt and into the Baltic, then up to the Gulf of Finland and Gulf of Bothnia. The first half of 2020 has been dominated by the industry's response to the Covid-19 pandemic which has severely impacted all operations.

The principal immediate impact of Covid has been two-fold: firstly, most operators ceased passenger traffic for all but the most essential of reasons. In practice, for most of the cruise ferry operations, this resulted in their entire networks being shut down from mid-March until late May although some operated skeleton services to keep essential goods flowing. The more freight-oriented services across the southern Baltic were less impacted. Secondly, as the industry now fights to return to some semblance of normality, several of the cruise ferry companies have chosen to experiment with a large number of ad hoc or semi-regular cruises linking various new destinations. Tallink in particular has adopted this strategy with some early success, although it remains to be seen whether the 2019 pattern of routes and frequencies will eventually return or whether the more fluid, cruise-based approach is here to stay.

Stena on the other hand took the opportunity to decisively shut down two of its operations permanently with both Frederikshavn - Oslo and Trelleborg - Sassnitz being closed. However, the long term ramifications of the crisis on the Scandinavian ferry industry and only just beginning to be felt and the future of many operators, services, vessels and most importantly employment prospects must surely now be in significant doubt.

FRISIAN ISLANDS & ELBE

The first Rederij Doeksen's new twin LNG-powered catamarans *Willem Barentsz* was finally inaugurated on 1 July 2020 and entered service between Harlingen and Terschelling two days later after lengthy delays in her construction and extensive damage caused during her delivery voyage which required her to be outfitted for a second time. Together with sister *Willem de Vlamingh*, which was due to be placed into service in September 2020, the new vessels replace the elderly *Midsland* and relegate *Friesland* to a spare vessel. The pair introduce new standards of comfort and quality onboard as well as a lower environmental footprint on the ecosystem of the Wadden Sea. Doeksen's stated strategy has been to introduce two smaller ferries to both reduce environmental impact but also to increase the frequency of departure.

The services to Vlieland and Terschelling were supplemented during the Spring of 2020 by the arrival of two former Doeksen vessels: the passenger ferry *Friesland* of 1956 (usually in use as a pleasure cruiser on the Ijsselmeer) and the 1951-built tug *Holland* (which had spent occasional summer seasons on charter to the ferry operator during the 1950s). Both vessels were chartered to provide additional passenger capacity on services to the islands during the period of social distancing which reduced the capacity of the regular vessels.

The SyltFähre operation between the Danish island of Rømø and the German island of Sylt introduced a second ferry in November 2019, the Fjord1 vessel *Tresfjord* which was renamed *RömöExpress* for the service between Havneby and List. The addition of the second ferry is partly due to the ongoing construction works on the Hindenburg dam that links Sylt with the German mainland, but also adds extra capacity during the peak season.

FAROE ISLANDS

Smyril Line acquired an additional ro-ro vessel in late 2019, purchasing Bore Line's *Bore Bank* which was renamed the *Akranes* and deployed on a new service between Thorlakshöfn (Iceland), Hirtshals (Denmark) and Tórshavn. Strandfaraskip Landsins acquired the Norwegian local ferry *Hasfjord* in December 2019. She was delivered in February 2020 and operates in freight-only mode. Also during 2020, the company are due to introduce a new small car carrying catamaran, the *Erla Kongsdóttir*.

Fynshav *(Frank Lose)*

Deutschland *(Frank Lose)*

Roblin Hood *(Frank Lose)*

Viking XPRS *(Miles Cowsill)*

NORWEGIAN DOMESTIC

Hurtigruten is to convert three of its current fleet to expedition cruise ships to expand this growing part of the business once the contract for the coastal express service is split with Havila from 2021. The three ships are the *Finnmarken* (2002), sisters *Trollfjord* (2002) and *Midnatsol* (2003). The vessels will receive battery packs to reduce emissions as well as capability for shore power. The engines will also be refurbished to cut emissions also. First to be converted will be the *Finnmarken* in late 2020 with the other two ships being refitted the following year. The *Finnmarken* will be renamed *Otto Sverdrup* with the *Midnatsol* being renamed *Maud*. The vessels are to be deployed on new Norwegian coastal cruises as from 2021, which are likely to focus on the more commercially lucrative destinations without the public-service requirement of the current contract. Hurtigruten will also offer in-depth expedition cruises to Norway from Dover (*Maud*), Hamburg (*Otto Sverdrup*) and Bergen (*Trollfjord*).

Havila Kystlink, the incoming operators of the Norwegian coastal express service, had two of its newbuild orders cancelled by the shipyard in late 2019 when the yard declared bankruptcy. The company subsequently replaced the contract with one at the Tersan Shipyard in Turkey, although these new vessels will miss the contract start in 2021 and Havila are seeking temporary replacement vessels. The company has announced that the new vessels are to be named *Havila Capella*, *Havila Castor*, *Havila Pollux* and *Havila Polaris*.

SKAGERRAK & KATTEGAT

The Covid crisis severely disrupted the ferry network for several months although the single biggest casualty was Stena's Frederikshavn – Oslo service which was permanently closed in late March and the *Stena Saga* laid up pending sale.

FjordLine's new Austal-built catamaran was launched as the *Fjord Fstr* at Cebu, Philippines, on 7 February and the vessel is expected to enter service in late August, replacing the *FjordCat*. During the Covid crisis, the company adopted a revised twice-weekly service, linking Hirtshals, Kristiansand and Stavanger.

Color Line's *Color Hybrid* experienced a successful first few months in operation until services were disrupted from mid-March. The ship she replaced, the *Bohus*, was sold to Red Star Ferries and is eventually likely to see service between Italy and Albania.

Stena inaugurated its new Grenaa – Halmstad service on 1 February when the *Stena Nautica* operated the first sailing having closed the route to Varberg the previous day, following the decision of the local authorities in the port to focus on leisure traffic.

SOUTHERN BALTIC

The southern Baltic routes experienced relatively little impact from the Covid crisis, being far more freight-oriented than the northern cruise ferry operations and therefore vital to trans-continental trade, although social distancing measures were naturally implemented. The single biggest casualty was Stena's Trelleborg – Sassnitz operation which was suspended when most of Europe went into lockdown in mid-March and in late April it was announced that the route was to close permanently and *Sassnitz* retired. There were discussions between Stena and the local authorities in Rügen and with a view to the operation passing into the ownership of the latter but this came to nothing. It was subsequently announced that FRS would restart the service from September 2020 albeit serving Ystad rather than Trelleborg. The company has acquired the *FjordCat* from Fjord Line for the new operation which will be branded FRS Baltic.

The keel for TT-Lines' new LNG-powered ro-pax vessel was laid on 3 July 2020 at the China Merchants Shipyard in Jinling. The new vessel will be delivered in 2022 and will measure 230 metres in length and offer capacity for 800 passengers and 4,600 metres of vehicle space.

TT-Line also acquired an additional ro-pax to service its routes to Świnoujscie and Klaipėda. The *Marco Polo*, formerly Moby Lines' *Barbara Krahulik*, was introduced in late January having been rebuilt at Gdańsk with the installation of an additional accommodation unit to increase its passenger capacity.

NORTHERN BALTIC

Grimaldi Group has placed an order for a new 'Superstar' class of ro-pax vessels with China Merchants Shipyard at Jinling. The €230 million order is for two vessels which will each carry 1,200 passengers and offer 5,100 lane metres of cargo. The vessels will be 230 metres in length and run on hybrid power. They will operate for Finnlines between Kapellskär and Naantali via Långnäs when introduced in 2023.

DFDS instigated a fleet reshuffle in early 2020 on the occasion of the return to service of the *Sirena Seaways* after its five-year charter to Brittany Ferries. The new vessel is partnered by the *Patria Seaways* on the Paldiski - Kapellskär service with the latter ship also replacing the *Sailor* on the Paldiski - Hanko operation. The *Sirena Seaways* displaced the *Optima Seaways*, which moved to provide additional capacity on the Klaipėda - Karlshamn service, whilst the chartered *Sailor* was sold by its owners to Tallink to operate on its own Paldiski - Kapellskär service, providing additional capacity at the height of the Covid crisis. The *Liverpool Viking* was sold to CMN and renamed the *Pelagos* for further service in the Mediterranean.

Having seen most of its fleet laid up from mid-March due to the pandemic, Tallink announced a series of innovative, semi-regular routes to be operated during the summer season. The *Silja Serenade* opened a new thrice-weekly Helsinki - Riga service whilst the *Baltic Queen* switched to a new weekly Turku - Tallinn route. Both services were designed to introduce customers to new destinations in an attempt to stimulate demand against the backdrop of the decimated passenger traffic on the services to Sweden - a country that was relatively slow in its reduction of the virus amongst the population. Several vessels were deployed to a number of ad-hoc cruises to Visby and Saaremaa from various Finnish or Estonian ports. All three routes from Stockholm were suspended with the *Silja Symphony* reopening Helsinki from late July. The *Victoria I* reopened Tallinn from early September whilst the Riga service remains suspended indefinitely.

Tallink has chosen the name *MyStar* for its new 'Shuttle' vessel that will partner the *Megastar* when it is introduced in 2022.

Also due to the pandemic, Moby SPL abandoned its entire summer season until late August with further cancellations likely. This was on top of a disrupted Autumn 2019 season when the *SPL Princess Anastasia* suffered a grounding, forcing her to miss the festive season. The *SPL Princess Anastasia* was deployed for most of summer 2020 on a long charter as an accommodation vessel near the Russian arctic port of Murmansk.

Destination Gotland's final Chinese newbuild, the *Thjelvar* arrived in Sweden in early February 2020. Prior to her entry into service in June, the ship was renamed the *Gotland* with the existing vessel of that name taking the name *Drotten*. The 2018-built *Visborg* and the 2003-built *Visby* will swap names later in the year.

Matthew Punter

Holger Danske *(Frank Lose)*

Stena Germanicia *(Frank Lose)*

SECTION 7 - NORTHERN EUROPE

ÆRØFÆRGERNE

THE COMPANY *Ærøfærgerne* is a Danish company, owned by the municipality of Ærø.

MANAGEMENT Managing Director Kelda Møller, **Marketing Coordinator** Jeanette Erikson.

ADDRESS Vestergade 1, 5970 Ærøskøbing, Denmark.

TELEPHONE Administration & Reservations +45 62 52 40 00.

INTERNET Email info@aeroe-ferry.dk **Website** www.aeroe-ferry.dk *(Danish, English, German)*

ROUTE OPERATED Ærøskøbing (Ærø) - Svendborg (Funen) (1hr 15mins; ***ÆRØSKØBING, MARSTAL***; every 1/2 hours), Søby (Ærø) - Faaborg (Funen) (1hr; ***SKJOLDNÆS***; 3 per day), Søby (Ærø) - Funenshav (Als) (1hr 10mins; ***ELLEN***; 3 per day).

1	ÆRØSKØBING	1617t	99	12.0k	49.0m	395P	42C	-	BA	DK	9199086
2	ELLEN	996t	18	13.0k	59.4m	198P	31C		BA	DK	9805374
3	MARSTAL	1617t	99	12.0k	49.0m	395P	42C	-	BA	DK	9199074
4	SKJOLDNÆS	986t	79	11.0k	47.1m	245P	31C	-	BA	DK	7925649

ÆRØSKØBING, MARSTAL Built by EOS, Esbjerg, Denmark for *Ærøfærgerne*.

ELLEN Built by Søby Vaerft, Søby, Ærø, Denmark for *Ærøfærgerne*. Hybrid electric powered.

SKJOLDNÆS Built as the SAM-SINE by Søren Larsen & Sønner Skibsværft A/S, Nykøbing Mors, Denmark for *Hou-Sælvig Ruten Aps* of Denmark. In 2001 she was lengthened by Ørskov Christensen's Staalskibsværft, Frederikshavn, Denmark. In 2009 sold to *Ærøfærgerne* and renamed the SKJOLDNÆS.

ÆRØXPRESSAN

THE COMPANY ÆrøX0L0Lpressan is a Danish private sector company.

ADDRESS Havnepladsen 8, 5960 Marstal, Ærø, Denmark.

TELEPHONE +45 73 70 78 00.

INTERNET Email info@aeroexpressen.dk **Website** www.aeroexpressen.dk *(Danish)*

ROUTE OPERATED Marstal (Ærø, Denmark) - Rudkøbing (Langeland, Denmark) (50 mins; ***ÆRØXPRESSAN***; up to 7 per day).

1	ÆRØXPRESSAN	600t	19	11.4k	50.0m	300P	30C	0L	BA	DK	9861500

ÆRØXPRESSAN Built by the Hvide Sande Shipyard, Denmark.

BASTØ FOSEN

THE COMPANY *Bastø Fosen* is a Norwegian private sector company, a subsidiary of *Torghatten ASA - Brønnøysund*.

MANAGEMENT Managing Director Øyvind Lund.

ADDRESS PO Box 94, 3191 Horten, Norway.

TELEPHONE Administration +47 33 03 17 40.

INTERNET Email post@fosen.no **Website** basto-fosen.no *(Norwegian, English)*

ROUTE OPERATED Moss - Horten (across Oslofjord, Norway) (30 mins; ***BASTØ I, BASTØ II, BASTØ IV***, ***BASTØ V, BASTØ VI***; up to every 15 mins).

1	BASTØ I	5505t	97	17.0k	109.0m	600P	200C	18L	BA	NO	9144081
2	BASTØ II	5505t	97	17.0k	109.0m	600P	200C	18L	BA	NO	9144093
3	BASTØ IV	7700t	16	18.0k	142.9m	600P	200C	30L	BA	NO	9771420
4	BASTØ V	7700t	17	18.0k	142.9m	600P	200C	30L	BA	NO	9771432

Ærøskøbing *(Frank Lose)*

Color Hybrid *(Miles Cowsill)*

5	BASTØ VI	7870t	16	18.0k	142.9m	600P	200C	30L	BA	NO	9769219

BASTØ I, BASTØ II Built by Fosen Mekaniske Verksteder, Frengen, Norway.

BASTØ IV, BASTØ V Built by Sefine Shipyard, Yalova, Turkey.

BASTØ VI Built by Cemre Shipyard, Yalova, Turkey.

Under construction

6	BASTØ ELECTRIC	7870t	21	18.0k	142.9m	600P	200C	24L	BA	NO	9878993

BASTØ ELECTRIC Under construction by Sefine Shipyard, Yalova, Turkey. Hybrid diesel/electric but will be able to operate in 100% electric mode when shore infrastructure is completed. Likely to be delivered in January 2021.

COLOR LINE

THE COMPANY *Color Line ASA* is a Norwegian private sector stock-listed limited company. The company merged with *Larvik Scandi Line* of Norway (which owned *Larvik Line* and *Scandi Line*) in 1996. In 1997 the operations of *Larvik Line* were incorporated into *Color Line*; *Scandi Line* continued as a separate subsidiary until 1998, when it was also incorporated into *Color Line*. The marketing name *Color Scandi Line* was dropped at the end of 2000.

MANAGEMENT CEO Trond Kleivdal.

ADDRESS *Commercial* Postboks 1422 Vika, 0115 Oslo, Norway, ***Technical Management*** Color Line Marine AS, PO Box 2090, 3210 Sandefjord, Norway.

TELEPHONE Administration & Reservations +45 99 56 19 00,

INTERNET Website www.colorline.com *(English, Danish, German, Norwegian, Swedish)*

ROUTES OPERATED Conventional Ferries Oslo (Norway) - Kiel (Germany) (19 hrs 30 mins; ***COLOR FANTASY, COLOR MAGIC***; 1 per day), Kristiansand (Norway) - Hirtshals (3 hrs 15 mins; ***SUPERSPEED 1***; 4 per day), Larvik (Norway) - Hirtshals (Denmark) (3 hrs 45 mins; ***SUPERSPEED 2***; up to 2 per day), Sandefjord (Norway) - Strömstad (Sweden) (2 hrs 30 mins; ***COLOR HYBRID, COLOR VIKING***; up to 4 per day). **Freight ferry** Oslo - Kiel (21 hrs; ***COLOR CARRIER***; 3 per week).

1F	COLOR CARRIER	12433t	98	20.0k	154.5m	12P	-	124T	A2	NO	9132002
2	COLOR FANTASY	74500t	04	22.3k	224.0m	2605P	750C	90T	BA	NO	9278234
3	COLOR HYBRID	27000t	19	25.3k	160.0m	2000P	500C	-	BA	NO	9824289
4	COLOR MAGIC	75100t	07	22.3k	224.0m	2812P	550C	90T	BA	NO	9349863
5	COLOR VIKING	19763t	85	16.4k	137.0m	1773P	370C	40T	BA2	NO	8317942
6	SUPERSPEED 1	36822t	08	27.0k	211.3m	2400P	750C	121T	BA2	NO	9374519
7	SUPERSPEED 2	33500t	08	27.0k	211.3m	2000P	764C	121T	BA2	NO	9378682

COLOR CARRIER Built as the UNITED CARRIER by Fosen Mekaniske Verksteder A/S, Rissa, Norway for *United Shipping* (a subsidiary of *Birka Shipping*) of Finland and chartered to *Transfennica*. During 2000 she was used on their Kemi - Oulu - Antwerpen - Felixstowe service. In 2001 the route was transferred to *Finnlines* and the vessel used sub-chartered to them (charter later transferred to *Finnlines*). In 2002 *United Shipping* was renamed *Birka Cargo* and the ship was renamed the BIRKA CARRIER. In 2006 the service ceased. In 2008 the charter was extended a further four years. In January 2013 chartered to *Transfennica*. In June 2013 she was renamed the CARRIER. In January 2015 sold to *Finnlines* but not delivered until the end of the year, when the charter ended. In January 2016 renamed the FINNCARRIER. In July 2018 sold to *Color Line* and chartered back to *Finnlines*. In January 2019 renamed the COLOR CARRIER and entered service between Oslo and Kiel.

COLOR FANTASY Built by Kværner Masa-Yards, Turku, Finland for *Color Line* to replace the PRINSESSE RAGNHILD on the Oslo - Kiel service.

COLOR HYBRID Built by Ulstein Verft A/S, Ulsteinvik, Norway, to replace the BOHUS on the Sandefjord - Strömstad route in August 2019. She is a hybrid vessel, operating in both battery and diesel-electric mode.

COLOR MAGIC Built by Aker Yards, Turku, Finland (hull construction) and Rauma, Finland (fitting out), for the Oslo - Kiel route.

COLOR VIKING Built as the PEDER PAARS by Nakskov Skibsværft A/S, Nakskov, Denmark for *DSB (Danish State Railways)* for their service between Kalundborg (Sjælland) and Århus (Jylland). In 1990 purchased by *Stena Line* of Sweden for delivery in 1991. In that year renamed the STENA INVICTA and entered service on the *Sealink Stena Line* Dover - Calais service. She was withdrawn from the route in February 1998, before the formation of *P&O Stena Line,* but ownership was transferred to that company. In Summer 1998, she was chartered to *Silja Line* to operate between Vaasa and Umeå under the marketing name 'WASA JUBILEE'. In Autumn 1998 she was laid up at Zeebrugge. She remained there until Autumn 1999 when she was chartered to *Stena Line* to operate between Holyhead and Dublin. In 2000 she was chartered to *Color Line*, renamed the COLOR VIKING and in April entered service on the Sandefjord - Strömstad service. In 2002 purchased by *Color Line*.

SUPERSPEED 1, SUPERSPEED 2 Built by Aker Yards, Rauma, Finland for the Kristiansand - Hirtshals and Larvik - Hirtshals routes. In January 2011, the SUPERSPEED 1 was modified to provide additional facilities and increase passenger capacity.

DESTINATION GOTLAND

THE COMPANY *Destination Gotland AB* is a Swedish private sector company owned by *Rederi AB Gotland.*

MANAGEMENT Managing Director Christer Bruzelius, **Marketing Manager** Adam Jacobsson.

ADDRESS Korsgatan 2, PO Box 1234, 621 23 Visby, Gotland, Sweden.

TELEPHONE Administration +46 (0)498-20 18 00, **Reservations** +46 (0)771-22 33 00.

FAX Administration +46 (0)498-20 18 90 **Reservations** +46 (0)498-20 13 96.

INTERNET Email info@destinationgotland.se **Website** www.destinationgotland.se *(Swedish, English, German)*

ROUTES OPERATED Fast Conventional Ferries Visby (Gotland) - Nynäshamn (Swedish mainland) (3 hrs 15 mins; ***DROTTEN, GOTLAND, VISBORG, VISBY***; up to 7 per day), Visby - Oskarshamn (Swedish mainland) (2 hrs 55 mins; ***DROTTEN, GOTLAND, VISBORG, VISBY***; up to 3 per day). **Fast Ferries (Summer only)** Visby (Gotland) - Nynäshamn (3 hrs 15 mins; ***GOTLANDIA II***; 1 per week), Visby - Vastervik (2 hrs 30 mins; ***GOTLANDIA II***; 1 per day).

1•	DROTTEN	29746t	03	28.5k	195.8m	1500P	500C	118T	BAS2	SE	9223796
4	GOTLAND	32000t	19	28.5k	200.0m	1650P	500C	110L	BAS2	SE	9783071
2»•	GOTLANDIA	5632t	99	35.0k	112.5m	700P	140C	-	A	SE	9171163
3»	GOTLANDIA II	6554t	06	36.0k	122.0m	780P	160C	-	A	SE	9328015
5	VISBY	29746t	03	28.5k	195.8m	1500P	500C	118T	BAS2	SE	9223784
6	VISBORG	32000t	18	28.5k	200.0m	1650P	500C	110L	BAS2	SE	9763655

DROTTEN Built as the GOTLAND by Guangzhou Shipyard International, Guangzhou, China for *Rederi AB Gotland* for use on *Destination Gotland* services. In February 2020 renamed the DROTTEN. In June 2020 laid up.

GOTLAND Built as the THJELVAR in 2019 by Guangzhou Shipyard International, Guangzhou, China for *Rederi AB Gotland* for use on *Destination Gotland* services. LNG powered. In May 2020 renamed the GOTLAND. Currently laid up.

GOTLANDIA Alstom Leroux Corsair 11500 monohull vessel built as the GOTLAND at Lorient, France for *Rederi AB Gotland* and chartered to *Destination Gotland*. In 2003 renamed the GOTLANDIA. Now laid up.

GOTLANDIA II Fincantieri SF700 monohull fast ferry built at Riva Trigoso, Italy for *Rederi AB Gotland* for use by *Destination Gotland*.

VISBY Built as the VISBORG by Guangzhou Shipyard International, Guangzhou, China for *Rederi AB Gotland* for use on *Destination Gotland* services. LNG powered. In due course to be renamed the VISBORG.

VISBORG Built as the VISBY by Guangzhou Shipyard International, Guangzhou, China for *Rederi AB Gotland* for use on *Destination Gotland* services. In due course to be renamed the VISBY.

DFDS SEAWAYS

THE COMPANY *DFDS Seaways* is a division of *DFDS A/S*, a Danish private sector company.

MANAGEMENT CEO DFDS A/S Torben Carlsen, **Executive Vice-President Shipping Division** Peder Gellert Pedersen, **Head of Business Unit Passenger** Kasper Moos, **Head of the Business Unit Baltic** Anders Refsgaard.

ADDRESS *København* Sundkrogsgade 11, 2100 København Ø, Denmark.

TELEPHONE Administration +45 33 42 33 42, **Reservations *Denmark*** +45 78 79 55 36, ***Germany*** +49 (0)40-389030, ***Lithuania*** +370 46 393616, ***Sweden*** +46 454 33680.

FAX Administration +45 33 42 33 41. **INTERNET Administration** incoming@dfdsseaways.dk, **Reservations *Denmark*** incoming@dfdsseaways.dk ***Germany*** service.de@dfds.com ***Lithuania*** booking.lt@dfds.com, ***Sweden*** pax@dfds.com

Website www.dfdsseaways.com *(English, Danish, Dutch, German, Italian, Japanese, Norwegian, Polish, Swedish)*

ROUTES OPERATED *Passenger services* København - Oslo (Norway) (16 hrs 30 mins; ***CROWN SEAWAYS, PEARL SEAWAYS***; 1 per day), Klaipėda (Lithuania) - Kiel (Germany) (21 hrs; ***REGINA SEAWAYS, VICTORIA SEAWAYS***; 7 per week), Klaipėda - Karlshamn (Sweden) (14 hrs; ***ATHENA SEAWAYS, OPTIMA SEAWAYS,***; 10 per week), Paldiski (Estonia) - Kapellskär (Sweden) (10 hrs; ***PATRIA SEAWAYS, SIRENA SEAWAYS***; 6 per week), Paldiski - Hanko (Finland) (3 hrs; ***PATRIA SEAWAYS***; 4 per week). ***Freight only service*** Fredericia - København - Klaipėda (***ARK FUTURA***; 2 per week).

See Section 1 for services operating to Britain.

1F	ARK FUTURA	18725t	96	19.7k	183.3m	12P	-	164T	AS	DK	9129598
2	ATHENA SEAWAYS	24950t	07	23.0k	199.1m	500P	-	190T	A	LT	9350680
3F	BOTNIA SEAWAYS	11530t	00	20.0k	162.2m	12P	-	140T	A	LT	9192129
4	CROWN SEAWAYS	35498t	94	22.0k	169.4m	1940P	450C	50T	BA	DK	8917613
5	OPTIMA SEAWAYS	25206t	99	21.5k	186.3m	327P	164C	150T	A	LT	9188427
6	PATRIA SEAWAYS	18332t	92	17.0k	154.0m	242P	-	114T	BA2	LT	8917390
7	PEARL SEAWAYS	40039t	89	21.0k	178.4m	2090P	350C	70T	BA	DK	8701674
8	REGINA SEAWAYS	25518t	10	24.0k	199.1m	600P	-	190T	A	LT	9458535
9	SIRENA SEAWAYS	22382t	03	22.0k	199.4m	596P	316C	154T	A	LT	9212163
10	VICTORIA SEAWAYS	24950t	09	23.0k	199.1m	600P	-	190T	A	LT	9350721

ARK FUTURA Built as the DANA FUTURA by C N Visentini di Visentini Francesco & C, Donada, Italy for *DFDS*. In 2001 she was renamed the TOR FUTURA. Initially operated mainly between Esbjerg and Harwich, but latterly operated mainly between Esbjerg and Immingham. In 2004 chartered to *Toll Shipping* of Australia. Later time-chartered to the *Danish MoD* for 5.5 years. However, when not required for military service she has been chartered to other operators such as *P&O Ferries*, *Cobelfret Ferries* and *Van Uden Ro-Ro* and used on *DFDS Tor Line* services. In 2006 sold to *DFDS Lys Line Rederi A/S* of Norway, a *DFDS* subsidiary and chartered back. In April 2011 renamed the ARK FUTURA. Currently operating on the Fredericia - København - Klaipėda service.

ATHENA SEAWAYS Built as the CORAGGIO by Nuovi Cantieri Apuani, Marina di Carrara, Italy. First of an order of eight vessels for *Grimaldi Holdings* of Italy. Used on *Grimaldi Lines* Mediterranean services. In September 2010, bare-boat chartered to *Stena Line* to operate

Patria Seaways *(Frank Lose)*

Athena Seaways *(Frank Lose)*

between Hoek van Holland and Killingholme. In November 2011 replaced by the new STENA TRANSIT and returned to Mediterranean service. In December 2013 renamed the ATHENA SEAWAYS, chartered to *DFDS* and replaced the LIVERPOOL SEAWAYS on the Klaipėda - Kiel service. In May 2016 purchased by *DFDS*.

BOTNIA SEAWAYS Built as the FINNMASTER by Jinling Shipyard, Nanjing, China for the *Macoma Shipping Group* and chartered to *Finncarriers*. In 2008 sold to *DFDS Lisco* and in January 2009 delivered, chartered to *DFDS Tor Line* and renamed the TOR BOTNIA. Operated on the Immingham - Rotterdam route until December 2010. In January 2011 moved to the Kiel - St Petersburg route. In January 2013 renamed the BOTNIA SEAWAYS. Currently operating on the Marseilles - Tunis service.

CROWN SEAWAYS Launched as the THOMAS MANN by Brodogradevna Industrija, Split, Croatia for *Euroway AB* for their Lübeck - Travemünde - Malmö service. However, political problems led to serious delays and, before delivery, the service had ceased. She was purchased by *DFDS*, renamed the CROWN OF SCANDINAVIA and introduced onto the København - Oslo service. In January 2013 renamed the CROWN SEAWAYS.

OPTIMA SEAWAYS Ro-pax vessel built as the ALYSSA by C N Visentini di Visentini Francesco & C Donada, Italy for *Levantina Trasporti* of Italy for charter. Initially chartered to *CoTuNav* of Tunisia for service between Marseilles, Génova and Tunis and in 2000 to *Trasmediterranea* of Spain for service between Barcelona and Palma de Mallorca. In 2001 chartered to *Stena Line Scandinavia AB*, renamed the SVEALAND and placed as second vessel on the *Scandlines AB* freight-only Trelleborg - Travemünde service. In 2003 sub-chartered to *Scandlines AG* and placed on the Kiel - Klaipėda route, replacing the ASK and PETERSBURG. In 2004 sold to *Rederia AB Hornet*, a *Stena* company. In late 2005 the *Scandlines* Kiel - Klaipėda service ended. In early 2006 she was chartered to *TT-Line* to cover for the rebuilding of the engines of their four newest vessels. Later sold to *DFDS*, renamed the LISCO OPTIMA. In April 2012 renamed the OPTIMA SEAWAYS.

PATRIA SEAWAYS Ro-pax vessel built as the STENA TRAVELLER by Fosen Mekaniske Verksteder, Trondheim, Norway for *Stena RoRo*. After a short period with *Stena Line* on the Hoek van Holland - Harwich service, she was chartered to *Sealink Stena Line* for their Southampton - Cherbourg route, initially for 28 weeks. At the end of the 1992 summer season she was chartered to *TT-Line* to operate between Travemünde and Trelleborg and was renamed the TT-TRAVELLER. In late 1995, she returned to *Stena Line*, resumed the name STENA TRAVELLER and inaugurated a new service between Holyhead and Dublin. In Autumn 1996 she was replaced by the STENA CHALLENGER (18523t, 1991). In early 1997 she was again chartered to *TT-Line* and renamed the TT-TRAVELLER. She operated on the Rostock - Trelleborg route. During Winter 1999/2000 her passenger capacity was increased to 250 and passenger facilities renovated. In early 2002 the charter ended and she was renamed the STENA TRAVELLER, chartered to *Stena Line* and placed on their Karlskrona - Gdynia service. This charter ended in May 2003 and she was sold to *Lisco Baltic Service* and renamed the LISCO PATRIA. Placed on the Klaipėda - Karlshamn service. In January 2006 transferred to the Klaipėda - Kiel service to replace the *Scandlines* vessel SVEALAND following that company's withdrawal from the joint route. In Spring 2006 returned to the Klaipėda - Karlshamn route. In May 2011 chartered to *Baltic Scandinavia Lines* and placed on their Paldiski - Kapellskär service. In September 2011 a controlling interest in this service was acquired by *DFDS Seaways*. In January 2012 renamed the PATRIA SEAWAYS. In September 2014 replaced by the SIRENA SEAWAYS and became a relief vessel. In April 2015 chartered as a windfarm accommodation vessel off Esbjerg. In January 2016 chartered to *P&O Ferries* to cover for refits on the Hull routes. In April 2016 became third vessel on the Klaipėda - Karlshamn route.

PEARL SEAWAYS Built as the ATHENA by Wärtsilä Marine, Turku, Finland for *Rederi AB Slite* of Sweden (part of *Viking Line*) and used on 24-hour cruises from Stockholm to Mariehamn (Åland). In 1993 the company went into liquidation and she was sold to *Star Cruises* of Malaysia for cruises in the Far East. She was renamed the STAR AQUARIUS. Later that year she was renamed the LANGKAPURI STAR AQUARIUS. In February 2001 sold to *DFDS* and renamed the AQUARIUS. After rebuilding, she was renamed the PEARL OF SCANDINAVIA and introduced onto the København - Oslo service. In January 2011 renamed the PEARL SEAWAYS.

REGINA SEAWAYS Built as the ENERGIA by Nuovi Cantieri Apuani, Marina di Carrara, Italy for *Grimaldi Holdings* of Italy. In August 2011 chartered to DFDS Seaways and moved to Klaipėda for modifications. In September 2011 renamed the REGINA SEAWAYS and placed on the Klaipėda - Kiel service.

SIRENA SEAWAYS Built as the GOLFO DEI DELFINI by Stocznia Szczecinska, Szczecin, Poland for *Lloyd Sardegna* of Italy for service between Italy and Sardinia. However, due to late delivery the order was cancelled. In 2002 purchased by *DFDS Seaways*, and, during Winter 2002/03, passenger accommodation was enlarged and refitted, increasing passenger capacity from 308 to 596. In June 2003, renamed the DANA SIRENA, she replaced unmodified sister vessel, the DANA GLORIA on the Esbjerg - Harwich service. In February 2013 she was renamed the SIRENA SEAWAYS. At the end of September 2014 the route ceased and she moved to the Paldiski (Estonia) - Kapellskär route, replacing the PATRIA SEAWAYS. In December she was replaced by the LIVERPOOL SEAWAYS and laid up. During the early part of 2015 she performed relief work in the Baltic. In April 2015 she was chartered to *Brittany Ferries* for five years and renamed the BAIE DE SEINE. She entered service in May 2015. In March 2020 returned to *DFDS* and in April renamed the SIRENA SEAWAYS and placed on the Klaipėda - Karlshamn route.

VICTORIA SEAWAYS Built by Nuovi Cantieri Apuani, Marina di Carrara, Italy. Launched as the FORZA. Fifth of an order of eight vessels for *Grimaldi Holdings* of Italy. Whilst under construction, sold to *DFDS Tor Line*. On delivery renamed the LISCO MAXIMA. In March/April 2012 renamed the VICTORIA SEAWAYS. Operates between Kiel and Klaipėda.

Under construction

12	NEWBUILDING 1	54900t	21	23.0k	230.0m	600P	-	270L	A2	DK	9851036
13	NEWBUILDING 2	54900t	21	23.0k	230.0m	600P	-	270L	A2	DK	9851048

NEWBUILDING 1, NEWBUILDING 2 Under construction by Guangzhou Shipyard International, Guangzhou, China. They will operate on Baltic routes from Klaipėda to Kiel and Karlshamn.

REDERIJ DOEKSEN

THE COMPANY *BV Rederij G. Doeksen en Zn BV* is a Dutch private sector company. Ferries are operated by subsidiary *Terschellinger Stoomboot Maatschappij*, trading as *Rederij Doeksen*.

MANAGEMENT Managing Director P J M Melles, **Manager Operations** R. de Vries, **Controller** R. Herrema, **Manager Hospitality & HR** D Spoor, **Manager Marketing & Communications** A. van Brummelen-van Dam.

ADDRESS Waddenpromenade 5, 8861 NT Harlingen, The Netherlands.

TELEPHONE *In The Netherlands* 088 - 9000 888, ***From abroad*** +31 562 442 002.

FAX +31 (0)517 413303.

INTERNET Email info@rederij-doeksen.nl **Website** www.rederij-doeksen.nl *(Dutch, English, German))* **Facebook** www.facebook.com/rederijdoeksen **Twitter** www.twitter.com/rederijdoeksen **Instagram** www.instagram.com/rederijdoeksen **LinkedIn** www.LinkedIn.com/company/rederijdoeksen

ROUTES OPERATED Conventional Ferries Harlingen (The Netherlands) - Terschelling (Frisian Islands) (2 hrs; ***FRIESLAND, WILLEM BARENTSZ, WILLEM DE VLAMINGH***; up to 6 per day), Harlingen - Vlieland (Frisian Islands) (1 hr 45 mins; ***VLIELAND***; 3 per day). **Fast Passenger Ferries** Harlingen - Terschelling (45 mins; ***KOEGELWIECK, TIGER***; 3 to 6 per day), Harlingen - Vlieland (45 mins; ***KOEGELWIECK, TIGER***; 2 per day), Vlieland - Terschelling (30 mins; ***KOEGELWIECK, TIGER***; 2 per day). **Freight Ferry** Harlingen - Terschelling (2 hrs; ***NOORD-NEDERLAND***), Harlingen - Vlieland (1hr 45 mins; ***NOORD-NEDERLAND***).

1	FRIESLAND	3583t	89	14.0k	69.0m	1100P	122C	12L	BA	NL	8801058
2»p	KOEGELWIECK	439t	92	33.0k	35.5m	315P	0C	0L	-	NL	9035527
3•	MIDSLAND	1812t	74	15.5k	77.9m	700P	55C	6L	BA	NL	7393066
4F	NOORD-NEDERLAND	361t	02	14.0k	68.0m	12P	-	-	BA	NL	9269611
5»p	TIGER	660t	02	37.0k	52.0m	414P	0C	0L	BA	NL	9179191

Europalink *(Frank Lose)*

Finnswan *(Frank Lose)*

6	VLIELAND	2726t	05	15.0k	64.1m	1950P	58C	4L	BA	NL	9303716
7	WILLEM BARENTSZ	3744t	19	14.0k	70.0m	700P	64C	-	BA	NL	9807578
8	WILLEM DE VLAMINGH	3744t	19	14.0k	70.0m	700P	64C	-	BA	NL	9807580

FRIESLAND Built by Van der Giessen de Noord, Krimpen aan den IJssel, Rotterdam, The Netherlands for *Rederij Doeksen*. Used on the Harlingen - Terschelling route.

KOEGELWIECK Harding 35m catamaran built at Rosendal, Norway for *Rederij Doeksen* to operate between Harlingen and Terschelling, Harlingen and Vlieland and Terschelling and Vlieland.

MIDSLAND Built as the RHEINLAND by Werftunion GmbH & Co, Cassens-Werft, Emden, Germany for *AG Ems* of Germany. In 1993 purchased by *Rederij Doeksen* and renamed the MIDSLAND. Used mainly on the Harlingen - Terschelling route but also used on the Harlingen - Vlieland service. She is now a reserve vessel.

NOORD-NEDERLAND Catamaran built by ASB, Harwood, New South Wales, Australia for *Rederij Doeksen*. Used on freight services from Harlingen to Terschelling and Vlieland. In spring 2017 lengthened by 20 metres.

TIGER Catamaran built as the SUPERCAT 2002 by FBMA Babcock Marine, Cebu, Philippines for *SuperCat* of the Philippines. In 2007 purchased by *Rederij Doeksen* and renamed the TIGER. Operates from Harlingen to Terschelling and Vlieland.

VLIELAND Catamaran built by FBMA Babcock Marine, Cebu, Philippines for *Rederij Doeksen* to operate between Harlingen and Vlieland.

WILLEM BARENTSZ, WILLEM DE VLAMINGH Built by Strategic Marine, Vung Tau, Vietnam and fitted out at Nesta Shipping, Harlingen, Netherlands. They are aluminium catamarans and LNG powered. They arrived in the Netherlands in May 2019 but entered service in July and October 2020 respectively. They have replaced the MIDSLAND. These vessels will be the first single fuel LNG ferries in the Netherlands and the very first ships in the world where single fuel LNG engines directly drive a fixed propeller.

REDERI AB ECKERÖ

THE COMPANY *Rederi AB Eckerö* is an Åland Islands company. It operates two ferry companiesa, a ro-ro time chartering company (*Eckerö Shipping*) and a bus company on Åland (*Williams*).

ADDRESS PO Box 158, AX-22101 Mariehamn, Åland, Finland.

TELEPHONE Administration +358 (0)18 28 030.

FAX Administration +358 (0)18 12 011.

INTERNET Email info@rederiabeckero.ax **Website** www.rederiabeckero.ax *(English, Swedish)*

ECKERÖ LINE

THE COMPANY *Eckerö Line Ab Oy* is a Finnish company, 100% owned by *Rederi Ab Eckerö* of Åland, Finland. Until January 1998, the company was called *Eestin-Linjat*.

MANAGEMENT Managing Director Taru Keronen, **Marketing Director** Ida Toikka-Everi.

ADDRESS PO Box 307, 00181 Helsinki, Finland.

TELEPHONE Administration & Reservations +358 9 (0) 6000 4300.

INTERNET Email info@eckeroline.fi **Website** www.eckeroline.fi www.finbocaro.com *(Swedish, Finnish, English)*

ROUTE OPERATED Passenger & Freight Service Helsinki (Jätkäsaari) - Tallinn (Estonia) (2 hrs 30 mins; ***FINLANDIA***; up to 2 per day), **Freight and Car Passengers only** Helsinki (Vuosaari Port) - Tallinn (Muuga); ***FINBO CARGO***; 2 per day.

1	FINBO CARGO	22152t	00	22.5k	180.0m	366P	-	120L	BA2	FI	9181106
2	FINLANDIA	36093t	01	27.0k	175.0m	1880P	665C	116T	BA	FI	9214379

FINBO CARGO Built as the MIDNIGHT MERCHANT by Astilleros Españoles SA, Sevilla, Spain for *Cenargo* (then owners of *NorseMerchant Ferries*). On delivery, chartered to *Norfolkline* to operate as second vessel on the Dover – Dunkerque (Ouest) service. In 2002 modified to allow two-deck loading. In 2006 chartered to *Acciona Trasmediterranea* of Spain and renamed the EL GRECO. Used on Mediterranean and Canary Island services. In 2007 sold to *P&O Ferries* and renamed the EUROPEAN ENDEAVOUR. Operated on The Dover – Calais route and as a re-fit relief vessel on Irish Sea routes. In May 2010 laid up. In February 2011 moved to the Liverpool – Dublin route. In May 2019 sold to *Rederi AB Eckerö*, renamed the FINBO CARGO and, in June 2019, placed on a new Helsinki – Muuga freight route. Between January and March 2020 converted to full 1A Ice Class at Öresund Drydocks in Landskrona.

FINLANDIA Built as the MOBY FREEDOM by Daewoo Shipbuilding & Heavy Machinery Ltd, Okpo, South Korea for *Moby SpA (Moby Line)* of Italy. Operated on their Génova/Civitavecchia/Livorno – Olbia routes. In March 2012 sold to *Eckerö Line*, and renamed the FREEDOM. Refitted at Landskrona and, in June, renamed the FINLANDIA. She entered service on 31st December 2012.

ECKERÖ LINJEN

THE COMPANY *Eckerö Linjen* is an Åland Islands company 100% owned by *Rederi AB Eckerö*.

MANAGEMENT Managing Director Björn Blomqvist, **Marketing Director** Maria Hellman Aarnio.

ADDRESS Torggatan 2, Box 158, AX-22100 Mariehamn, Åland.

TELEPHONE Administration +358 (0)18 28 000, **Reservations** 358 (0)50 597 2255.

FAX Administration +358 (0)18 28 380. **Reservations** +358 (0)18 28 230.

INTERNET Email info@eckerolinjen.ax **Website** www.eckerolinjen.se *(Swedish, Finnish, English)*

ROUTE OPERATED Eckerö (Åland) – Grisslehamn (Sweden) (2 hrs; ***ECKERÖ***; 3 per day).

1	ECKERÖ	12358t	79	19.5k	121.1m	1500P	265C	34T	BA	SE	7633155

ECKERÖ Built as the JENS KOFOED by Aalborg Værft A/S, Aalborg, Denmark for *Bornholmstrafikken*. Used on the Rønne – København, Rønne – Ystad and (until December 2002) Rønne – Sassnitz services. Rønne – København service became Rønne – Køge in September 2004. In October 2004 sold to *Eckerö Linjen* for delivery in May 2005. Renamed the ECKERÖ and substantially rebuilt before entering service in early 2006. In January 2009 transferred from the Finnish to the Swedish flag.

AG EMS

THE COMPANY *AG Ems* is a German public sector company.

MANAGEMENT Managing Director & Chief Executive Dr Bernhard Brons, **Marine Superintendent** Knut Gerdes, **Operations Manager** Hans-Jörg Oltmanns.

ADDRESS Zum Borkumanleger 6, 26723 Emden, Germany.

TELEPHONE Administration & Reservations +49 (0)1805-180182.

FAX Administration & Reservations +49 (0)4921-890740.

INTERNET Email info@ag-ems.de **Website** www.ag-ems.de *(German)* www.borkumlijn.nl *(Dutch)* www.helgolandlinie.de *(German)*

ROUTES OPERATED Conventional Ferries Emden (Germany) – Borkum (German Frisian Islands) (2 hrs; ***GRONINGERLAND, MÜNSTERLAND, OSTFRIESLAND, WESTFALEN***; up to 4 per day), Eemshaven (The Netherlands) – Borkum (55 mins; ***GRONINGERLAND, MÜNSTERLAND, OSTFRIESLAND, WESTFALEN***; up to 4 per day). **Fast Ferry** Emden – Borkum (1 hr; ***NORDLICH***; up to 4 per day), Eemshaven – Borkum (30 mins; ***NORDLICHT***; 1 per week in summer).

1	GRONINGERLAND	1070t	91	12.0k	44.4m	621P	30C	-	BA	DE	9002465
2	MÜNSTERLAND	1859t	86	15.5k	78.7m	1200P	70C	10L	BA	DE	8601989
3p»	NORDLICHT	435t	89	33.0k	38.8m	272P	0C	0L	-	DE	8816015

4	OSTFRIESLAND	1859t	85	16.0k	78.7m	1200P	70C	10L	BA	DE	8324622
5p	WAPPEN VON BORKUM	287t	76	11.5k	42.8m	358P	0C	0L	-	DE	7525918
6	WESTFALEN	1812t	72	15.5k	77.9m	1200P	65C	10L	BA	DE	7217004

GRONINGERLAND Built by Husumer Schiffswerft, Husum, Germany as the HILLIGENLEI for *Wyker Dampfschiffs-Reederei Föhr-Amrum GmbH* of Germany. Operated Schlüttsiel - Halligen - Wittdün (North Frisian Islands). In 2004 laid up. In late 2005 sold to *AG Ems*. In 2006 renamed the GRONINGERLAND.

MÜNSTERLAND Built by Martin Jansen GmbH & Co KG Schiffswerft, Leer, Germany for *AG Ems*. During winter 2020/21 do be converted to LNG propulsion and a new stern section fitted by Royal Niestern Sander, Farmsum, Netherlands. Expected to re-enter service Easter 2021.

NORDLICHT Fjellstrand 38m passenger-only catamaran built at Mandal, Norway for *AG Ems*.

OSTFRIESLAND Built by Martin Jansen GmbH & Co KG Schiffswerft, Leer, Germany for *AG Ems*. In 2015 lengthened by 15.4 m by BVT Brenn-und Verformtechnik GmbH, Bremen, Germany.

WAPPEN VON BORKUM Built as the HANNOVER by Schiffswerft Schlömer GmbH & Co KG, Oldersum, Germany for *Friesland Fahrlinie* of Germany. In 1979 sold to *AG Ems* and renamed the STADT BORKUM. In 1988 sold to *ST-Line* of Finland, operating day trips from Rauma and renamed the PRINCESS ISABELLA. In 1994 returned to *AG Ems* and renamed the WAPPEN VON BORKUM.

WESTFALEN Built by as the WESTFALEN by C Cassens Schiffswerft, Emden, Germany for *AG Ems*. Rebuilt in 1994. In 2006 renamed the HELGOLAND and inaugurated a new Wilhelmshaven - Helgoland service for subsidiary *Helgoland Linie*. In January 2016 reverted to the name WESTFALEN and used on service from Borkum.

FINNLINES

THE COMPANY *Finnlines Plc* is a Finnish private sector company owned by the Grimaldi Group. It operates three passenger brands: *Finnlines HansaLink*, *Finnlines NordöLink* and *FinnLink*.

MANAGEMENT President and CEO Emanuele Grimaldi, **Head of Passenger Services and Line Manager HansaLink & Hanko-Rostock** Kielo Vesikko, **Line Manager NordöLink, Finnlink and Russia** Antonio Raimo.

ADDRESS PO Box 197, 00181 Helsinki, Finland.

TELEPHONE Administration +358 (0)10 343 50, **Passenger Reservations** +358 9 231 43 100, +49 451 1507 443, +46 771 340 900.

INTERNET *Finnlines* Email info.fi@finnlines.com **Website *Finnlines*** www.finnlines.com *(English, Finnish, German, Swedish, Russian)*

ROUTES OPERATED *Finnlines Hansalink branded routes* Helsinki (Vuosaari) - Travemünde (27 hrs; ***FINNLADY, FINNMAID, FINNSTAR***; 7 per week).

Finnlines NordöLink branded route Malmö - Travemünde (9 hrs; ***EUROPALINK, FINNPARTNER, FINNTRADER;*** up to 3 per day).

FinnLink branded route Naantali (Finland) - Långnäs - Kapellskär (Sweden) (6 hrs; ***FINNFELLOW, FINNSWAN***; 2 per day).

1	EUROPALINK	46119t	07	22.0k	218.8m	554P	-	300T	BA2	SE	9319454
2	FINNFELLOW	33769t	00	22.0k	188.3m	440P	-	220T	BA	FI	9145164
3	FINNLADY	45923t	07	22.0k	218.8m	500P	-	300T	BA2	FI	9336268
4	FINNMAID	45923t	06	22.0k	218.8m	500P	-	300T	BA2	FI	9319466
5	FINNPARTNER	33313t	94	21.3k	183.0m	280P	-	236T	A2	SE	9010163
6	FINNSTAR	45923t	06	22.0k	218.8m	500P	-	300T	BA2	FI	9319442
7	FINNSWAN	45923t	07	22.0k	218.8m	500P	-	300T	BA2	FI	9336256
8	FINNTRADER	33313t	95	21.3k	183.0m	280P	-	220T	BA2	SE	9017769
9	ROSALIND FRANKLIN	33724t	99	22.0k	188.3m	440P	-	210T	BA2	CY	9137997

EUROPALINK Built by Fincantieri-Cantieri Navali Italiani SpA, Castellamare, Italy for *Finnlines* to operate for *Finnlines NordöLink* between Travemünde and Malmö. Launched as the FINNLADY but name changed before delivery. In April 2009 transferred to *Finnlines HansaLink*. In October 2012 sold to *Atlantica Navigazione* of Italy, another company within the *Grimaldi Group*, for Mediterranean service. In January 2018 repurchased by *NordöLink* (a subsidiary of *Finnlines*) and returned to the Travemünde and Malmö service.

FINNFELLOW 'Ro-pax' ferry built as the STENA BRITANNICA by Astilleros Españoles, Cadiz, Spain for *Stena RoRo* and chartered to *Stena Line BV* to operate between Hoek van Holland and Harwich. In 2003 replaced by a new STENA BRITANNICA, sold to *Finnlines*, renamed the FINNFELLOW and placed on the Helsinki – Travemünde route. In 2004 transferred to *FinnLink*.

FINNLADY, FINNMAID Built by Fincantieri-Cantieri Navali Italiani SpA, Ancona, Italy to operate between Helsinki and Travemünde.

FINNPARTNER 'Ro-pax' vessel built by Stocznia Gdańska SA, Gdańsk, Poland for *Finnlines Oy* of Finland to provide a daily service conveying both freight and a limited number of cars and passengers on the previously freight-only route between Helsinki and Travemünde. In February 2007 replaced by the FINNLADY and placed on the Turku – Travemünde freight service; in May sent to the Remontowa Shipyard in Gdańsk for rebuilding to increase passenger capacity and allow for two-deck through loading. Currently operating on the Travemünde – Malmö and Lübeck – St Petersburg services.

FINNSWAN Built by Fincantieri-Cantieri Navali Italiani SpA, Castellamare, Italy as the NORDLINK for *Finnlines* to operate for *Finnlines NordöLink* between Travemünde and Malmö. In February 2018 renamed the FINNSWAN and in May moved to the Naantali – Långnäs – Kapellskär route.

FINNTRADER 'Ro-pax' vessel built by Stocznia Gdańska SA, Gdańsk, Poland for *Finnlines Oy* of Finland to provide a daily service conveying both freight and a limited number of cars and passengers on the previously freight-only route between Helsinki and Travemünde. In 2006/07 rebuilt to increase passenger capacity and allow for two-deck through loading. In 2007 transferred to the Malmö – Travemünde route.

ROSALIND FRANKLIN 'Ro-pax' ferry built by Astilleros Españoles, Cadiz, Spain. Ordered by *Stena RoRo* of Sweden and launched as the STENA SEAPACER 1. In 1998 sold, before delivery, to *Finnlines* and renamed the FINNCLIPPER. Entered service on the Helsinki – Travemünde route in 1999. During Winter 1999/2000 she was converted to double-deck loading. In 2003 transferred to *FinnLink*. In 2007 an additional freight deck was added. In May 2018 chartered to *Baleària* of Spain and renamed the ROSALIND FRANKLIN.

Under Construction

10	NEWBUILDING 1	-	23	25.0k	229.5m	1100P	-	370T	BA2	FI	-
11	NEWBUILDING 2	-	23	25.0k	229.5m	1100P	-	370T	BA2	FI	-

NEWBUILDING 1, NEWBUILDING 2 Under construction by CMI Jinling Weihai Shipyard, Weihai, China. To operate on the Kapellskär-Långnäs-Naantali route, replacing FINNSWAN and FINNFELLOW. When these vessels are delivered the route will have a much greater passenger focus.

FJORD LINE

THE COMPANY *Fjord Line* is a Norwegian company. During 2007 most of the shares of the company were purchased by *Frode and Ole Teigen*. The company bought and merged with *Master Ferries* during December 2007 and all operations are branded as *Fjord Line*.

MANAGEMENT CEO Rickard Ternblom, **Communications Director** Eva Sørås Mellgren.

ADDRESS PO Box 513, 4379 Egersund, Norway.

TELEPHONE Administration & Reservations +47 51 46 40 00.

INTERNET Email info@fjordline.com freight@fjordline.com **Website** www.fjordline.com *(English, Danish, German, Dutch, Norwegian)*

Finlandia *(Miles Cowsill)*

Stavangerfjord *(Miles Cowsill)*

ROUTES OPERATED Conventional Ferry Bergen (Norway) – Stavanger – Hirtshals (Denmark) (17 hrs; ***BERGENSFJORD, STAVANGERFJORD***; daily), Langesund (Norway) – Hirtshals (4 hrs 30 mins; ***BERGENSFJORD, STAVANGERFJORD***; daily), Sandefjord (Norway) – Strömstad (Sweden) (2 hrs 30 mins; ***OSLOFJORD***; 2 per day), **Fast Ferry *May-August*** Kristiansand (Norway) – Hirtshals (Denmark) (2 hrs 15 min; ***FJORD FSTR***; up to 3 per day).

1	BERGENSFJORD	31678t	13	21.5k	170.0m	1500P	600C	90T	BA	DK	9586617
2»	FJORD FSTR	12000t	20	37.0k	109.0m	1200P	404C	30L	A	DK	9837339
3	OSLOFJORD	16794t	93	19.0k	134.4m	882P	350C	44T	BA	DK	9058995
4	STAVANGERFJORD	31678t	13	21.5k	170.0m	1500P	600C	90T	BA	DK	9586605

BERGENSFJORD, STAVANGERFJORD Built by Bergen Group Fosen AS, Rissa, Norway for *Fjord Line*. They operate on LNG.

FJORD FSTR Austal 109m catamaran built by Austal Ships, Cebu, Philippines.

OSLOFJORD Built by Fosen Mekaniske Verksteder, Rissa, Norway for *Rutelaget Askøy-Bergen* as the BERGEN and used on the *Fjord Line* Bergen – Egersund – Hanstholm service. In April 2003 chartered to *DFDS Seaways*, renamed the DUCHESS OF SCANDINAVIA and, after modifications, introduced onto the Harwich – Cuxhaven service. In 2004 sold to *Bergensfjord KS* of Norway and chartered to *DFDS Seaways*. In 2005 sub-chartered to *Fjord Line* for 5 months (with *DFDS* officers and deck-crew) and renamed the ATLANTIC TRAVELLER. In 2006 chartered directly to *Fjord Line*. In March 2008 purchased by *Fjord Line* and renamed the BERGENSFJORD. In January 2014 renamed the OSLOFJORD, rebuilt as a day ferry by STX Finland, Rauma, Finland and, in June 2014, inaugurated a new service between Sandefjord and Strömstad.

FORSEA

THE COMPANY *ForSea* (formerly *Scandlines Helsingør – Helsingborg*) is the trading name of *HH Ferries Group*, a Swedish private sector company owned by First State Investments. Previously a joint venture between *Scandlines* and *Stena Line*, it was acquired by First State Investments in January 2015 and until 2018 operated as part of the *Scandlines* network.

MANAGEMENT CEO Kristian Durhuus.

ADDRESS Bredgatan 5, 252 25 Helsingborg, Sweden.

TELEPHONE Administration & Reservations +46 42 18 61 00.

INTERNET Email customerservice@forseaferries.com **Website** www.forsea.dk *(Danish)*, www.forseaferries.com *(English)*, www.forsea.se *(Swedish)*.

ROUTES OPERATED Helsingør (Sjælland, Denmark) – Helsingborg (Sweden) (20 mins; ***AURORA AF HELSINGBORG, MERCANDIA IV, MERCANDIA VIII, HAMLET, TYCHO BRAHE***; up to every 15 mins)

1	AURORA AF HELSINGBORG	10918t	92	14.0k	111.2m	1250P	225C	25Lr	BA	SE	9007128
2	HAMLET	10067t	97	13.5k	111.2m	1000P	244C	34L	BA	DK	9150030
3	MERCANDIA IV	4296t	89	13.0k	95.0m	420P	170C	18L	BA	DK	8611685
4	MERCANDIA VIII	4296t	87	13.0k	95.0m	420P	170C	18L	BA	DK	8611623
5	TYCHO BRAHE	11148t	91	14.5k	111.2m	1250P	240C	35Lr	BA	DK	9007116

AURORA AF HELSINGBORG Train/vehicle ferry built by Langsten Verft A/S, Tomrefjord, Norway for *SweFerry* for *ScandLines* joint *DSB/SweFerry* service between Helsingør and Helsingborg. In autumn 2018 converted to full battery electric operation with shoreside power supply. She can also operate in hybrid and diesel electric mode, although the last is only used in emergency.

HAMLET Road vehicle ferry built by Finnyards, Rauma, Finland for *Scandlines* (50% owned by *Scandlines AG* and 50% owned by *Scandlines AB* of Sweden) for the Helsingør – Helsingborg service. Sister vessel of the TYCHO BRAHE but without rail tracks.

MERCANDIA IV Built as the SUPERFLEX NOVEMBER by North East Shipbuilders Ltd, Sunderland, UK for *Vognmandsruten* of Denmark. In 1989 sold to *Mercandia* and renamed the MERCANDIA IV. In 1990 she began operating on their *Kattegatbroen* Juelsminde – Kalundborg service. In

1996 she was transferred to their *Sundbroen* Helsingør – Helsingborg service. In 1997 the service and vessel were leased to *HH-Ferries*. In 1999 she was purchased by *HH-Ferries*. She has been equipped to carry dangerous cargo.

MERCANDIA VIII Built as the SUPERFLEX BRAVO by North East Shipbuilders Ltd, Sunderland, UK for *Vognmandsruten* of Denmark and used on their services between Nyborg and Korsør and København (Tuborg Havn) and Landskrona (Sweden). In 1991 she was chartered to *Scarlett Line* to operate on the København and Landskrona route. In 1993 she was renamed the SVEA SCARLETT but later in the year the service ceased and she was laid up. In 1996 she was purchased by *Mercandia*, renamed the MERCANDIA VIII and placed on their *Sundbroen* Helsingør – Helsingborg service. In 1997 the service and vessel were leased to *HH-Ferries*. In 1999 she was purchased by *HH-Ferries*. Now reserve vessel. Between April and July 2015 she operated between Puttgarden and Rødby for *Scandlines*, following damage sustained by the PRINSESSE BENEDIKTE at Gdańsk during a refit. In summer 2018 and summer 2019 chartered to *Praamid* of Estonia to act as spare vessel.

TYCHO BRAHE Train/vehicle ferry, built by Tangen Verft A/S, Tomrefjord, Norway for *DSB* for the *ScandLines* joint *DSB/SweFerry* service between Helsingør and Helsingborg.

FRS BALTIC

THE COMPANY *FRS Baltic* is a trading name of FRS (Förde Reederei Seetouristik) a German private sector company. The company which took over the Sassnitz-Trelleborg service, previously operated by *Stena Line* in September 2020. The route was traditionally known as the 'King's Line' - 'Königslinie' in German and 'Kungslinjen' in Swedish..

ADDRESS Jasmunder Landstrasse 2, 18546 Sassnitz / Neu Mukran, Germany.

TELEPHONE +49 (0)461 864-608.

INTERNET Email info@frs-baltic.com **Website** www.frs-baltic.com *(English, German)*

ROUTE OPERATED Sassnitz (Germany) – Ystad (Sweden) (2 hrs 30 mins; ***SKANE JET***; 1 per day (2 per day from Spring 2021)). Service starts September 2020.

1»	SKANE JET	5619t	98	43.0k	91.3m	663P	220C	-	A	CY	9176060

SKANE JET Incat 91-metre catamaran, built speculatively by Incat, Hobart, Tasmania, Australia. In Spring 1998, following *Incat's* acquisition of a 50% share in *Scandlines Cat-Link A/S*, she was chartered by *Nordic Catamaran Ferries K/S* to that company, operating between Århus and Kalundborg and named the CAT-LINK V. She is the current holder of the Hales Trophy for fastest crossing of the Atlantic during her delivery voyage between the USA and Falmouth, UK (although this claim is disputed because it was not a genuine commercial service). In 1999 the charter was transferred to *Mols-Linien*, she was renamed the MADS MOLS and operated between Århus and Odden. Charter ended in July 2005. Laid up and renamed the INCAT 049. In 2006 sold to *Gabriel Scott Rederi (Master Ferries)* and renamed the MASTER CAT. In December 2008 purchased by *Fjord Line* renamed the FJORD CAT. Did not operate in 2009 but service resumed in 2010. *FRS Baltic* and renamed the SKANE JET..

HAVILA VOYAGES

THE COMPANY *Havila Voyages* is a trading name of *Havila Shipping ASA*, a Norwegian private sector company, In March 2018 it won a ten-year concession to operate, with *Hurtigruten*, the coastal route between Bergen and Kirkenes from January 2021.

MANAGEMENT CEO Arild Myrvoll, **Marketing Manager** Tonje Alvestad Ytrebø.

ADDRESS P.O.Box 215, N-6099 Fosnavaag, Norway.

TELEPHONE +47 70 00 70 70.

INTERNET Email office@havila.no **Website** www.havilavoyages.com *(English, German, Norwegian)*

ROUTE OPERATED Bergen – Kirkenes (from January 2021).

Under Construction

1	HAVILA CAPELLA	15776t	20	15.5k	124.1m	640P	9C	0L	S	NO	9865570
2	HAVILA CASTOR	15776t	20	15.5k	124.1m	640P	9C	0L	S	NO	9865582
3	HAVILA POLARIS	15776t	21	15.5k	124.1m	640P	9C	0L	S	NO	9873759
4	HAVILA POLLUX	15776t	21	15.5k	124.1m	640P	9C	0L	S	NO	9873761

HAVILA CAPELLA, HAVILA CASTOR, HAVILA POLARIS, HAVILA POLLUX Hybrid vessels under construction by Tersan Shipyard, Yalova, Turkey. To run on LNG and batteries.

HURTIGRUTEN

THE COMPANY *Hurtigruten AS* is a Norwegian private sector company. The service was originally provided by a consortium of companies. By 2006, through mergers and withdrawal from the operation, there were just two companies – *Troms Fylkes D/S* and *Ofotens og Vesteraalens D/S* and in that year *Hurtigruten ASA* was formed. In September 2015 it was taken over by *Silk Bidco AS* of Norway and the company changed its name to *Hurtigruten AS*.

MANAGEMENT Chairman Trygve Hegnar, **Chief Executive Officer** Daniel Skjeldam.

ADDRESS Hurtigruten AS, Fredrik Lamges gate 14, Postboks 6144, 9291 Tromsø, Norway.

TELEPHONE Administration +47 970 57 030, **Reservations *Norway*** +47 810 03 030,

UK +44 (0)2036 037112.

INTERNET Email firmapost@hurtigruten.com uk.sales@hurtigruten.com

Websites www.hurtigruten.co.uk *(English)* www.hurtigruten.no *(Norwegian)* www.hurtigruten.de *(German)* www.hurtigruten.fr *(French)* www.hurtigruten.us *(US English)*

ROUTE OPERATED 'Hurtigruten' sail every day throughout the year from Bergen and calls at 34 ports up to Kirkenes and takes you along one of the world's most exciting coast lines, where you will find yourself close to nature, people and traditions. Daily departures throughout the year. The round trip takes just under 11 days.

1	FINNMARKEN	15539t	02	18.0k	138.5m	1000P	47C	0L	S	NO	9231951
2p	FRAM	11647t	07	18.0k	110.0m	500P	0C	0L	-	NO	9370018
3p	FRIDTJOF NANSEN	20889t	19	15k	140.0m	530P	0C	0L	S	NO	9813084
4	KONG HARALD	11204t	93	18.0k	121.8m	691P	45C	0L	S	NO	9039119
5	LOFOTEN	2621t	64	16.0k	87.4m	410P	0C	0L	C	NO	5424562
6	MIDNATSOL	16151t	03	18.0k	135.7m	1000P	45C	0L	S	NO	9247728
7	NORDKAPP	11386t	96	18.0k	123.3m	691P	45C	0L	S	NO	9107772
8	NORDLYS	11204t	94	18.0k	121.8m	691P	45C	0L	S	NO	9048914
9	NORDNORGE	11384t	97	18.0k	123.3m	691P	45C	0L	S	NO	9107784
10	POLARLYS	11341t	96	18.0k	123.0m	737P	35C	0L	S	NO	9107796
11	RICHARD WITH	11205t	93	18.0k	121.8m	691P	45C	0L	S	NO	9040429
12p	ROALD AMUNDSEN	20889t	19	15k	140.0m	530P	0C	0L	S	NO	9813072
13p	SPITSBERGEN	7344t	09	16.0k	100.5m	335P	0C	0L	-	NO	9434060
14	TROLLFJORD	16140t	02	18.0k	135.7m	822P	45C	0L	S	NO	9233258
15	VESTERÅLEN	6262t	83	18.0k	108.6m	560P	35C	0L	S	NO	8019368

FINNMARKEN Built by Kværner Kleven Skeppsvarv, Ulsteinvik, Norway for *Ofotens og Vesteraalens D/S*. In October 2009 chartered as a support vessel for the Gorgon Project (natural gas) in Western Australia. In November 2011 returned to *Hurtigruten* and, in February 2012, returned to service. In January 2021 to be converted to hybrid propulsion, moved to the company's expedition fleet and renamed the OTTO SVERDRUP.

FRAM Built by Fincantieri-Cantieri Navali Italiani SpA at Trieste for *Hurtigruten Group ASA* (ordered by *OVDS*). Since 2007 she has operated cruises around Greenland and Svalbad during the summer period and in South America during the winter and this has been the pattern since. She is named after Fridtjof Nansen's expedition ship FRAM and has ice class 1A/1B.

Mercandia IV *(Uwe Jakob)*

Trollfjord *(Uwe Jakob)*

FRIDTJOF NANSEN, ROALD AMUNDSEN Built by Kleven Verft, Ulsteinvik, Norway. They are designed to cope with both polar waters (for cruising) and service on the regular routes along the Norwegian coastline.

KONG HARALD Built by Volkswerft, Stralsund, Germany for *Troms Fylkes D/S*.

LOFOTEN Built by A/S Aker Mekaniske Verksted, Oslo, Norway for *Vesteraalens D/S*. In 1988 she was sold to *Finnmark Fylkesrederi og Ruteselskap*. In 1996 she was sold to *Ofotens og Vesteraalens D/S*. In 2002 she was replaced by the FINNMARKEN but she then operated summer cruises and in the winter months substituted for the NORDNORGE when that vessel was sailing in the Chilean Fjords and Antarctica. Since 2008 she has operated on the main Hurtigruten roster.

MIDNATSOL Built by Fosen Mekaniske Verksteder, Rissa, Norway for *Troms Fylkes D/S*. From 2016 also used as an expedition ship in the Antarctic. In January 2021 to be converted to hybrid propulsion, moved to the company's expedition fleet and renamed the MAUD.

NORDKAPP Built by Kværner Kleven Skeppsvarv, Ulsteinvik, Norway for *Ofotens og Vesteraalens D/S*. During the winters of 2005/06 and 2006/07 she operated cruises in South America but following the delivery of the FRAM she now remains on the Hurtigruten throughout the year.

NORDLYS Built by Volkswerft, Stralsund, Germany for *Troms Fylkes D/S*. In 2002 sold to *Kilberg Shipping KS* of Norway and leased back on 15 year bareboat charter with options to repurchase. She was laid up during winter 2008/09 until required to replace the damaged RICHARD WITH from the end of January. She now operates full-time on the Hurtigruten roster.

NORDNORGE Built by Kværner Kleven, Ulsteinvik, Norway for *Ofotens og Vesteraalens D/S*. During winters 2002/03 - 2007/08 she operated cruises in South America. During most of Winter 2008/09 she was used as an accommodation vessel for a liquefied natural gas field. Laid up at Bremerhaven during winter 2009/10.

POLARLYS Built by Ulstein Verft A/S, Ulsteinvik, Norway for *Troms Fylkes D/S*.

RICHARD WITH Built by Volkswerft, Stralsund, Norway for *Ofotens og Vesteraalens D/S*. In 2002 sold to *Kystruten KS*, of Norway and leased back on 15 year bareboat charter with options to re-purchase.

SPITSBERGEN Built as the ATLANTIDA by Estaleiros Navais de Viana do Castelo, Viana do Castelo, Portugal for *Atlanticoline* of Portugal as a ro-ro ferry to operate in the Azores. Although completed in 2009, she was never delivered because she did not meet the required specification. In June 2015 purchased by *Hurtigruten* and renamed the NORWAY EXPLORER. Taken to the Öresund Drydocks shipyard, Landskrona, Sweden for rebuilding to make her suitable for *Hurtigruten* service and cruising in polar waters. In May 2016 renamed the SPITSBERGEN and entered service on the *Hurtigruten*, running along-side the LOFOTEN. Unlike most other *Hurtigruten* vessels, no cars can be conveyed. In January 2021 to be moved to the company's expedition fleet.

TROLLFJORD Built by Fosen Mekaniske Verksteder, Rissa, Norway for *Troms Fylkes D/S*. In 2021 to be converted to hybrid propulsion and moved to the company's expedition fleet. It appears that she will retain her name, at least for 2021.

VESTERÅLEN Built by Kaarbös Mekaniske Verksted A/S, Harstad, Norway for *Vesteraalens D/S*. From 1987 owned by *Ofotens og Vesteraalens D/S* and from 2006 by *Hurtigruten Group ASA*.

Under Construction

16p	NEWBUILDING	20889t	21	15k	140.0m	530P	0C	0L	S	NO	9871189

NEWBUILDING Under construction by Kleven Verft, Ulsteinvik, Norway. Other details as FRIDTJOF NANSEN and ROALD AMUNDSEN.

FÆRGESELSKABET LÆSØ

THE COMPANY *Færgeselskabet Læsø K/S* is a Danish public sector company, 50% owned by the county of North Jylland and 50% by the municipality of Læsø.

MANAGEMENT Managing Director Lars Ricks, **Marketing Manager** Bente Faurholt.

ADDRESS Havnepladsen 1, 9940 Læsø, Denmark.

TELEPHONE Administration & Reservations +45 98 49 90 22

INTERNET Email info@laesoe-line.dk **Website** www.laesoe-line.dk *(English, Danish, German)*

ROUTE OPERATED Læsø - Frederikshavn (Jylland) (1 hr 30 mins; ***ANE LÆSØ***, ***MARGRETE LÆSØ***; up 7 per day).

1	ANE LÆSØ	2208t	95	12.0k	53.8m	440P	72C	-	BA	DK	9107370
2	MARGRETE LÆSØ	3668t	97	13.5k	68.5m	586P	76C	12L	BA	DK	9139438t

ANE LÆSØ Built as the VESBORG by Ørskov Stålskibsværft, Ørskov, Denmark for *Samsø Linien*. In March2012 sold to *Læsø Færgen*. Rebuilt by Soby Yard, Aerø, Denmark and renamed the ANE LÆSØ. Between September 2014 and February 2015 she operated on the Hou - Sælvig (Samsø) service which had been taken over by *Samsø Rederi* before their new SAMSØ (now PRINSESSE ISABELLA) was delivered. She will continue to act as reserve vessel on this route.

MARGRETE LÆSØ Built as the LÆSØ FÆRGEN by A/S Norsdsøværftet, Ringkøbing, Denmark for *Andelsfærgeselskabet Læsø* of Denmark. In June 1997 renamed the MARGRETE LÆSØ. In July 1999 transferred to *Færgeselskabet Læsø*.

MOBY SPL

THE COMPANY *Moby SPL* is a joint venture between *Moby Lines* of Italy and *St. Peter Line*, a EU registered private sector company.

MANAGEMENT CEO Sergei Kotenev.

ADDRESS 18/2 South Street, Valetta, VLT 1102, Malta; **Representative office in St. Petersburg** Russia - 199106, St. Petersburg, Maritime Glory Plaza, 1.

TELEPHONE *Russia* +7 (812) 7020777, ***Finland*** +358 (0)9 6187 2000

INTERNET Email sales@stpeterline.com **Website** www.stpeterline.com *(Russian, Chinese, English, Estonian, Finnish, Swedish)*

ROUTES OPERATED St Petersburg - Tallinn - Stockholm - Helsinki - St Petersburg ***SPL PRINCESS ANASTASIA***; 1 per week), St Petersburg - Helsinki - St Petersburg. ***SPL PRINCESS ANASTASIA***; 1 per week).

1	SPL PRINCESS ANASTASIA	37583t	86	15.0k	176.8 m	2500P	318C	63L	BA2	IT	8414582

SPL PRINCESS ANASTASIA Built as the OLYMPIA by Oy Wärtsilä Ab, Turku, Finland for *Rederi AB Slite* of Sweden for *Viking Line* service between Stockholm and Helsinki. In 1993 she was chartered to *P&O European Ferries* to inaugurate a new service between Portsmouth and Bilbao. Renamed the PRIDE OF BILBAO. During the summer period she also operated, at weekends, a round trip between Portsmouth and Cherbourg. In 1994 she was purchased by the *Irish Continental Group* and re-registered in the Bahamas. In 2002 her charter was extended for a further five years and again for a further three years from October 2007. The Cherbourg service ended at the end of 2004. In September 2010 redelivered to *Irish Continental Group*. In October 2010 renamed the BILBAO. In November 2010 chartered to *St. Peter Line*, in February 2011 renamed the SPL PRINCESS ANASTASIA and in April 2011 inaugurated a new Stockholm - St Petersburg service. In February 2011 purchased by an associated company of *St. Peter Line*. During January and February 2014 she served as a floating hotel at the Winter Olympics in Sochi, Russia. In November 2016 sold to *Moby Lines* of Italy and chartered to *Moby SPL*. The service did not operate in 2020 due to the Covid-19 pandemic.

MOLSLINJEN

THE COMPANY *Molslinjen A/S* (formerly *Mols-Linien A/S*) is a Danish private sector company. In October 2018 they were authorised to acquire all the vessels and services of *Danske Færger A/S*.

MANAGEMENT CEO Søren Jespersen, **Communications Manager** Jesper Maack, **Marketing Manager** Mikkel Hybel.

ADDRESS Hveensgade 4, 8000 Aarhus C, Denmark.

TELEPHONE Administration +45 89 52 52 00, **Reservations *Bornholmslinjen*** +45 70 900 100, ***Other Routes*** +45 70 10 14 18 (press 1).

INTERNET Email molslinjen@molslinjen.dk **Websites** www.molslinjen.dk www.bornholmslinjen.com *(Danish)*

ROUTES OPERATED

Alslinjen Fynshav (Als) - Bøjden (Funen) (50 mins; ***FRIGG SYDFYEN, FYNSHAV***; hourly (summer) two-hourly (winter)), ***Bornholmslinjen*** Rønne (Bornholm, Denmark) - Køge (5 hrs 30 mins; ***HAMMERSHUS***; 1 per day, Rønne - Sassnitz (Germany) (3 hrs 20 mins; ***HAMMERSHUS***; 1 per day). **Fast Ferry** Rønne - Ystad (Sweden) (1 hr 20 mins; ***EXPRESS 1, MAX***; up to 8 per day).

Fanølinjen Esbjerg (Jylland) - Nordby (Fanø) (12 mins; ***FENJA, MENJA, SØNDERHO***; every 20-40 mins), ***Langelandslinjen*** Spodsbjerg (Langeland) - Tårs (Lolland) (45 mins; ***LANGELAND, LOLLAND***; hourly), ***Molslinjen* (all services fast ferry) *All year*** Århus (Jylland) - Odden (Sjælland) (1 hr 5 mins; ***EXPRESS 2, EXPRESS 3, EXPRESS 4***; up to 12 per day), ***April – October- weekends only*** Ebeltoft (Jylland) - Odden (45 mins; ***EXPRESS 2***; 1 per day), ***Samsølinjen*** Kalundborg - Ballen (Samsø) (1 hr 15 min; ***SAMSØ***; up to 4 per day).

1»	EXPRESS 1	10504t	09	40.0k	112.6m	1200P	417C	34L	A	DK	9501590
2»	EXPRESS 2	10500t	13	40.0k	112.6m	1000P	417C	34L	A	DK	9561356
3»	EXPRESS 3	10842t	17	40.0k	109.4m	1000P	411C	34L	A	DK	9793064
4»	EXPRESS 4	12450t	19	37.0k	109.0m	1006P	425C	36L	A	DK	9824564
5	FENJA	751t	98	11.5k	49.9m	396P	34C	4L	BA	DK	9189378
6	FRIGG SYDFYEN	1676t	84	13.5k	70.1m	338P	50C	8L	BA	DK	8222824
7	FYNSHAV	3380t	98	14.5k	69.2m	450P	96C	8L	BA	DK	9183025
8	HAMMERSHUS	18500	18	17.7k	158.0m	720P	-	90L	BA	DK	9812107
9	LANGELAND	4500t	12	16.0k	99.9m	600P	122C	36L	BA	DK	9596428
10	LOLLAND	4500t	12	16.0k	99.9m	600P	122C	36L	BA	DK	9594690
11»	MAX	5617t	98	43.0k	91.3m	800P	220C	-	A	DK	9176058
12	MENJA	751t	98	11.5k	49.9m	396P	34C	4L	BA	DK	9189380
13	POVL ANKER	12131t	78	19.5k	121.0m	1500P	262C	26T	BA	DK	7633143
14	SAMSØ	4250t	08	16.0k	91.4m	600P	122C	30L	BA	DK	9548562
15p	SØNDERHO	93t	62	10.0k	26.3m	163P	0C	0L	-	DK	

EXPRESS 1 Incat 112m catamaran built by Incat Tasmania Pty Ltd for *MGC Chartering* of the Irish Republic. Launched as the INCAT 066. On completion, sold to for *MGC Chartering* of the Irish Republic and renamed the MGC 66. In April 2009 chartered to *LD Lines*, renamed the NORMAN ARROW and, in June, placed on the Dover - Boulogne route. In November 2009 withdrawn and laid up for the winter. In April 2010 began operating on the Portsmouth Le Havre - route. In March 2012 chartered to *Mols-Linien* and renamed the KATEXPRESS 1 (Note: in upper and lower case spelt 'KatExpress 1'). Entered service in May 2012. In January 2017 renamed the EXPRESS 1. In September 2018 moved to the *Bornholmslinjen* service.

EXPRESS 2 Incat 112m catamaran built by Incat Tasmania Pty Ltd. Launched as INCAT 067. In March 2013 chartered to *Mols-Linien* and renamed the KATEXPRESS 2 for ten years with a purchase option. (Note: in upper and lower case spelt 'KatExpress 2'). Entered service in May 2013. In March 2017 renamed the EXPRESS 2.

EXPRESS 3 Incat 109m catamaran built by Incat Tasmania Pty Ltd, Hobart, Australia.

Express 3 *(Uwe Jakob)*

Express 4 *(Frank Lose)*

EXPRESS 4 Austal 109m catamaran built by Austal Ships, Fremantle, Australia.

FENJA Built by Morsø Værft A/S, Nykøbing Mors, Denmark for *Scandlines Sydfyenske A/S* for the Esbjerg - Nordby service.

FRIGG SYDFYEN Built by Svendborg Skibsværft A/S, Svendborg, Denmark for *Sydfyenske Dampskibsselskab (SFDS)* of Denmark for the service between Spodsbjerg and Tårs. In June 2012 moved to the Fynshav - Bøjden route.

FYNSHAV Built as the KYHOLM by Ørskov Staalskibsværft, Frederikshavn, Denmark for *Samsø Linien* of Denmark. In October 2008 chartered to *Nordic Ferry Services* and in July 2009 sold to them. Used on the Kalundborg - Koby Kås service. In March 2015 renamed the FYNSHAV and moved to the Fynshav - Bøjden service.

HAMMERSHUS Built by Rauma Marine Constructions Oy, Rauma, Finland. Delivered in July 2018. She has operated between Rønne and Køge (Bornholm) and Rønne and Sassnitz from 1st September 2018.

LANGELAND Built by Sietas Werft, Hamburg, Germany for the Spodsbjerg - Tårs route.

LOLLAND Built by Sietas Werft, Hamburg, Germany. She was launched as the SAMSØ and it was intended that she would be operated on the Hou - Sælvig service, being owned by *Samsø Linien* and operated by *Færgen*. However, these plans were dropped and in February 2012 she was renamed the LOLLAND. After delivery in March 2012 she was, in April, placed on the Spodsbjerg - Tårs route.

MAX Incat 91-metre catamaran, built speculatively at Hobart, Tasmania, Australia. In Spring 1998, following *Incat's* acquisition of a 50% share in *Scandlines Cat-Link A/S,* she was sold to that company and named the CAT-LINK IV. In 1999 purchased by *Mols-Linien* and renamed the MAX MOLS. In 2000 chartered to *Marine Atlantic* of Canada to operate between Port aux Basques (Newfoundland) and North Sydney (Nova Scotia). Returned to *Mols-Linien* in Autumn 2000. In Summer 2002 chartered to *Riga Sea Lines* to operate between Riga and Nynäshamn. Returned to *Mols-Linien* in Autumn 2002. In 2004 chartered to *P&O Ferries* to operate between Portsmouth and Caen. Operated under the marketing name 'Caen Express'. In November 2004 returned to *Mols-Linien* and placed on the Århus - Odden route to enhance the service. In June 2017 transferred to the Ebeltoft - Odden route. In January 2019 renamed the MAX. In April transferred to the *Bornholmslinjen* service.

MENJA Built by Morsø Værft A/S, Nykøbing Mors, Denmark for *Scandlines Sydfyenske A/S* for the Esbjerg - Nordby service.

POVL ANKER Built by Aalborg Værft A/S, Denmark for *Bornholmstrafikken*. Used on the Rønne - København (until September 2004), Rønne - Køge (October 2004-date), Rønne - Ystad and Rønne - Sassnitz services. In recent years she has operated between Rønne and Sassnitz and Rønne and Ystad in the peak summer period. In July 2016 sold to *Mols-Linien A/S* and chartered back. Delivered to *Mols-Linien* at the end of August 2018.

SAMSØ Built as the KANHAVE by Frantzis Shipyard, Perama, Greece. Used on the Hou - Sælvig route. In January 2015 transferred to the Kalundborg - Koby Kås (Samsø) service. Later in January 2015 the Samsø terminal was moved to Ballen. In August 2015 renamed the SAMSØ.

SØNDERHO Passenger-only ferry built by Esbjerg Jernstøberi & Maskinfabrik A/S, Esbjerg, Denmark for *Post & Telegrafvæsenet* (Danish Post Office). In 1977 taken over by *DSB (Danish State Railways)*. Used on extra peak sailings and late night and early morning sailings between Esbjerg and Nordby.

Under Construction

16»	EXPRESS 5	13859t	22	37.0k	115.0m	1600P	450C	28L	A	DK	9913286
17	NEWBUILDING	751t	21	11.5k	49.9m	396P	34C	4L	BA	DK	9909429

EXPRESS 5 Austal 115m catamaran under construction by Austal Ships, Fremantle, Australia. To operate between Rønne and Ystad.

NEWBUILDING Under construction by Hvide Sande Shipyard, Denmark to replace the SØNDERHO on the Esbjerg - Nordby service. Of similar dimensions and capacity to the FENJA and MENJA but electrically powered.

REEDEREI NORDEN-FRISIA

THE COMPANY *Aktiengesellschaft Reederei Norden-Frisia* is a German public sector company.

MANAGEMENT President/CEO C U Stegmann, **Managing Director/CFO** Prok. Harms, **Technical Manager** Prok. de Vries.

ADDRESS Am Hafen 1, 26534 Norderney, Germany.

TELEPHONE *Administration* +49 (0)4931 987 0.

FAX *Administration* +49 (0)4931 987 1131.

INTERNET *Email* info@reederei-frisia.de ***Website*** www.reederei-frisia.de *(German)*

ROUTES OPERATED Car Ferries & Passenger Ferries Norddeich (Germany) - Norderney (German Frisian Islands) (1 hr; ***FRISIA I, FRISIA III, FRISIA IV, FRISIA VI***; up to 15 per day), Norddeich - Juist (German Frisian Islands) (1 hr 20 mins; ***FRISIA II, FRISIA VII***; up to 15 per day). **Excursion Vessels** *(**FRISIA IX, FRISIA X, WAPPEN VON NORDENEY**; varies).*

1	FRISIA I	1020t	70	12.3k	63.7m	1500P	53C	-	BA	DE	7018604
2	FRISIA II	1125t	78	12.0k	63.3m	1340P	53C	-	BA	DE	7723974
3	FRISIA III	1786t	15	12.0k	74.3m	1342P	58C	-	BA	DE	9732450
4	FRISIA IV	1574t	02	12.0k	71.7m	1342P	58C	-	BA	DE	9246839
5	FRISIA VI	768t	68	12.0k	54.9m	1096P	35C	-	BA	DE	8827179
6F	FRISIA VII	363t	84	10.0k	53.0m	12P	30C	-	BA	DE	8891807
7F	FRISIA VIII	581t	10	10.0k	54,5m	12P	35C	-	BA	DE	9578127
8p	FRISIA IX	571t	80	11.0k	57.0m	785P	0C	-	-	DE	7924310
9p	FRISIA X	187t	72	12.0k	36.3m	290P	0C	-	-	DE	7222308
10p	FRISIA XI	105t	69	12.0k	35.4m	940P	0C	-	-	DE	8137237
11p	WAPPEN VON JUIST	54t	68	10.0k	20.2m	80P	0C	-	-	DE	-

FRISIA I, FRISIA II, FRISIA VI Built by Jos L Meyer Werft, Papenburg, Germany for *Reederei Norden-Frisia*. Passenger capacities relate to the summer season. Capacity is reduced during the winter.

FRISIA III Built by Cassen-Werft, Emden, Germany.

FRISIA IV Built by Schiffswerft und Maschinenfabrik Cassens GmbH, Emden, Germany for *Reederei Norden-Frisia* to replace the FRISIA VIII.

FRISIA VII Built by Schlömer Werft, Oldersum, Germany for *Reederei Norden-Frisia.* Conveys ro-ro freight to Norderney and Juist.

FRISIA VIII Built by Sietas Werft, Hamburg, Germany for AG Reederei Norden-Frisia. Conveys ro-ro freight to Norderney and Juist.

FRISIA IX, FRISIA X Built by Schiffswerft Julius Diedrich GmbH & Co. KG, Oldersum, Germany for *Reederei Norden-Frisia*. The FRISIA IX was built to convey 9 cars at the bow end but is now used in passenger-only mode. These ships are generally used for excursions.

FRISIA XI Built by Julius Diedrich Schiffswerft, Odersum, Germany as the BALTRUM IV for *Baltrum-Linie* of Germany. In November 1982 sold to *Wyker Dampfschiffs-Reederei* and renamed the RÜM HART. In March 2014 sold to *Reederei Norden-Frisia*. In October renamed to FRISIA XI.

WAPPEN VON JUIST Built by Lübbe Voss-Werft, Westerende, Germany for private owner. Sold in April 2019 to *AG Reederei Norden-Frisia* subsidy *Cassen Tours GmbH*, Norderney. Generally used for excursions.

Under Construction

11	FRISIA V	1786t	20	12.0k	74.3m	1338P	58C	-	BA	DE	9886122

FRISIA V Under construction by Pella Sietas Werft, Hamburg. To operate on the Norddeich-Norderney service. A sister vessel of the FRISIA III.

POLFERRIES

THE COMPANY *Polferries* is the trading name of *Polska Zegluga Baltycka SA (Polish Baltic Shipping Company)*, a Polish state-owned company.

MANAGEMENT President Piotr Redmerski.

ADDRESS ul Portowa 41, 78-100 Kolobrzeg, Poland.

TELEPHONE Administration & Reservations *Poland* +48 22 230 2222, ***Sweden*** +46 (0)40 12 17 00.

INTERNET Email info@polferries.pl **Website** www.polferries.pl *(Polish, Danish, English, German, Swedish)*

ROUTES OPERATED Świnoujście - Ystad (7 hrs; ***BALTIVIA, CRACOVIA, MAZOVIA***; up to 3 per day), Gdańsk - Nynäshamn (Sweden) (18 hrs; ***NOVA STAR, WAWEL***; up to 6 per week.

1	BALTIVIA	17790t	81	19.0k	146.9m	250P	30C	80L	BA	BS	7931997
2	CRACOVIA	25028t	02	22.8k	180.0m	550P	-	150T	BA	BS	9237242
3	MAZOVIA	25996t	96	21.0k	168.0m	200P	-	154T	BA2	BS	9010814
4	NOVA STAR	27744t	11	19.0k	162.0m	1215P	400C	90L	A	BS	9462067
5	WAWEL	25318t	80	19.0k	163.9m	900P	550C	75L	A2	BS	7814462

BALTIVIA Built as the SAGA STAR by Fartygsentreprenader AB, Kalmar, Sweden for *TT-Saga-Line* and, from 1982, used on freight services between Travemünde and Trelleborg/Malmö. (Originally ordered by *Rederi AB Svea* as the SAGALAND). In 1989 sold to *Cie Meridionale* of France, renamed the GIROLATA and used on *SNCM* (later *CMR*) services in the Mediterranean. In 1993 she was chartered back to *TT-Line*, resumed her original name and was used on the Travemünde - Trelleborg service. Following delivery of the ROBIN HOOD and the NILS DACKE in 1995, she was transferred to the Rostock - Trelleborg route. In July 1997 she was purchased by *TT-Line* and in 1998 passenger facilities were completely renovated to full ro-pax format; following the delivery of the TOM SAWYER she was transferred back to the Travemünde - Trelleborg route, operating additional freight sailings. Briefly transferred back to Rostock - Trelleborg when the charter of the TT-TRAVELLER ended. Withdrawn in 2002, sold to *Transmanche Ferries* and renamed the DIEPPE. In 2006 replaced by the SEVEN SISTERS, sold to *Polferries*, renamed the BALTIVIA and, in 2007, placed on the Gdańsk - Nynäshamn route. In February 2013 transferred to the Świnoujście - Ystad service.

CRACOVIA Built as the MURILLO by Astilleros Españoles SA, Seville, Spain for *Trasmediterranea* of Spain. Used mainly on the service between Cadiz and Canary Islands. In June 2014 sold to *Bulgaria West Port* of Bulgaria and renamed the DRUJBA. She operated between Bourgas, Bulgaria, Batumi (Georgia) and Novorossiysk (Russia). In March 2017 sold to *Polferries* and, in June 2017, renamed the CRACOVIA. In September 2017 introduced onto the Świnoujście - Ystad route.

MAZOVIA Built as the GOTLAND by Pt Dok Kodja Bahri, Kodja, Indonesia for *Rederi AB Gotland* for charter. In 1997 briefly chartered to *Tor Line* and then to *Nordic Trucker Line*, to operate between Oxelösund and St Petersburg (a ro-ro freight service). In June 1997 she was chartered to *SeaWind Line*, enabling a twice-daily passenger service to be operated. In late 1997 she was sold to *Finnlines* and renamed the FINNARROW. She started operating twice weekly between Helsinki and Travemünde. During Summer 1998 she was transferred to *FinnLink*; a bow door was fitted and she was modified to allow for two-level loading. In 2003 transferred to *Nordö Link*. In 2005 returned to *FinnLink*. In 2006 transferred to *Finnlines Nordö Link* again. In 2007 chartered to *Stena Line* to operate between Karlskrona and Gdynia. In December 2011 transferred to the Hoek van Holland - Killingholme route. In March 2011 returned to *Finnlines* and placed on the Travemünde - Malmö service. In October 2011 transferred to *FinnLink*. Between January and March 2013 chartered to *Stena Line* to cover Irish Sea routes during the refit period but withdrawn from service prematurely following an accident. In April 2013 chartered to *Grimaldi Line* of Italy for five years and renamed the EUROFERRY BRINDISI. In October 2014 sold to the *Grimaldi Group* of Italy. In November sold to *Polferries* and renamed the MAZOVIA. Entered service in June 2015 on the Świnoujście - Ystad service.

NOVA STAR Built as the NORMAN LEADER by St Marine Shipyard, Singapore for *LD Lines* of France. However, delivery was not taken as she did not meet the design specification. She was registered to *Singapore Technologies Marine* and remained laid up until February 2014 when she was chartered to *Nova Star Cruises* of Canada and renamed the NOVA STAR. She operated between Portland, Maine USA and Yarmouth, Nova Scotia, Canada. In October 2015 she was arrested in Portland Maine due to unpaid bills and the service ceased. In February 2016 she was chartered to *Inter Shipping* of Morocco and placed on their Algeciras (Spain) - Tangier Morocco service. In November 2017 chartered to *Polferries* and sub-charted to *Inter Shipping* until February 2018 when she was taken over by *Polferries*. She began operating between Gdańsk and Nynäshamn in September 2018. In October 2019 purchased by *Polferries*.

WAWEL Built as the SCANDINAVIA by Kockums Varvet AB, Malmö, Sweden for *Rederi AB Nordö* of Sweden. After service in the Mediterranean for *UMEF*, she was, in 1981, sold to *SOMAT* of Bulgaria, renamed the TZAREVETZ and used on *Medlink* services between Bulgaria and the Middle East, later on other routes. In 1986 she was chartered to *Callitzis* of Greece for a service between Italy and Greece. In 1988 she was sold to *Sealink*, re-registered in The Bahamas and renamed the FIESTA. She was then chartered to *OT Africa Line*. During Autumn 1989 she was rebuilt at Bremerhaven to convert her for passenger use and in March 1990 she was renamed the FANTASIA and placed on the Dover - Calais service. Later in 1990 she was renamed the STENA FANTASIA. In 1998 transferred to *P&O Stena Line*. In 1999 she was renamed the P&OSL CANTERBURY. In 2002, following *Stena Line's* puling out of the joint company, she was renamed the PO CANTERBURY. In Spring 2003 replaced by the PRIDE OF CANTERBURY and laid up at Dunkerque. Later in the year sold to *GA Ferries* and renamed the ALKMINI A. In 2004 moved to Greece and, after a partial rebuild (including the welding up of the bow door) placed on the Igoumenitsa - Brindisi route. Later in 2004 sold to *Polferries* and renamed the WAWEL; rebuilt to increase the number of cabins. In 2005 placed on the Świnoujście - Ystad service. In May 2015 transferred to the Gdańsk - Nynäshamn route.

PRAAMID

THE COMPANY *Praamid* is the trading name of the ferry operation of the *TS Laevad*, a company owned by the Republic of Estonia. It took over the operation of services to the islands of Hiiumaa and Saaremaa in October 2016.

ADDRESS Sadama 25, Tallinn 15051, Estonia.

TELEPHONE +372 618 1310.

INTERNET Email info@praamid.ee **Website** www.praamid.ee *(Estonia, English)*

ROUTES OPERATED Kuivastu - Virtsu (Saaremaa) (28 mins; ***PIRET, REGULA, TÕLL***; up to 25 per day), Rohuküla - Heltermaa (Hiiumaa) (1 hr 30 mins; ***LEIGER, TIIU***; up to 11 per day).

1	LEIGER	4012t	16	10.0k	114.0m	700P	150C	-	BA	EE	9762675
2	PIRET	4012t	17	10.0k	114.0m	700P	150C	-	BA	EE	9762663
3	REGULA	3774t	71	14.5k	71.2m	580P	105C	20L	BA2	EE	7051058
4	TIIU	4012t	17	10.0k	114.0m	700P	150C	-	BA	EE	9762687
5	TÕLL	4012t	17	10.0k	114.0m	700P	150C	-	BA	EE	9762651

LEIGER, TIIU Built by Sefine Shipyard, Yalova, Turkey. LNG powered.

PIRET, TÕLL Built by Remontowa Shipyard, Gdańsk, Poland (The PIRET's hull was subcontracted to Irko, Gdańsk, Poland). LNG powered.

REGULA Built by Jos L Meyer, Papenburg, Germany for *Stockholms Rederi AB Svea* of Sweden for the service between Helsingborg and Helsingør operated by *Linjebuss International AB* (a

Cracovia *(Frank Lose)*

Nova Star *(Uwe Jakob)*

subsidiary company). In 1980 she was sold to *Scandinavian Ferry Lines*. During Winter 1984/85 she was rebuilt to increase vehicle and passenger capacity. In 1991 ownership was transferred to *SweFerry* and operations to *ScandLines* on the Helsingborg - Helsingør service. Ownership later transferred to *Scandlines AB*. In 1997 sold to *Saaremaa Laevakompanii*. In October 2016 chartered to *Praamid*. Following delivery of new vessels, she was retained as spare vessel. However, in summer 2017 she was used on regular service and the MERCANDIA VIII of *HH Ferries* was chartered as spare vessel. In September 2017 purchased by *TS Laevad*.

SAMSØ REDERI

THE COMPANY *Samsø Rederi* is a Danish public sector company owned by the Samsø Municipality.

MANAGEMENT Managing Director Carsten Kruse.

ADDRESS Sælvig 64, 8305 Samsø, Denmark.

TELEPHONE Administration and Reservations + 45 70 22 59 00.

INTERNET Email tilsamsoe@samsoe.dk **Website** www.tilsamsoe.dk *(Danish, German, English).*

ROUTE OPERATED Sælvig (Samsø) - Hou (Jylland) (1 hr; ***PRINSESSE ISABELLA***; up to 7 per day).

1	PRINSESSE ISABELLA	5478t	15	9.9k	100.0m	600P	160C	16T	BA	DK	9692806

PRINSESSE ISABELLA Built as the SAMSØ by Stocznia Remontowa, Gdańsk, Poland. Entered service in March 2015. In June 2015 renamed the PRINSESSE ISABELLA.

SCANDLINES

THE COMPANY In 2007, the owners of *Scandlines AG*, the Danish Ministry of Transport and Energy and Deutsche Bahn AG, decided to sell their shares. The new owner was a consortium of the 3i Group (UK), Allianz Capital Partners GmbH (Germany) (40% of the shares each) and *Deutsche Seereederei GmbH* (Germany) (20% of the shares). The company was subsequently transformed into a private limited company and now trades under the name Scandlines GmbH, uniting the companies *Scandlines Deutschland GmbH* and *Scandlines Danmark A/S*. With *Deutsche Seereederei GmbH* selling its shares in *Scandlines GmbH* in 2010, 3i and Allianz Capital Partners held 50% of the shares each. During 2012 *Stena Line* took over the Travemünde - Ventspils, Travemünde - Liepaja and Nynäshamn - Ventspils routes, took full control of the joint routes - Rostock - Trelleborg and Sassnitz - Trelleborg services and took over the vessels used. The freight-only route between Rostock and Hanko passed to *SOL*. In November 2013 3i Group purchased Allianz Capital Partners' share and now control 100% of the company. In March 2016 3i sold a majority share in the company to First State Investments and Hermes Investment Management.

MANAGEMENT CEO Søren Poulsgaard Jensen, **Managing Director & Chief Customer Officer** Morten Haure-Petersen.

ADDRESS Am Bahnhof 3a, 18119 Rostock, Germany.

TELEPHONE Administration & Reservations *Denmark* +45 33 15 15 15, ***Germany*** +49 (0)381-77 88 77 66.

INTERNET Email servcecenter.germany@scandlines.com **Website** www.scandlines.com *(Danish, English, German, Polish, Swedish)*

ROUTES OPERATED Rødby (Lolland, Denmark) - Puttgarden (Germany) (45 mins; ***DEUTSCHLAND, HOLGER DANSKE, KRONPRINS FREDERIK, PRINS RICHARD, PRINSESSE BENEDIKTE, SCHLESWIG-HOLSTEIN*** (***HOLGER DANSKE*** *specially for dangerous goods)*; half-hourly train/vehicle ferry + additional road freight-only sailings), Gedser (Falster, Denmark) - Rostock (Germany) (2 hours; ***BERLIN, COPENHAGEN***; every 2 hours).

1	BERLIN	22319t	16	20.5k	169.5m	1300P	460C	96L	BA2	DE	9587855
2	COPENHAGEN	22319t	16	20.5k	169.5m	1300P	460C	96L	BA2	DK	9587867

3	DEUTSCHLAND	15187t	97	18.5k	142.0m	1200P	364C	30Lr	BA2	DE	9151541
4F	HOLGER DANSKE	2779t	76	14.9k	86.8m	12P	-	12L	BA	DK	7432202
5	KRONPRINS FREDERIK	16071t	81	20.5k	152.0m	1082P	210C	46T	BA	DE	7803205
6	PRINS RICHARD	14822t	97	18.5k	142.0m	1100P	364C	36Lr	BA2	DK	9144419
7	PRINSESSE BENEDIKTE	14822t	97	18.5k	142.0m	1100P	364C	36Lr	BA2	DK	9144421
8	SCHLESWIG-HOLSTEIN	15187t	97	18.5k	142.0m	1200P	364C	30Lr	BA2	DE	9151539

BERLIN Partly built by Volkswerft Stralsund, Stralsund, Germany for *Scandlines* to operate on the Gedser – Rostock route. The propulsion system allows for adaption to LNG. Originally due to enter service in Spring 2012, construction was seriously delayed. It was then found that she did not meet the specification and the order was cancelled. She was 90% finished and had undertaken sea trials. In March 2014, purchased by *Scandferries ApS* of Denmark (an associated company) and towed, firstly to Blohm + Voss Shipyards, Hamburg and then to Fayard Shipyard, Odense to be completed with an almost completely new superstructure. Her engines were also modified straight diesel to diesel-electric hybrid. In May 2016 chartered to *Scandlines* and entered service on the Gedser – Rostock route.

COPENHAGEN As the BERLIN except that at the time of purchase by *Scandlines*, she had been launched but was only 50% finished. Entered service in Autumn 2016.

DEUTSCHLAND Train/vehicle ferry built by Van der Giessen de Noord, Krimpen aan den IJssel, Rotterdam, The Netherlands for *DFO* for the Puttgarden – Rødby service. During Winter 2003/04 a new hoistable deck was added for cars by Neptun Yard Rostock, (Germany).

HOLGER DANSKE Built by Aalborg Værft A/S, Aalborg, Denmark as a train/vehicle ferry for *DSB* for the Helsingør – Helsingborg service. In 1991 transferred to the Kalundborg – Samsø route (no rail facilities). In 1997 transferred to subsidiary *SFDS A/S*. Withdrawn at the end of November 1998 when the service passed to *Samsø Linien*. In 1999 began operating between Rødby and Puttgarden as a road-freight-only vessel, carrying, among others, loads which cannot be conveyed on passenger vessels.

KRONPRINS FREDERIK Train/vehicle ferry built by Nakskov Skibsværft A/S, Nakskov, Denmark for *DSB* for the Nyborg – Korsør service. Withdrawn in 1997. After conversion to a car/lorry ferry, she was transferred to the Gedser – Rostock route (no rail facilities). In March 2017, following modifications, transferred to the Rødby – Puttgarden route to provide extra capacity for lorry traffic. Also serves as reserve vessel on Gedser – Rostock service.

PRINS RICHARD, PRINSESSE BENEDIKTE Train/vehicle ferries, built by Ørskov Christensen Staalskibsværft A/S, Frederikshavn, Denmark for *Scandlines A/S* for the Rødby – Puttgarden service. During Winter 2003/04 a new hoistable deck was added for cars by Neptun Yard Rostock, (Germany).

SCHLESWIG-HOLSTEIN Train/vehicle ferry built by Van der Giessen de Noord, Krimpen aan den IJssel, Rotterdam, The Netherlands for *DFO* for the Puttgarden – Rødby service. During Winter 2003/04 a new hoistable deck was added for cars by Neptun Yard Rostock, (Germany).

SMYRIL LINE

THE COMPANY *Smyril Line* is a Faroe Islands company.

MANAGEMENT Adm. Director Rúni Vang Poulsen, **Accounting and Department Manager** Nina Djurhuus.

ADDRESS Yviri við Strond 1, 110 Tórshavn, Faroe Islands.

TELEPHONE Administration & Reservations +298-34 59 00.

INTERNET Email office@smyrilline.com **Website** www.smyrilline.com *(English, Danish, Dutch, Faroese, French, German, Icelandic, Norwegian, Swedish)*

ROUTES OPERATED *Winter/Early Spring* Tórshavn (Faroes) – Hirtshals (Denmark) (36 hrs; ***NORRÖNA***; 1 per week), ***Spring/Early Summer/Autumn*** Tórshavn – Hirtshals (36 hrs; ***NORRÖNA***; 1 per week), Tórshavn – Seyðisfjördur (Iceland) (19 hrs; ***NORRÖNA***; 1 per week), ***Summer*** Tórshavn – Hirtshals (Denmark) (30 hrs; ***NORRÖNA***; 2 per week), Tórshavn –

Seyðisfjördur (Iceland) (19 hrs; ***NORRÖNA***; 2 per week). ***Freight services*** Tórshavn (Faroe Islands) - Scrabster (UK) - Hirtshals (Denmark) - St. Petersburg (Russia) (***EYSTNES***, ***HVITANES***), Thorlakshöfn (Iceland) - Hirtshals (Denmark) - Tórshavn (***MISTRAL***), Thorlakshöfn (Iceland) - Tórshavn - Rotterdam (***MYKINES***), Rotterdam - Stavanger (Norway) - Trondheim (Norway) - Rørvik (Norway) - Hitra (***AKRANES***).

1F	AKRANES	10585t	96	20.0k	138.8m	12P	-	105T	A2	FO	9160774
2F	EYSTNES	4610t	81	15.0k	102.2m	0P	-	24T	AS	FO	7922166
3F	HVITANES	4636t	80	12.0k	77.3m	0P	-	14T	AS	FO	7915541
4F	MISTRAL	10471t	98	22.0k	153.5m	12P	-	112T	A	FI	9183788
5F	MYKINES	18979t	96	20.0k	138.5m	12P	1452C	105T	A2	FO	9121998
6	NORRÖNA	35966t	03	21.0k	164.0m	1482P	800C	134T	BA	FO	9227390

AKRANES Built as the SERENADEN by Umoe Sterkoder AS, Kristiansund, Norway for *Rederi AB Engship* of Finland and chartered to *Transfennica*. In 2006 *Rederi AB Engship* was taken over by *Rettig Group Bore*. In 2007 converted at COSCO Shipyard, Nantong, China to add a garage on top of the weather deck, renamed AUTO BANK and placed on long-term charter to *UECC*. Generally used on the Baltic or Iberian services. In December 2016 converted back to a conventional ro-ro freighter by Öresundwerft, Landskrona, Sweden and renamed the BORE BANK. Chartered to *Transfennica*. In December 2019 sold to *Smyril Line* and renamed the AKRANES.

EYSTNES Con-ro vessel (only the main deck can take trailers) built as the COMETA by Fosen Mekaniske Verksteder, Rissa, Norway for *Nor-Cargo*. Until 2010 she operated for *Sea-Cargo* between Norwegian ports and Immingham; afterwards she operated on *Nor-Cargo* Norwegian domestic services. In September 2015 sold to *Smyril Line* and renamed the EYSTNES.

HVITANES Con-ro vessel (only the main deck can take trailers) built as the TANAGER by Bergen Mekaniske Verksteder, Bergen, Norway for *NorCargo* of Norway. In September 2015 sold to *Smyril Line* and renamed the HVITANES.

MISTRAL Built by J J Sietas KG, Hamburg, Germany for *Godby Shipping AB* of Finland. Chartered to *Transfennica*. In 2003 chartered to *UPM-Kymmene Oy* of Finland and operated between Rauma and Santander. In 2005 chartered to *Finnlines*. Until the end of 2007 used on a Helsinki - Hamina - Zeebrugge service only available northbound for general traffic. From January 2008 operated on *UPM-Kymmene Seaways'* service from Hamina to Lübeck, Amsterdam and Tilbury. In June 2013 charter ended. During the ensuing period she undertook several short charters. In October 2014 chartered to *P&O Ferries* as second ship on the Zeebrugge - Middlesbrough (Teesport) service; she has also operated between Tilbury and Zeebrugge. In early June 2018 replaced by the *Estraden* and at the end of the month sub-chartered to *Stena Line* to operate between Rotterdam and Harwich. In August 2018 returned to *P&O Ferries* and operated between Teesport and Rotterdam. In March 2019 moved to the Liverpool - Dublin route. In December 2019 charter ended. Chartered to *Balieria* of Spain and used on the 'Canary Bridge' Huelva-Tenerife-Las Palmas service until end of May. In August 2020 chartered to *Smyril Line*.

MYKINES Built as the TRANSGARD by Umoe Sterkoder, Kristiansund, Norway for *Bror Husell Chartering* of Finland for long-term charter to *Transfennica* and used between Rauma and Antwerpen and Hamina and Lübeck. Later chartered to *Finncarriers*. In 2005 she underwent conversion in Poland to add a garage on top of the original weather deck and was placed on long-term charter to *UECC*. She was generally used on the Baltic or Iberian services. In 2007 renamed AUTO BALTIC. In January 2016 chartered to *Flotta Suardiaz*. In April 2017 sold to *Smyril Line* to inaugurate a new service between Thorlakshofn (Iceland), Tórshavn and Rotterdam and renamed the MYKINES.

NORRÖNA Built by Flender Werft, Lübeck, Germany for *Smyril Line*, to replace the existing NORRÖNA. Originally due to enter service in Summer 2002, start of building was delayed by financing difficulties. She was to have been built at Flensburger Schiffbau-Gesellschaft, Flensburg, Germany, but delays in arranging finance led to change of shipyard.

STENA LINE

THE COMPANY *Stena Line Scandinavia AB* is a Swedish private sector company. During 2012, the operations of subsidiary *Scandlines AB* of Sweden were absorbed and some of the Baltic operations and vessels of *Scandlines GmbH* of Germany were taken over. In *2015 Stena Line Scandinavia's* share in *Scandlines AB* where sold and the route Helsingborg – Helsingør sold to new owners.

MANAGEMENT CEO Niclas Mårtensson, **Chief Operating Officer** Peter Arvidsson.

ADDRESS Danmarksterminalen, 405 19 Göteborg, Sweden.

TELEPHONE Administration +46 (0)31-85 80 00, **Reservations** +46 (0)770 57 57 00.

INTERNET Email info@stenaline.com **Website** www.stenaline.com

ROUTES OPERATED Passenger Ferries Göteborg (Sweden) – Frederikshavn (Denmark) (3 hrs 15 mins; ***STENA DANICA, STENA JUTLANDICA, STENA VINGA***; up to 6 per day), Göteborg – Kiel (Germany) (14 hrs; ***STENA GERMANICA, STENA SCANDINAVICA***; 1 per day), Halmstad (Sweden) – Grenaa (Denmark) (4 hrs 35 mins; ***STENA NAUTICA***; 2 per day), Karlskrona (Sweden) – Gdynia (Poland) (10 hrs 30 mins; ***STENA BALTICA***, ***STENA NORDICA, STENA SPIRIT, STENA VISION***; 3/4 per day), Rostock (Germany) – Trelleborg (Sweden) (7 hrs); ***MECKLENBURG-VORPOMMERN, SKÅNE***; 3/4 per day), Travemünde (Germany) – Karlskrona – Liepaja (Latvia) (27 hrs; ***STENA GOTHICA, URD***; 5 per week)(one westbound journey per week calls at Karlskrona, adding 5 hours to the journey time), Nynäshamn (Sweden) – Ventspils (Latvia) (12 hrs; ***SCOTTISH VIKING, STENA FLAVIA***; 12 per week).

1	MECKLENBURG- VORPOMMERN	36185t	96	22.0k	199.9m	600P	445C	230Tr	A2	DE	9131797
2	SCOTTISH VIKING	26500t	09	24.0k	186.5m	800P	185C	120L	A	IT	9435454
3	SKÅNE	42705t	98	21.0k	200.2m	600P	520C	240Tr	AS2	SE	9133915
4	STENA BALTICA	22542t	07	23.0k	167.0m	160P	-	140L	BA2	UK	9364978
5»•	STENA CARISMA	8631t	97	40.0k	88.0m	900P	210C	-	A	SE	9127760
6	STENA DANICA	28727t	83	19.5k	154.9m	2274P	555C	120T	BAS2	SE	7907245
7	STENA FLAVIA	26904t	08	24.0k	186.5m	852P	185C	120L	A	DK	9417919
8	STENA GERMANICA	44372t	01	22.0k	240.1m	900P	-	250L	BA	SE	9145176
9F	STENA GOTHICA	13144t	82	18.0k	171.0m	186P	-	104T	AS	DK	7826867
10	STENA JUTLANDICA	29691t	96	21.5k	183.7m	1500P	550C	156T	BAS2	SE	9125944
11	STENA NAUTICA	19504t	86	19.4k	134.0m	700P	330C	70T	BA2	SE	8317954
12	STENA NORDICA	24206t	01	25.7k	169.8m	405P	375C	90L	BA2	BS	9215505
13•	STENA SAGA	33750t	81	22.0k	166.1m	2000P	510C	76T	BA	SE	7911545
14	STENA SCANDINAVICA	55050t	03	22.0k	240.1m	900P	-	260L	BA	SE	9235517
15	STENA SPIRIT	39169t	88	20.0k	175.4m	2400P	550C	120T	BAS2	BS	7907661
16	STENA VINGA	13906t	05	18.5k	124.9m	400P	342C	106T	A	SE	9323699
17	STENA VISION	39178t	87	20.0k	175.4m	2400P	550C	120T	BAS2	SE	7907659
18	URD	13144t	81	17.5k	171.0m	186P	-	104T	AS	DK	7826855

MECKLENBURG-VORPOMMERN Train/vehicle ferry built by Schichau Seebeckwerft, Bremerhaven, Germany for *DFO* for the Rostock – Trelleborg service. During Winter 2002/03 modified to increase freight capacity and reduce passenger capacity. In September 2012 sold to *Stena Line*.

SCOTTISH VIKING Built by CN Visentini, Porto Viro, Italy for *Epic Shipping* of the UK and chartered to *Norfolkline*. Operated between Zeebrugge and Rosyth until December 2010. In January 2010 chartered to *Scandlines* and placed on the Nynäshamn – Ventspils service. In September 2012 charter transferred to *Stena Line*.

SKÅNE Train/vehicle ferry built by Astilleros Españoles, Cadiz, Spain for an American trust and chartered to *Scandlines*. She is used on the Trelleborg – Rostock service.

STENA BALTICA Built as the COTENTIN by STX Finland, Helsinki, Finland for *Brittany Ferries*. Used on freight service from Poole to Cherbourg and Santander. In March 2013 replaced by the BARFLEUR (operating to Cherbourg only). During summer 2013 operated twice weekly from Poole to Bilbao and Santander. In October 2013 chartered to *Stena RoRo* and renamed the

Norröna *(Uwe Jakob)*

Stena Vinga *(Miles Cowsill)*

Stena Vision *(Frank Lose)*

Stena Danica *(Miles Cowsill)*

STENA BALTICA. In November 2013 chartered to *Stena Line* and replaced the STENA ALEGRA on the Karlskrona - Gdynia route.

STENA CARISMA Westamarin HSS 900 craft built at Kristiansand, Norway for *Stena Line* for the Göteborg - Frederikshavn service. Work on a sister vessel, approximately 30% completed, was ceased. She has not operated since 2013.

STENA DANICA Built by Chantiers du Nord et de la Méditerranée, Dunkerque, France for *Stena Line* for the Göteborg - Frederikshavn service.

STENA FLAVIA Built by CN Visentini, Porto Viro, Italy for *Epic Shipping* of the UK. Launched as the WATLING STREET. On delivery, chartered to *ISCOMAR* of Spain and renamed the PILAR DEL MAR. In 2009 laid up until February 2010 when she was chartered to *Acciona Trasmediterranea* of Spain and operated between Barcelona and Tangiers. Later that month, chartered to *T-Link* and resumed the name WATLING STREET. In May 2011 chartered to *Scandlines* and placed on the Travemünde - Ventspils service. In April 2012, sold to *Stena RoRo*; she continued to be chartered to *Scandlines*. In September 2012 charter transferred to *Stena Line*. In April 2013 renamed the STENA FLAVIA. She now operates between Nynäshamn and Ventspils.

STENA GERMANICA Ro-pax ferry built as the STENA HOLLANDICA by Astilleros Españoles, Cadiz, Spain for *Stena RoRo* and chartered to *Stena Line BV* to operate between Hoek van Holland and Harwich. In 2007 lengthened by 50m at Lloyd Werft, Bremerhaven and passenger capacity increased to 900. Between May and August 2010 refurbished at Gdańsk and had an 100 additional cabins added. At the end of August entered service on the Göteborg - Kiel route, renamed the STENA GERMANICA III. In September, after the previous STENA GERMANICA had been renamed the STENA VISION, she was renamed the STENA GERMANICA.

STENA GOTHICA Built as the LUCKY RIDER by Nuovi Cantieri Apuania S.P.A., Marina De Carrara, Italy, a ro-ro freight ferry, for *Delpa Maritime* of Greece. In 1985 she was acquired by *Stena Line* and renamed the STENA DRIVER. Later that year she was acquired by *Sealink British Ferries* and renamed the SEAFREIGHT FREEWAY to operate freight-only services between Dover and Dunkerque. In 1988 she was sold to *SOMAT* of Bulgaria for use on *Medlink* services in the Mediterranean and renamed the SERDICA. In 1990 she was sold and renamed the NORTHERN HUNTER. In 1991 she was sold to *Blæsbjerg* of Denmark, renamed the ARKA MARINE and chartered to *DSB*. She was then converted into a ro-pax vessel, renamed the ASK and introduced onto the Århus - Kalundborg service. Purchased by *Scandlines A/S* of Denmark in 1997. In 1999 she was, after some modification, transferred to *Scandlines Euroseabridge* and placed on the Travemünde - Klaipėda route. In 2000 she was transferred to the Rostock - Liepaja route. Lengthened by 20m in 2001 and, in late 2001, chartered to *Nordö Link* to operate between Travemünde and Malmö. In late 2002 replaced by the FINNARROW and returned to *Scandlines*. She was transferred to the Rostock - Trelleborg route whilst the MECKLENBURG-VORPOMMERN was being rebuilt. She was then transferred to the Kiel - Klaipėda route. In 2003 chartered to *Scandlines AB* to operate on the Trelleborg - Travemünde route. In April 2005 the charter ended and she returned to *Scandlines AG*. Initially she was due to replace the FELLOW on the Nynäshamn - Ventspils route during her annual refit. In Autumn 2005 moved to the Rostock - Ventspils route. In January 2009 moved to the Nynäshamn - Ventspils route. In January 2011 moved to the Travemünde - Liepaja route. In May 2011 laid up. In November introduced as second vessel. In September 2012 sold to *Stena Line*. In September 2015 moved to the Göteborg - Frederikshavn freight service and renamed the STENA GOTHICA. In September to be 2018 moved to the Travemünde - Liepaja route.

STENA JUTLANDICA Train/vehicle 'ro-pax' vessel built by Van der Giessen de Noord, Krimpen aan den IJssel, Rotterdam, The Netherlands for *Stena Line* to operate between Göteborg and Frederikshavn. She was launched as the STENA JUTLANDICA III and renamed on entry into service.

STENA NAUTICA Built as the NIELS KLIM by Nakskov Skibsværft A/S, Nakskov, Denmark for *DSB (Danish State Railways)* for their service between Århus (Jylland) and Kalundborg (Sjælland). In 1990 she was purchased by *Stena Rederi* of Sweden and renamed the STENA NAUTICA. In 1992 she was chartered to *B&I Line*, renamed the ISLE OF INNISFREE and introduced onto the Rosslare - Pembroke Dock service, replacing the MUNSTER (8093t, 1970). In 1993 she was transferred to the Dublin – Holyhead service. In early 1995 she was chartered to *Lion Ferry*. She was renamed the LION KING. In 1996 she was replaced by a new LION KING and renamed the STENA NAUTICA. During Summer 1996 she was chartered to *Transmediterranea* of Spain but returned to *Stena RoRo* in the autumn and remained laid up during 1997. In December 1997 she was chartered to *Stena Line* and placed on the Halmstad – Grenaa route. This route ended on 31st January 1999 and she was transferred to the Varberg – Grenaa route. During Winter 2001/02 she was rebuilt to heighten the upper vehicle deck and allow separate loading of vehicle decks; passenger capacity was reduced. On 16th February 2004 she was hit by the coaster JOANNA and holed. Returned to service at the end of May 2004 after repairs at Göteborg and Gdańsk.

STENA NORDICA Built as the EUROPEAN AMBASSADOR by Mitsubishi Heavy Industries, Shimonoseki, Japan for *P&O Irish Sea* for their Liverpool – Dublin service. Service transferred to from Liverpool to Mostyn in November 2001. Also operated between Dublin and Cherbourg once a week. In 2004 the Mostyn route closed and she was sold to *Stena RoRo*. Chartered to *Stena Line* to operate between Karlskrona and Gdynia and renamed the STENA NORDICA. In 2008 transferred to the Holyhead – Dublin service. In February 2015 replaced by the STENA SUPERFAST X and chartered to *DFDS Seaways*. She was renamed the MALO SEAWAYS and, in April 2015, placed on the Dover – Calais route. Withdrawn from traffic in February 2016 and laid up. In June 2016 charter ended. Renamed the STENA NORDICA and chartered to *GNV* of Italy to operate between Sicily and the Italian mainland. In January 2017 chartered to *Stena Line* and performed refit relief duties in the Irish Sea. In April placed on the Travemünde – Liepāja service. In October 2018 to be moved back to the Karlskrona – Gdynia route. In March 2019 replaced the STENA EUROPE on the Fishguard – Rosslare route for six months.

STENA SAGA Built as the SILVIA REGINA by Oy Wärtsilä Ab, Turku, Finland for *Stockholms Rederi AB Svea* of Sweden. She was registered with subsidiary company *Svea Line* of Turku, Finland and was used on *Silja Line* services between Stockholm and Helsinki. In 1981 she was sold to *Johnson Line* and in 1984 sold to a Finnish Bank and chartered back. In 1990 she was purchased by *Stena RoRo* of Sweden for delivery in 1991. In 1991 she was renamed the STENA BRITANNICA and took up service on the Hoek van Holland – Harwich service for Dutch subsidiary *Stena Line BV*, operating with a British crew. In 1994 she was transferred to the Oslo – Frederikshavn route and renamed the STENA SAGA. During Winter 2002/03 rebuilt to increase passenger capacity by 200. In March 2020 withdrawn following the permanent ending of the service and laid up.

STENA SCANDINAVICA Ro-pax vessel built by Hyundai Heavy Industries, Ulsan, South Korea, for *Stena RoRo*. Launched and delivered in January 2003 as the STENA BRITANNICA II. Chartered to *Stena Line* for use on the Hoek van Holland – Harwich service, replacing the 2000-built STENA BRITANNICA, now the FINNFELLOW of *FinnLink*. In March 2003 renamed the STENA BRITANNICA. In 2007 lengthened at Lloyd Werft, Bremerhaven. In September 2010 renamed the BRITANNICA. Between October 2010 and April 2011 refurbished and had 100 additional cabins added at Gdańsk. In April 2011 renamed the STENA SCANDINAVICA IV and entered service on the Göteborg – Kiel route. In May, after the previous STENA SCANDINAVICA had been renamed the STENA SPIRIT, she was renamed the STENA SCANDINAVICA.

STENA SPIRIT Built as the STENA SCANDINAVICA by Stocznia i Komuni Paryski, Gdynia, Poland for *Stena Line* for the Göteborg – Kiel service (launched as the STENA GERMANICA and names swapped with sister vessel before delivery). There were originally intended to be four vessels. Only two were delivered to *Stena Line*. The third (due to be called the STENA POLONICA) was sold by the builders as an unfinished hull to *Fred. Olsen Lines* of Norway and then resold to *ANEK* of Greece who had her completed at Perama and delivered as EL VENIZELOS for service between Greece and Italy. The fourth hull (due to be called the STENA BALTICA) was sold to *A Lelakis* of Greece and was to be rebuilt as a cruise ship to be called REGENT SKY; however, the project was never completed. The hull was broken up in 2004. During the summer period on some days, the vessel arriving in Göteborg overnight from Kiel operates a round trip to Frederikshavn before departing for Kiel the following evening. During Winter 1998/99 she was modified to increase freight capacity and reduce the number of cabins. In April 2011 replaced by the former STENA BRITANNICA (renamed the STENA SCANDINAVICA IV) and entered CityVarvet in Göteborg for refurbishment. In June 2011 she was renamed the STENA SPIRIT and, in July 2011, transferred to the Karlskrona - Gydnia route.

STENA VINGA Built as the HAMMERODDE by Merwede Shipyard, Hardinxveld-Giessendam, The Netherlands for *Bornholmstrafikken*. In Winter 2010 an additional vehicle deck was added for freight and some additional cabins. In November 2017 sold to *Stena RoRo* and chartered back. In September 2018 delivered to *Stena Line*, renamed the STENA VINGA and placed on the Göteborg - Frederikshavn service, replacing the STENA GOTHICA.

STENA VISION Built as the STENA GERMANICA by Stocznia im Lenina, Gdańsk, Poland for *Stena Line* for the Göteborg - Kiel service. During the summer period on some days, the vessel arriving in Göteborg overnight from Kiel operates a round trip to Frederikshavn before departing for Kiel the following evening. During Winter 1998/99 modified to increase freight capacity and reduce the number of cabins. In August 2010 replaced by the former STENA HOLLANDICA (renamed the STENA GERMANICA III initially) and entered CityVarvet in Göteborg for refurbishment. In September she was renamed the STENA VISION and, in November, transferred to the Karlskrona - Gydnia route.

URD Built as the EASY RIDER by Nouvi Cantieri Aquania SpA, Venice, Italy, a ro-ro freight ferry, for *Delpa Maritime* of Greece and used on Mediterranean services. In 1985 she was acquired by *Sealink British Ferries* and renamed the SEAFREIGHT HIGHWAY to operate a freight-only service between Dover and Dunkerque. In 1988 she was sold to *SOMAT* of Bulgaria for use on *Medlink* services in the Mediterranean and renamed the BOYANA. In 1990 she was sold to *Blæsbjerg* of Denmark, renamed the AKTIV MARINE and chartered to *DSB*. In 1991 she was converted into a ro-pax vessel, renamed the URD and introduced onto the Århus - Kalundborg service. Purchased by *Scandlines* in 1997. Withdrawn at the end of May 1999 and, after modification, transferred to the *Balticum Seaways* (later *Scandlines Balticum Seaways*) Århus - Aabenraa - Klaipėda route. In 2001 lengthened and moved to the Rostock - Liepaja route. In Autumn 2005 this route became Rostock - Ventspils. Withdrawn from Rostock - Ventspils in November 2009. Vessel inaugurated new service Travemünde - Ventspils in January 2010. Replaced by the WATLING STREET in May 2011 and moved to the Travemünde - Liepaja route. In October 2012 sold to *Sol Dru A/S* (a subsidiary of *Swedish Orient Line*) and chartered to *Stena Line*. In August 2013 sold to *Stena Line*.

Under Construction

20	E-FLEXER 7	-	22	22k	239.7m	1200P	300C	220L	BA2	-	-
21	E-FLEXER 8	-	22	22k	239.7m	1200P	300C	220L	BA2	-	-

E-FLEXER 7, E-FLEXER 8 Two lengthened vessels of E-Flexer model under construction by CMI Jinling Weihai Shipyard, Weihai, China. It has been announced they will operate for *Stena Line* but on what route is subject to confirmation. There is also a E-FLEXER 9 which is to be chartered to *Brittany Ferries* and named the SANTOÑA. *Stena RoRo* have options for more vessels.

STRANDFARASKIP LANDSINS

THE COMPANY *Strandfaraskip Landsins* is owned by the Faroe Islands Government.

ADDRESS Sjógøta 5, Postsmoga 30, 810 Tvøroyri, Faroe Islands.

TELEPHONE Administration & Reservations +298 34 30 00.

FAX Administration & Reservations +298 34 30 01.

INTERNET Email firstssl.fo **Website** www.ssl.fo *(Faroese)*

ROUTES OPERATED Passenger and Car Ferries Tórshavn (Streymoy) - Tvøroyri (Suduroy) (1 hr 50 mins; ***SMYRIL***; up to 3 per day), Klaksvík - Sydradali (20 min; ***SAM***; up to 6 per day), Skopun - Gamlarætt (30 mins; ***TEISTIN***; up to 9 per day). **Passenger-only Ferries** Sørvágur - Mykines (1 hr 15 mins; ***JÒSUP (chartered ship)***; up to 3 per day, May to August only), Hvannasund - Svínoy (40 mins) - Kirkja (20 mins) - Hattarvik (10 mins) - Svínoy (30 mins; ***RITAN***; up to 4 per day), Sandur - Skúvoy (35 mins; ***SILDBERIN***; up to 5 per day), Tórshavn - Nólsoy (25 mins; ***TERNAN***; up to 5 per day.

1	ERLA KONGSDÓTTIR	185t	20	-	27.0m	97P	3C	0L	BA	FO	9905526
2F	HASFJORD	686t	75	8.2k	40.8m	12P	0C	0L	BA	FO	7383542
3p	RITAN	81t	71	10.5k	22.1m	125P	0C	0L	-	FO	
4	SAM	217t	75	9.7k	30.2m	115P	17C	-	A	FO	7602168
5p	SILDBERIN	34t	79	7.5k	11.2m	30P	0C	0L	-	FO	
6	SMYRIL	12670t	05	21.0k	135.0m	976P	200C	32L	A	FO	9275218
7	TEISTIN	1260t	01	11.0k	45.0m	288P	33C	2L	BA	FO	9226102
8p	TERNAN	927t	80	12.0k	39.7m	319P	0C	0L	BA	FO	7947154

ERLA KONGSDÓTTIR Catamaran built by GS Marine, Gursken, Norway.

HASFJORD Built by Einar S Nielsen Mek. Verksted AS, Harstad, Norway for *Finnmark Fylkesrederi* of Norway to operate in the Hammerfest area. In 2003 the company was sold to *Veolia Transport Norge*, a subsidiary of the French *Veolia* group. In 2007 the group's Norwegian interests became *Veolia Transport Nord* and in May 2007 *Boreal Transport Nord*. In December 2019 the HASFJORD was sold to *Strandfaraskip Landsins* and delivered in February 2020. Now operates in freight-only mode, with 12 passenger maximum.

RITAN Built by Monnickenda, Volendam, The Netherlands. Used on the Hvannasund - Svínoy-Kirkja- Hattarvik service.

SAM Built by Blaalid Slip & Mek Verksted, Raudeberg, Norway. Used on the Klaksvik - Syòradali route and the Leirvik - Syòradali route.

SILDBERIN Built at Tvøroyri, Faroe Islands. Used on the Sandur - Skúvoy route.

SMYRIL Built by IZAR, San Fernando, Spain for *Strandfaraskip Landsins*. Operates on the Tórshavn - Tvøroyri service.

SÚLAN Built by Faaborg Værft A/S, Faaborg, Denmark. Used on the Sørvágur - Mykines service. Now conveys freight to Skúvoy.

TEISTIN Built by P/F Skipasmidjan a Skala, Skala, Faroe Islands for *Strandfaraskip Landsins*. Used on the Skopun - Gamlarætt service.

TERNAN Built by Tórshavnar Skipasmidja P/f, Tórshavn, Faroe Islands for *Strandfaraskip Landsins*. Used on the Tórshavn - Nólsoy service.

SYLTFÄHRE

THE COMPANY *Syltfähre* (*Syltfærge* in Danish) is the trading name of *Römö-Sylt Linie GmbH & Co. KG*, a German private sector company, a subsidiary of *FRS (Förde Reederei Seetouristik)* of Flensburg.

MANAGEMENT Managing Director RSL Birte Dettmers, Tim Kunstmann.

ADDRESS *Germany* Norderhofenden 19-20, 24937 Flensburg, Germany, ***Denmark*** Kilebryggen, 6792 Rømø, Denmark.

TELEPHONE Administration +49 (0)461 864 0, **Reservations *Germany*** +49 (0)461 864 601, ***Denmark*** +49 461 864 601.

INTERNET Email info@syltfaehre.de **Website** www.syltfaehre.de *(Danish, English, German)*

ROUTE OPERATED List auf Sylt (Sylt, Germany) - Havneby (Rømø, Denmark) (approx. 40 mins; ***RÖMÖ EXPRESS, SYLT EXPRESS***; variable - approx two-hourly). **Note**: The Danish island of Rømø is linked to the Danish mainland by a toll-free road causeway; the German island of Sylt is linked to the German mainland by the Hindenburgdamm, a rail-only causeway on which cars are conveyed on shuttle wagons.

1	RÖMÖ EXPRESS	3423t	91	15.0k	96.95m	345P	127C	-	BA	CY	9008794
2	SYLT EXPRESS	3650t	05	16.0k	88.2m	600P	80C	10L	BA	CY	9321823

RÖMÖ EXPRESS Built as the TRESFJORD by Fiskerstrand Verft A/S of Norway for *Møre og Romsdal Fylkesbåtar AS (MRF)* of Molde, Norway. In 2005 transferred to *Fjord1 MRF AS* of Molde, Norway. In October 2012 transferred to *Fjord 1 AS* of Florø, Norway. Until 2010 operated between Molde and Vestnes. She was then converted to LNG propulsion. Between February 2011 and January 2019 operated between Flakk and Rørvik. In January 2019 became a reserve vessel on the Molde and Vestnes route. In September 2019 purchased by *Römö-Sylt Linie* and renamed the RÖMÖ EXPRESS.

SYLT EXPRESS Built by Fiskerstrand Verft A/S, Aalesund, Norway for *Römö-Sylt Linie*.

TALLINK/SILJA LINE

THE COMPANY *AS Tallink Grupp* is an Estonian private sector company. *Tallink Silja Oy* is a Finnish subsidiary, *Tallink Silja AB* is a Swedish subsidiary.

MANAGEMENT *AS Tallink Grupp:* Chairman of Management Board Paavo Nõgene, **Communications Director** Katri Link, ***Tallink Silja Oy* Managing Director** Margus Schults, ***Tallink Silja AB* Managing Director** Marcus Risberg.

ADDRESSES *AS Tallink Grupp* Sadama 5/7, Tallinn 10111, Estonia, ***Tallink Silja Oy*** P.O. Box 100, 00181 Helsinki, Finland, ***Tallink Silja AB*** Box 27295, 10253 Stockholm, Sweden.

TELEPHONE *AS Tallink Grupp* +372 (0)640 9800, ***Tallink Silja Oy* Administration** +358 (0)9 18041, **Reservations** +49 (0)40 547 541 222**.**

FAX *AS Tallink Grupp* Administration + 372 (0)640 9810, ***Tallink Silja Oy* Administration** +358 (0)9 180 4262.

INTERNET Email info@tallink.ee **Websites** www.tallinksilja.com *(17 languages, see the internet page)*, www.tallink.com (corporate site) *(English)*

ROUTES OPERATED Tallink branded services *Passenger Ferries* Helsinki - Tallinn: ***Shuttle*** (2 hrs; ***MEGASTAR, STAR***; up to 6 per day), ***Cruise Ferries*** (3 hrs 30 - 4hrs 30 mins; ***SILJA EUROPA***; normally 2 per day), Stockholm - Mariehamn (Åland) - Tallinn (14 hrs; ***BALTIC QUEEN, VICTORIA I***; daily), Stockholm - Riga (Latvia) (16 hrs; ***ISABELLE, ROMANTIKA***; daily). ***Freight and Car Passengers Ferry*** Helsinki (Vuosaari) - Tallinn (Muuga) (3 hrs 30 mins; ***SEA WIND***; 2 per day). ***Freight-only Ferry*** Kapellskär - Paldiski (9 hrs - 11 hrs; ***REGAL STAR, SAILOR***; 6 per week).

Silja Line branded services Helsinki (Finland) - Mariehamn (Åland) - Stockholm (Sweden) (16 hrs; ***SILJA SERENADE, SILJA SYMPHONY***; 1 per day), Turku (Finland) - Mariehamn (Åland) (day)/Långnäs (Åland) (night) - Stockholm (11 hrs; ***BALTIC PRINCESS***, ***GALAXY***; 2 per day).

1	ATLANTIC VISION	30285t	02	27.9k	203.3m	728P	695C	110L	BA2	CA	9211509
2	BALTIC PRINCESS	48300t	08	24.5k	212.0m	2800P	300C	82T	BA	FI	9354284
3	BALTIC QUEEN	48300t	09	24.5k	212.0m	2800P	300C	82T	BA	EE	9443255
4	GALAXY	48915t	06	22.0k	212.0m	2800P	300C	82T	BA	SE	9333694
5	ISABELLE	35154t	89	21.5k	170.9m	2420P	364C	30T	BA	LV	8700723
6	MEGASTAR	49000t	16	27.0k	212m	2800P	300C	120L	BA2	EE	9773064
7F+	REGAL STAR	15281t	00	17.5k	156.6m	100P	-	120T	A	EE	9087116
8	ROMANTIKA	40803t	02	22.0k	193.8m	2178P	300C	82T	BA	LV	9237589
9F+	SAILOR	20921t	87	19.0k	157.6m	119P	50C	82L	A2	EE	8401444
10F+	SEA WIND	15879t	72	17.5k	154.4m	260P	55C	88T	BAS	EE	7128332
11	SILJA EUROPA	59912t	93	21.5k	201.8m	3000P	400C	68T	BA	EE	8919805
12	SILJA SERENADE	58376t	90	21.0k	203.0m	2800P	410C	70T	BA	FI	8715259
13	SILJA SYMPHONY	58377t	91	21.0k	203.0m	2800P	410C	70T	BA	SE	8803769
14	STAR	36249t	07	27.5k	185.0m	1900P	450C	120L	BA2	EE	9364722
15	VICTORIA I	40975t	04	22.0k	193.8m	2500P	300C	82T	BA	EE	9281281

ATLANTIC VISION Built as the SUPERFAST IX by Howaldtswerke Deutsche Werft AG, Kiel, Germany for *Attica Enterprises* for use by *Superfast Ferries*. She operated between Rostock and Södertälje from January until April 2002. In May 2002 she began operating between Rosyth and Zeebrugge (with the SUPERFAST X (now the A NEPITA)). In 2004 fitted with additional cabins and conference/seating areas. In 2005 transferred to the Rostock - Hanko (later Helsinki) route. In 2006 sold to *Tallink*. In October 2008 chartered to *Marine Atlantic* of Canada to operate on the North Sydney-Port aux Basques service and renamed the ATLANTIC VISION.

BALTIC PRINCESS Built by Aker Yards, Helsinki. A large part of the hull was built at St Nazaire, France. In August 2008 replaced the GALAXY on the Tallinn - Helsinki route. In February 2013 transferred to the Stockholm - Turku service.

BALTIC QUEEN Built by STX Europe, Rauma, Finland. Currently operates between Stockholm and Tallinn.

GALAXY Built by Aker Yards, Rauma, Finland to operate as a cruise ferry on the Tallinn - Helsinki route. In July 2008 transferred to the Stockholm - Turku route and rebranded as a *Silja Line* vessel.

ISABELLE Built as the ISABELLA by Brodogradevna Industrija, Split, Yugoslavia for *SF Line*. Used on the *Viking Line* Stockholm - Naantali service until 1992 when she was switched to operating 24-hour cruises from Helsinki and in 1995 she was transferred to the Stockholm - Helsinki route. During 1996 she additionally operated day cruises to Muuga in Estonia during the 'layover' period in Helsinki. In 1997 she was transferred to the Stockholm - Turku route. in January 2013 she was replaced by the VIKING GRACE. After covering for the AMORELLA during her refit period she was laid up. In April 2013 sold to *Hansa Link Limited*, a subsidiary of *AS Tallink Grupp* and renamed the ISABELLE. In May placed on the Stockholm - Riga service, replacing the SILJA FESTIVAL. Between June and August 2020 she operated between Paldiski and Kapellskär whilst the Riga service became a single ship operation.

MEGASTAR Built by Meyer Turku, Turku, Finland to operate on the Tallinn - Helsinki Shuttle. She is LNG/diesel dual powered. An option on a second vessel was allowed to lapse in March 2016.

REGAL STAR Partly built by Sudostroitelnyy Zavod Severnaya Verf, St Petersburg. Work started in 1993 (as a deep-sea ro-ro) but was never completed. In 1999 the vessel was purchased, taken to Palumba SpA, Naples and completed as a short-sea ro-ro with accommodation for 80 drivers. In 2000 she was delivered to *MCL* of Italy and placed on a route between Savona and Catania. In September of that year she was chartered to *Grimaldi Ferries* and operated on a route Salerno - Palermo - Valencia. In late 2003 she was sold to *Hansatee Shipping* of Estonia and, in 2004, placed on the Kapellskär - Paldiski route, replacing the KAPELLA. From February 2006 she was transferred to the Helsinki - Tallinn service, replacing the KAPELLA due to the hard ice conditions. She continued in this service for the summer, but the returned to the Paldiski - Kapellskär service. In June 2010 moved to the *SeaWind Line* Stockholm - Turku service for the summer seasons and returned to the Kapellskär - Paldiski route in the autumn.

ROMANTIKA Built by Aker Finnyards, Rauma, Finland for *Tallink Grupp* to operate for *Tallink* between Tallinn and Helsinki. Currently operating between Stockholm and Riga.

SAILOR Built as the FINNSAILOR by Gdańsk Shipyard, Gdańsk, Poland for *Finnlines* of Finland for freight service between Finland and Germany. In 1996 converted to ro-pax format to inaugurate a new passenger/freight service between Helsinki and Norrköping (Sweden) for subsidiary *FinnLink*. In 1997 this service was transferred to the Kapellskär - Naantali route and passengers (other than lorry drivers) ceased to be conveyed. In 2000 she was chartered to *Nordö-Link* to operate between Travemünde and Malmö. In 2002 she returned to *FinnLink*. In 2004 transferred to *Nordö-Link*. In 2007 returned to *FinnLink* as fourth ship. In early 2009 transferred to *Finnlines'* freight service operating between Helsinki, Turku and Travemünde but in April transferred back. In March 2011 moved back to *Finnlines Nordö-Link*. In November 2013 chartered to *Navirail* of Estonia to operate between Paldiski and Hanko. In January 2014 returned to *Finnlines* and placed on the Naantali - Kapellskär route. In January 2015 time chartered again to *Navirail*. In February 2015 demise chartered to *Navirail* and renamed the SAILOR. In October 2016 time chartered to *DFDS Seaways*, following their take over of the Hanko and Paldiski route. In May 2020 transferred to the Kapellskär-Paldiski route. In July 2020 sold to a subsidiary of *Tallink* and operated on the same route.

SEA WIND Train/vehicle ferry built as the SVEALAND by Helsingørs Skipsværft, Helsingør, Denmark for *Stockholms Rederi AB Svea* and used on the *Trave Line* Helsingborg (Sweden) - København (Tuborg Havn) - Travemünde freight service. In 1981 she was sold to *TT-Saga Line* and operated between Travemünde and Malmö. In 1984 she was rebuilt to increase capacity and renamed the SAGA WIND. In 1989 she was acquired by *Silja Line* subsidiary *SeaWind Line*,

Silja Euorpa *(Frank Lose)*

Slija Symphony *(Frank Lose)*

renamed the SEA WIND and inaugurated a combined rail freight, trailer and lower-priced passenger service between Stockholm and Turku. This route later became freight-only. In January 2015 transferred to the Tallinn – Helsinki freight service.

SILJA EUROPA Built by Jos L Meyer, Papenburg, Germany. Ordered by *Rederi AB Slite* of Sweden for *Viking Line* service between Stockholm and Helsinki and due to be called EUROPA. In 1993, shortly before delivery was due, *Rederi AB Slite* went into liquidation and the order was cancelled. A charter agreement with her builders was then signed by *Silja Line* and she was introduced onto the Stockholm – Helsinki route as SILJA EUROPA. In early 1995 she was transferred to the Stockholm – Turku service. In January 2013 she was transferred to the Helsinki – Tallinn route. In August 2014 chartered to an Australian company as an accommodation vessel. In March 2016 joined the BALTIC PRINCESS as second vessel on the Helsinki – Tallinn 'Cruise' service. In December 2016 resumed the role of sole cruise vessel on the route.

SILJA SERENADE, SILJA SYMPHONY Built by Masa-Yards Oy, Turku, Finland for *Silja Line* for the Stockholm – Helsinki service. In 1993, SILJA SERENADE was transferred to the Stockholm – Turku service but in early 1995 she was transferred back to the Helsinki route.

STAR Built by Aker Yards, Helsinki, Finland for *Tallink* to operate on the Tallinn – Helsinki route. In January 2017 modified at Vene Balti Shipyard, Tallinn to allow for two deck loading. Between March and April 2020 operated between Sassnitz and Paldiski, during the Covid-19 pandemic as the Polish border was shut.

VICTORIA I Built by Aker Finnyards, Rauma, Finland for *Tallink*. Operates between Tallinn and Stockholm. Starting in June 2020 she has operated between Helsinki and Tallinn on a temporary basis.

Under Construction

16	MySTAR	49000t	22	27.0k	212.0m	2800P	750C	180L	BA2	EE	9878319

MySTAR Under construction by Rauma Marine Constructions of Finland to operate on the Helsinki – Tallinn 'Shuttle' service.

TESO

THE COMPANY *TESO (Texels Eigen Stoomboot Onderneming)* is a Dutch private company, with most shares owned by inhabitants of Texel.

MANAGEMENT Managing Director Cees de Waal.

ADDRESS Pontweg 1, 1797 SN Den Hoorn, The Netherlands.

TELEPHONE Administration +31 (0)222 36 96 00, **Reservations** Not applicable.

INTERNET Email info@teso.nl **Website** www.teso.nl *(Dutch, English, German)*

ROUTE OPERATED Den Helder (The Netherlands) – Texel (Dutch Frisian Islands) (20 minutes; ***DOKTER WAGEMAKER***, ***TEXELSTROOM***; hourly).

1	DOKTER WAGEMAKER	13256t	05	15.6k	130.4m	1750P	320C	44L	BA2	NL	9294070
2	TEXELSTROOM	16400t	16	15.0k	135.4m	1750P	350C	44L	BA2	NL	9741918

DOKTER WAGEMAKER Built at Galatz, Romania (hull and superstructure) and Royal Schelde, Vlissingen (fitting out) for *TESO*.

TEXELSTROOM Built by La Naval Shipyard, Sestao, Spain.

TT-LINE

THE COMPANY *TT-Line GmbH & Co KG* is a German private sector company.

MANAGEMENT Managing Directors Hanns Heinrich Conzen & Jens Aurel Scharner, **Sales Manager** Dirk Lifke.

ADDRESS Zum Hafenplatz 1, 23570, Lübeck-Travemünde, Germany.

TELEPHONE +49 (0)4502 801-81.

INTERNET Email info@ttline.com **Website** www.ttline.com *(English, German, Lithuanian, Polish, Swedish)*

ROUTES OPERATED ***Passenger Ferries*** Travemünde (Germany) - Trelleborg (Sweden) (8 hrs 30 mins/9 hrs 30 mins; ***NILS HOLGERSSON, PETER PAN***; 2 per day). ***Ro-pax Ferries*** Travemünde (Germany) - Trelleborg (Sweden) (7 hrs 30 mins/8 hrs 15 mins; ***ROBIN HOOD***; 1 per day), Rostock (Germany) - Trelleborg (Sweden) (5 hrs 30 mins/6 hrs 30 mins/7 hrs 30 mins; ***HUCKLEBERRY FINN, TOM SAWYER***; 3 per day, Świnoujście (Poland) - Trelleborg (Sweden) (7 hrs; ***NILS DACKE***; 1 per day), Trelleborg - Klaipėda (Lithuania) (15 hrs; ***MARCO POLO***, 5 per week), Świnoujście (Poland) - Rønne (Bornholm, Denmark) (5 hrs (day), 6 hrs 30 mins (night); ***NILS DACKE***; 1 per week) (summer only),

1	HUCKLEBERRY FINN	26391t	88	18.0k	177.2m	400P	280C	121T	BAS2	SE	8618358
2	MARCO POLO	14398t	93	19.0k	150.3m	130P	-	130T	A2	CY	9019080
3	NILS DACKE	26796t	95	18.5k	179.7m	300P	-	157T	BA	CY	9087465
4	NILS HOLGERSSON	36468t	01	18.0k	190.8m	744P	-	171T	BAS2	DE	9217230
5	PETER PAN	44245t	01	18.0k	220.0m	744P	-	210T	BAS2	SE	9217242
6	ROBIN HOOD	26790t	95	18.5k	179.7m	317P	-	157T	BA	DE	9087477
7	TOM SAWYER	26478t	89	18.0k	177.2m	400P	280C	121T	BAS2	DE	8703232

HUCKLEBERRY FINN Built as the NILS DACKE by Schichau Seebeckwerft AG, Bremerhaven, Germany, as a ro-pax vessel. During Summer 1993 rebuilt to transform her into a passenger/car ferry and renamed the PETER PAN, replacing a similarly named vessel (31356t, 1986). On arrival of the new PETER PAN in Autumn 2001 she was renamed the PETER PAN IV. She was then converted back to ro-pax format, renamed the HUCKLEBERRY FINN and, in early 2002, transferred to the Rostock -Trelleborg route.

MARCO POLO Built as the VIA IONIO by Van der Giessen de Noord, Krimpen-a d Ijssel, Netherlands at their Welgelegen shipyard for *Viamare di Navigazione SpA* of Italy. Between April and August 1993 chartered to *TT-Line* and operated between Travemünde and Trelleborg. In August, placed on Mediterranean service. In April 1994 sold to *Adriatica di Navigazione SpA* of Italy and renamed the ESPRESSO RAVENNA. Operated between Ravenna - Catania. In July 2012 sold to *Compagnia Italiana Di Navigaz* of Italy and in January 2017 renamed the BARBARA KRAHULIK. In July 2019 sold to *TT-Line* and chartered back. Operated for *Tirennae* of Italy, mainly between Naples and Catania Delivered in November 2019 and renamed the MARCO POLO. In January 2020, after a major rebuild, placed on the Trelleborg - Klaipėda service.

NILS DACKE, Ro-pax vessels built as the ROBIN HOOD by Finnyards, Rauma, Finland. She operated on the Travemünde - Trelleborg and Travemünde - Helsingborg routes. In December 2014 she was renamed the NILS DACKE and transferred to Cypriot registry. Moved to the Trelleborg - Świnoujście route.

NILS HOLGERSSON, PETER PAN Built by SSW Fähr und Spezialschiffbau GmbH, Bremerhaven, Germany for the Travemünde - Trelleborg route. In January and February 2018 the PETER PAN was lengthened at MWB Motorenwerke Bremerhaven AG, Germany by 30 metres.

ROBIN HOOD Ro-pax vessels built as the NILS DACKE, by Finnyards, Rauma, Finland. She operated on the Travemünde - Trelleborg and Travemünde - Helsingborg routes. In January 2014, she was transferred to a new Trelleborg - Świnoujście service and changed to Polish registry. In December 2014 she was renamed the ROBIN HOOD and transferred German Registry. Moved to the Travemünde - Trelleborg route.

TOM SAWYER Built as the ROBIN HOOD by Schichau Seebeckwerft AG, Bremerhaven, Germany, as a ro-pax vessel. During Winter 1992/93 rebuilt to transform her into a passenger/car ferry and renamed the NILS HOLGERSSON, replacing a similarly named vessel (31395t, 1987) which had been sold to *Brittany Ferries* and renamed the VAL DE LOIRE. In 2001 converted back to ro-pax format and renamed the TOM SAWYER. Transferred to the Rostock - Trelleborg route.

Under Construction

8	NEWBUILDING 1	24500	22	21.0k	177.0m	900P	-	160T	BAS2	-	-

Polonia *(Frank Lose)*

Copernicus *(Uwe Jakob)*

9	NEWBUILDING 2	24500	22	21.0k	177.0m	900P	-	160T	BAS2	-	-

NEWBUILDING1, NEWBUILDING 2 Under construction by the CMI Jinling Shipyard, Nanjing, China. It is likely that they will replace the HUCKLEBERRY FINN and TOM SAWYER.

UNITY LINE

THE COMPANY *Unity Line* is a Polish company owned by *Polish Steamship Company (Polsteam)*. The operator manages seven ferries on two routes: Świnoujście - Ystad and Świnoujście - Trelleborg. Three ships are owned by *Euroafrica Shipping* which was previously a partner in the company; the ships continue to be operationally managed by to *Unity Line*.

MANAGEMENT Managing Director Jarosław Kotarski.

ADDRESS Plac Rodla 8, 70-419 Szczecin, Poland.

TELEPHONE Administration& Reservations +48 (0)91 88 02 909.

FAX Administration +48 91 35 95 885.

INTERNET Email rezerwacje@unityline.pl **Website** www.unityline.pl *(English, German, Polish, Swedish)*

ROUTES OPERATED Passenger Service Świnoujście (Poland) - Ystad (Sweden) (6 hrs 30 mins (day), 9 hrs (night); ***POLONIA, SKANIA***; 2 per day). **Freight Services** Świnoujście (Poland) - Ystad (Sweden) (8 hrs (day), 9 hrs (night); ***JAN ŚNIADECKI***; 1 per day), Świnoujście (Poland) - Trelleborg (Sweden) (6 hrs 30 mins (day), 9 hrs (night); ***COPERNICUS, GALILEUSZ, GRYF, WOLIN***; 4 per day).

1F+	COPERNICUS	14398t	96	19.0k	150.4m	50P	-	122T	A	CY	9031703
2F+	GALILEUSZ	15848t	92	17.0k	150.4m	160P	-	115L	A	CY	9019078
3F+	GRYF	18653t	90	16.0k	158.0m	180P	-	125L	BA	CY	8818300
4F+	JAN ŚNIADECKI	14417t	88	17.0k	155.1m	57P	-	70Lr	SA2	CY	8604711
5	POLONIA	29875t	95	17.2k	169.9m	920P	440C	145Lr	SA2	CY	9108350
6	SKANIA	23933t	95	22.5k	173.7m	1400P	430C	140L	BA	CY	9086588
7F+	WOLIN	22874t	86	17.5k	188.9m	370P	-	110Lr	SA	CY	8420842

COPERNICUS Built as the PUGLIA by Fincantieri-Cantieri Navali Italiani SpA, Ancona, Italy for *Tirrenia di Navigazione SpA.* of Italy. In 2016 rebranded as *Moby Cargo*. In December 2017 sold to *Euroafrica Shipping*, renamed the COPERNICUS and, in September 2018, placed on the Świnoujście - Trelleborg route.

GALILEUSZ Built as the VIA TIRRENO by Van der Giessen de Noord, Krimpen aan den IJssel, The Netherlands for *Viamare di Navigazione SpA* of Italy. Initially operated between Voltri and Termini Imerese. In 1998 transferred to the Génova - Termini Imerese route and in 2001 to the Génova - Palermo route. In 2006 sold to *Euroafrica Shipping*, renamed the GALILEUSZ and in November introduced onto the *Unity Line* Świnoujście - Ystad service. In February 2007 transferred to the new Świnoujście - Trelleborg route.

GRYF Built as the KAPTAN BURHANETTIN ISIM by Fosen Mekaniske Verksteder, Fevag, Norway for *Turkish Cargo Lines* of Turkey to operate between Trieste (Italy) and Derince (Turkey). In 2002 chartered to *Latlines* to operate between Lübeck and Riga (Latvia). In 2003 chartered to *VentLines* to inaugurate a new service between Travemünde and Ventspils. In 2004 sold to *Polsteam*, managed by *Unity Line* and renamed the GRYF. Entered service in 2005. In February 2007 transferred to the new Świnoujście - Trelleborg route.

JAN ŚNIADECKI Built by Falkenbergs Varv AB, Falkenberg, Sweden for *Polish Ocean Lines* to operate between Świnoujście and Ystad. Now operates for *Unity Line* on this route.

POLONIA Train/vehicle ferry built by Langsten Slip & Båtbyggeri A/S, Tomrefjord, Norway for *Polonia Line Ltd* and managed by *Unity Line*.

SKANIA Built as the SUPERFAST I by Schichau Seebeckwerft, Bremerhaven, Germany for *Superfast Ferries* of Greece. Operated between Patras and Ancona (Italy). In 1998 transferred to the Patras - Igoumenitsa (Greece) - Bari (Italy) route. In 2004 sold to a subsidiary of *Grimaldi*

Lines, renamed the EUROSTAR ROMA and placed on the Civitavecchia (Italy) - Barcelona (Spain) service. In 2008 sold to *Polsteam* and renamed the SKANIA. After modifications, she was placed on the *Unity Line* Świnoujście - Ystad service as second passenger vessel. In during the peak summer period in 2010 operated a round trip between Ystad and Rønne for *Bornholmstrafikken*.

WOLIN Train/vehicle ferry built as the ÖRESUND by Moss Rosenberg Værft, Moss, Norway for *Statens Järnvägar (Swedish State Railways)* for the 'DanLink' service between Helsingborg and København. Has 817 metres of rail track. Service ceased in July 2000 and vessel laid up. In 2001 sold to *Sea Containers Ferries* and in 2002 converted at Gdańsk, Poland to a passenger ferry. She was chartered to *SeaWind Line*, renamed the SKY WIND and in Autumn 2002 replaced the STAR WIND on the Stockholm - Turku service. In 2007 sold to *Polsteam*, renamed the WOLIN and placed on the *Unity Line* Świnoujście - Trelleborg service.

VIKING LINE

THE COMPANY *Viking Line Abp* is a Finnish company Listed on the Helsinki Stock Exchange since 1995.

MANAGEMENT President & CEO Jan Hanses, **Executive Vice President/Deputy CEO and Chief Financial Officer at Viking Line Abp** Mats Engblom.

ADDRESS Box 166, AX-22100 Mariehamn, Åland, Finland.

TELEPHONE Administration +358 (0)18 27000, **Reservations** +358 (0)600 41577.

INTERNET Email international.sales@vikingline.com **Websites** www.vikingline.com *(English)* www.vikingline.fi *(Finnish)* www.vikingline.se *(Swedish)* www.vikingline.ee *(Estonian)* www.vikingline.de *(German)*

ROUTES OPERATED *Conventional Ferries - all year* Stockholm (Sweden) - Mariehamn (Åland) - Helsinki (Finland) (14 hrs; ***GABRIELLA, MARIELLA***; 1 per day), Stockholm - Mariehamn (day)/Långnäs (Åland) (night) - Turku (Finland) (9 hrs 10 mins; ***AMORELLA, VIKING GRACE***; 2 per day), Kapellskär (Sweden) - Mariehamn (Åland) (2 hrs 15 mins; ***ROSELLA***; up to 3 per day), Helsinki - Tallinn (2 hrs 30 mins; ***VIKING XPRS***; 2 per day), Cruises from Stockholm to Mariehamn (21 hrs - 24 hrs round trip (most 22 hrs 30 mins); ***VIKING CINDERELLA***; 1 per day),

1	AMORELLA	34384t	88	21.5k	169.4m	2450P	450C	53T	BA	FI	8601915
2	GABRIELLA	35492t	92	21.5k	171.2m	2420P	400C	50T	BA	FI	8917601
3	MARIELLA	37799t	85	22.0k	176.9m	2500P	400C	60T	BA	FI	8320573
4	ROSELLA	16850t	80	21.3k	136.0m	1700P	340C	40T	BA	AX	7901265
5	VIKING CINDERELLA	46398t	89	21.5k	191.0m	2500P	100C	-	BA	SE	8719188
6	VIKING GRACE	57000t	13	23.0k	214.0m	2800P	556C	90L	BA	FI	9606900
7	VIKING XPRS	34000t	08	25.0k	185.0m	2500P	250C	60L	BA	EE	9375654

AMORELLA Built by Brodogradevna Industrija, Split, Yugoslavia for *SF Line* for the Stockholm - Mariehamn - Turku service.

GABRIELLA Built as the FRANS SUELL by Brodogradiliste Industrija, Split, Croatia for *Sea-Link AB* of Sweden to operate for subsidiary company *Euroway AB*, who established a service between Lübeck, Travemünde and Malmö. In 1994 this service ceased and she was chartered to *Silja Line*, renamed the SILJA SCANDINAVIA and transferred to the Stockholm - Turku service. In 1997 she was sold to *Viking Line* to operate between Stockholm and Helsinki. She was renamed the GABRIELLA.

MARIELLA Built by Oy Wärtsilä Ab, Turku, Finland for *SF Line*. Used on the Stockholm - Helsinki service. During 1996 additionally operated short cruises to Muuga in Estonia during the 'layover' period in Helsinki. In 2014, a daytime sailing during summer from Helsinki to Tallinn was introduced.

ROSELLA Built by Oy Wärtsilä Ab, Turku, Finland for *SF Line*. Used mainly on the Stockholm - Turku and Kapellskär - Naantali services until 1997. From 1997 operated 21 to 24-hour cruises from Stockholm to Mariehamn under the marketing name 'The Dancing Queen', except in the peak summer period when she operated between Kapellskär and Turku. In Autumn 2003 transferred to a new twice-daily Helsinki - Tallinn ferry service. In May 2008 placed on the Mariehamn - Kapellskär route under the Swedish flag. In 2011 she was extensively rebuilt at Balti Laevaremondi Tehas in Tallinn, Estonia. Cabin capacity was lowered from 1184 to 418 and the restaurant and shop areas were increased. In January 2014 placed under the Finnish flag.

VIKING CINDERELLA Built as the CINDERELLA by Wärtsilä Marine Ab, Turku, Finland for *SF Line*. Until 1993 provided additional capacity between Stockholm and Helsinki and undertook weekend cruises from Helsinki. In 1993 she replaced the OLYMPIA (a sister vessel of the MARIELLA) as the main Stockholm - Helsinki vessel after the OLYMPIA had been chartered to *P&O European Ferries* and renamed the PRIDE OF BILBAO. In 1995 switched to operating 20-hour cruises from Helsinki to Estonia in the off peak and the Stockholm - Mariehamn - Turku service during the peak summer period (end of May to end of August). From 1997 she remained cruising throughout the year. In Autumn 2003 she was transferred to the Swedish flag, renamed the VIKING CINDERELLA and transferred to Stockholm - Mariehamn cruises. She operates these cruises all year round.

VIKING GRACE Built by STX Europe, Turku, Finland. She operates between Stockholm and Turku. She is powered by LNG. Entered service in January 2013.

VIKING XPRS Built by Aker Yards, Helsinki to operate between Helsinki and Tallinn. In January 2014 placed under the Estonian flag.

Under construction

8	VIKING GLORY	63800t	21	23.0k	225.5m	2800P	556C	90L	BA	FI	9827877

VIKING GLORY Under construction by Xiamen Shipbuilding Industry Co. Ltd, Xiamen, China. She will be LNG powered and will replace the AMORELLA on the Stockholm - Mariehamn - Turku service.

WAGENBORG

THE COMPANY *Wagenborg Passagiersdiensten BV* is a Dutch private sector company.

MANAGEMENT Managing Director Ger van Langen.

ADDRESS Reeweg 4, 9163 ZM Nes, Ameland, The Netherlands.

TELEPHONE Administration & Reservations *International* +31 88 1031000, ***Netherlands*** 0900 9238.

INTERNET Email info@wpd.nl **Website** www.wpd.nl *(Dutch, English, German)*

ROUTES OPERATED *Car Ferries* Holwerd (The Netherlands) - Ameland (Frisian Islands) (45 minutes; ***OERD, SIER***; up to 14 per day), Lauwersoog (The Netherlands) - Schiermonnikoog (Frisian Islands) (45 minutes; ***MONNIK, ROTTUM***; up to 6 per day).

1	MONNIK	1121t	85	12.2k	58.0m	1000P	46C	9L	BA	NL	8408961
2	OERD	2286t	03	11.2k	73.2m	1200P	72C	22L	BA	NL	9269673
3	ROTTUM	1121t	85	12.2k	58.0m	1000P	46C	9L	BA	NL	8408959
4	SIER	2286t	95	11.2k	73.2m	1200P	72C	22L	BA	NL	9075761

MONNIK Built by Scheepswerf Hoogezand, Hoogezand, The Netherlands for *Wagenborg Passagiersdiensten BV* as the OERD. In 2003, on delivery of the new OERD, she was renamed the MONNIK. Used on the Lauwersoog - Schiermonnikoog route.

OERD Built by Scheepswerf Bijlsma Lemmer, Lemmer, The Netherlands for *Wagenborg Passagiersdiensten BV*. Used on the Ameland - Holwerd route.

ROTTUM Built as the SIER by Scheepswerf Hoogezand, Hoogezand, The Netherlands for *Wagenborg Passagiersdiensten BV* and used on the Holwerd - Ameland route. In 1995 renamed the ROTTUM and transferred to the Lauwersoog - Schiermonnikoog route.

SIER Built by Shipyard Bijlsma, Wartena, The Netherlands for *Wagenborg Passagiersdiensten BV*. Used on the Ameland - Holwerd route.

WASALINE

THE COMPANY *Wasaline* is the trading name of *NLC Ferry Oy Ab*, a Finnish company, jointly owned by the cities of Vaasa and Umeå.

MANAGEMENT Managing Director Peter Ståhlberg.

ADDRESS *Finland* Skeppsredaregatan 3, 65170 Vasa, Finland ***Sweden*** Blå Vägen 4, 91322 Holmsund, Sweden.

TELEPHONE Administration & Reservations *Finland* +358 (0)207 716 810, ***Sweden*** +46 (0)90 185 200.

INTERNET *Email* info@wasaline.com ***Website*** www.wasaline.com *(English, Finnish, Swedish)*

ROUTE OPERATED Vaasa (Finland) - Umeå (Sweden) (4 hrs; ***WASA EXPRESS***; 1/2 per day).

1	WASA EXPRESS	17053t	81	17.0k	140.8m	1100P	450C	84T	BAS2	FI	8000226

WASA EXPRESS Built by Oy Wärtsilä AB, Helsinki, Finland as the TRAVEMÜNDE for *Gedser-Travemünde Ruten* of Denmark for their service between Gedser (Denmark) and Travemünde (Germany). In 1986 the company's trading name was changed to *GT Linien* and in 1987, following the takeover by *Sea-Link AB* of Sweden, it was further changed to *GT Link*. The vessel's name was changed to the TRAVEMÜNDE LINK. In 1988 she was purchased by *Rederi AB Gotland* of Sweden, although remaining in service with *GT Link*. Later in 1988 she was chartered to *Sally Ferries* and entered service in December on the Ramsgate - Dunkerque service. She was renamed the SALLY STAR. In 1997 she was transferred to *Silja Line* to operate between Vaasa and Umeå during the summer period, under the marketing name WASA EXPRESS (although not renamed). She returned to *Rederi AB Gotland* in Autumn 1997, was renamed the THJELVAR and entered service with *Destination Gotland* in January 1998. Withdrawn and laid up in December 2003. In 2004 chartered to *Color Line* to inaugurate a new service between Larvik and Hirtshals. Renamed the COLOR TRAVELLER. Operated in reduced passenger mode on this service but in summer peak period operated between Frederikshavn and Larvik in full passenger mode. In December 2006 returned to *Rederi AB Gotland*. In 2007 renamed the THJELVAR, chartered to *Scandlines* and placed on the Gedser - Rostock route. Renamed the ROSTOCK. In Autumn 2008 withdrawn and laid up. In June 2009 sub-chartered to *Comarit* of Morocco for two months. In September she resumed the name THJELVAR. In August 2008 she was chartered to *Fred. Olsen SA* of Spain, renamed the BETANCURIA and placed on the Las Palmas - Puerto del Rosario - Arrecife service. In September 2012 laid up. In October 2012 purchased by *NLC Ferry Oy Ab* and, in November, renamed the WASA EXPRESS. Entered service in January 2013.

Under Construction

2	AURORA BOTNIA	23970t	21	20.0k	150.0m	800P	-	105T	BA	FI	9878319

AURORA BOTNIA Under construction by Rauma Marine Constructions, Rauma, Finland.

WYKER DAMPFSCHIFFS-REEDEREI

THE COMPANY *Wyker Dampfschiffs-Reederei* is a German company.

MANAGEMENT CEO Axel Meynköhn.

ADDRESS PO Box 1540, 25933 Wyk auf Föhr, Germany.

TELEPHONE Administration & Reservations +49 (0)4681 800.

INTERNET *Email* info@faehre.de ***Website*** www.faehre.de *(Danish, English, German)*

ROUTES OPERATED Dagebüll - Föhr (50min; ***NORDERAUE, NORDFRIESLAND, RUNGHOLT***; ***SCHLESWIG-HOLSTEIN, UTHLANDE***; up to 14 per day), Dagebüll - Amrun (90 min (120 min via Föhr); ***NORDERAUE, NORDFRIESLAND, RUNGHOLT, SCHLESWIG-HOLSTEIN***, ***UTHLANDE***; 7 per day), Föhr - Amrum (1 hr; ***NORDERAUE, NORDFRIESLAND, RUNGHOLT***; ***SCHLESWIG-HOLSTEIN, UTHLANDE***; up to 4 per day), Schlüttsiel - Hooge - Langeness (2 hrs; ***HILLIGENLEI***; up to 2 per day).

Gabriella *(Frank Lose)*

Mariella *(Miles Cowsill)*

1	HILLIGENLEI	467t	85	19.0k	38.3m	200P	22C	-	BA	DE	8411217
2	NORDERAUE	3250t	18	12.0k	75.9m	1200P	75C	-	BA	DE	9796121
3	NORDFRIESLAND	2287t	95	12.0k	67.0m	1200P	55C	-	BA	DE	9102758
4	SCHLESWIG-HOLSTEIN	3202t	11	12.0k	75.9m	1200P	75C	-	BA	DE	9604378
5	UTHLANDE	1960t	10	12.0k	75.9m	1200P	75C	-	BA	DE	9548407

HILLIGENLEI Built as the PELLWORM by Husumer Schiffswerft, Husum, Germany for *Neue Pellwormer Dampfschiffahrtsgesellschaft* of Germany and operated between Pellworm and Strucklahnungshörn. In 1996 sold to Sven Paulsen, Altwarp, Germany and renamed the ADLER POLONIA. Operated between Altwarp and Novo Warpno (Poland). In 2002 sold to *Wyker Dampfschiffsreederei* and renamed the HILLIGENLEI I. In February 2010 renamed the HILLIGENLEI.

NORDERAUE Built by Neptun Werft GmbH, Rostock, Germany for *Wyker Dampfschiffsreederei*.

NORDFRIESLAND Built by Husumer Schiffswerft, Husum, Germany for *Wyker Dampfschiffsreederei*.

SCHLESWIG-HOLSTEIN Built by Neptun Werft GmbH, Rostock, Germany for *Wyker Dampfschiffsreederei*.

UTHLANDE Built by J.J. Sietas GmbH & Co KG, Hamburg, Germany for *Wyker Dampfschiffsreederei*.

SECTION 8 – OTHER VESSELS

The following passenger vessels are, at the time of going to print, not operating and are owned by companies which do not currently operate services or are used on freight -only services. They are therefore available for possible re-deployment, either in the area covered by this book or elsewhere. Passenger vessels operating freight-only services outside the scope of this book are also included here. Exceptionally we have included two freight-only vessels possibly to be chartered to an operator serving the UK. Withdrawn vessels not yet disposed of and owned by operating companies are shown under the appropriate company and marked '•'.

Rederi AB Gotland

1	GUTE	7616t	79	15.0k	138.8m	88P	-	60T	A	SE	7802794

GUTE Built as the GUTE by Falkenbergs Varv AB, Falkenberg, Sweden for *Rederi AB Gotland* of Sweden. Used on service between Gotland and the Swedish mainland. In 1988 chartered to *Brambles Shipping* of Australia and used between Port Melbourne (Victoria) and Burnie (Tasmania). In 1992 she was renamed the SALLY SUN and chartered to *Sally Ferries*, operating between Ramsgate and Dunkerque. In 1994 she inaugurated a Ramsgate – Vlissingen service, which was later changed to Dartford – Vlissingen. In 1995 she was chartered to *SeaWind Line*, renamed the SEAWIND II and operated between Stockholm and Turku. In 1997 she was chartered to *Nordic Trucker Line* for the Oxelösund – St Petersburg service and in 1998 she returned to *SeaWind Line*. In 1998, after *Rederi AB Gotland*-owned *Destination Gotland* regained the franchise to operate to Gotland, she was renamed the GUTE and resumed her summer role of providing summer freight back-up to the passenger vessels, but with a number of short charters during the winter. In Autumn 2002 chartered to *Amber Lines* for the Karlshamn – Liepaja service. In February 2003 chartered to *NATO* for the Iraq crisis. Returned to *Destination Gotland* in Summer 2003. In Autumn 2003 chartered to *Scandlines Amber Lines* to operate between Karlshamn and Liepaja. In 2004 lengthened by 20.3m by Nauta Shiprepair, Gdynia, Poland. In Autumn 2004 chartered to *Riga Sea Line* to inaugurate a freight service between Riga and Nynäshamn. In Autumn 2005 the service ended and the vessel was laid up. In January 2006 chartered to *Lisco* and placed on the Klaipėda – Karlshamn route, also undertaking two trips from Klaipėda to Baltiysk. In May 2006 chartered to *SeaWind Line*. In March 2007 chartered to *Baltic Scandinavian Line*. Charter ended September 2007. Apart from a trip to Cameroon, conveying Swedish UN Troops for Chad, she remained laid up until October 2008 when she was chartered to *Baltic Scandinavian Line* to operate between Härnösand and Kaskinen. In 2009 this service closed and she was laid up. At the end of March 2015 she was chartered to *Færgen* to operate between Køge and Rønne covering for the HAMMERODDE. She returned to layup in May. In August 2017 chartered to *Stena Line* to operate as fourth ship on the Karlskrona - Gdynia route. In September 2018 replaced by the STENA NORDICA and the charter ended. During July 2019 replaced the PETER PAN of *TT Line* following a fire.

Saaremaa Laevakompanii (Estonia)

1	HARILAID	1028t	85	9.9k	49.9m	120P	35C	5L	BA	EE	8727367
2	KÖRGELAID	1028t	87	9.9k	49.9m	190P	35C	5L	BA	EE	8725577

HARILAID, KÖRGELAID Built by Riga Shiprepair Yard, Riga, Latvia (USSR) for *ESCO* of Estonia. In 1994 transferred to *Saaremaa Laevakompanii*. In October 2016 transferred to *Praamid* until new vessels were delivered. Then laid up in Tallinn.

Siem Industries

1	HONFLEUR	42400t	-	22.0k	187.4m	1680P	550C	150L	BA	-	9832119

HONFLEUR Under construction by Flensburger Schiffbau-Gesellschaft, Flensburg for *Brittany Ferries*, Germany to operate on the Portsmouth - Caen route, replacing the NORMANDIE. LNG powered. Construction has been heavily delayed, with fitting out still incomplete, and in June 2020 the contract was cancelled. In July 2020 sold to *Seim Industries* of Norway, former owner of the yard. The future of the vessel is uncertain; she may be purchased by *Brittany Ferries* under new terms and may be completed at a different yard.

Stena RoRo

1	SASSNITZ	21154t	89	18.5k	171.5m	875P	314C	50Tr	BA2	CY	8705383

SASSNITZ Train/vehicle ferry built by Danyard A/S, Frederikshavn, Denmark for *Deutsche Reichsbahn*. In 1993 ownership transferred to *DFO*. Used on the Sassnitz - Trelleborg service. In September 2012 sold to *Stena Line*. In April 2020 laid up and handed over to *Stena RoRo* following the ending of the Trelleborg - Sassnitz route.

Sassnitz *(Frank Lose)*

9 – SISTERS – A LIST OF SISTER (OR NEAR SISTER) VESSELS IN THIS BOOK

The following vessels are sisters or near sisters. This refers to 'as built' condition; some ships will subsequently have been modified and become different from their sister vessels.

ÆRØSKØBING, MARSTAL *(Ærøfærgerne)*

AMORELLA, GABRIELLA *(Viking Line)*, ISABELLE *(Tallink Silja Line)*, CROWN OF SCANDINAVIA *(DFDS Seaways)*.

ARGYLE, BUTE *(Caledonian MacBrayne)*.

ATHENA SEAWAYS, REGINA SEAWAYS, VICTORIA SEAWAYS *(DFDS Seaways)*.

ATLANTIC VISION *(Tallink)*, STENA SUPERFAST VII, STENA SUPERFAST VIII *(Stena Line)*.

AURORA AF HELSINGBORG, HAMLET, TYCHO BRAHE *(ForSea)*.

BALTIC QUEEN, BALTIC PRINCESS, GALAXY *(Tallink Silja Line)*.

BASTØ I, BASTØ II *(Bastø Fosen)*.

BASTØ IV, BASTØ V, BASTØ VI *(Bastø Fosen)*.

BEN-MY-CHREE *(Isle of Man Steam Packet Company)*, COMMODORE CLIPPER *(Condor Ferries)*, STENA VINGA *(Stena Line)* (Near sisters).

BEN WOOLLACOTT, DAME VERA LYNN *(Woolwich Free Ferry)*.

BERGENSFJORD, STAVANGERFJORD *(Fjord Line)*.

BERLIN, COPENHAGEN *(Scandlines)*.

CANNA *(Arranmore Fast Ferries)*, CLEW BAY QUEEN (*Clare Island Ferry Company)*, COLL *(Arranmore Island Ferries)*, EIGG *(Clare Island Ferry Company)*, MORVERN *(Arranmore Fast Ferries)*, RAASAY *(Inishbofin Island Discovery)*, RHUM *(Arranmore Island Ferries)*.

CARRIGALOE, GLENBROOK *(Cross River Ferries)*.

CATRIONA, HALLAIG, LOCHINVAR *(Caledonian MacBrayne)*

COLOR FANTASY, COLOR MAGIC *(Color Line)*.

COLOR VIKING *(Color Line)*, STENA NAUTICA *(Stena Line)*.

CONNEMARA *(Brittany Ferries)*, EPSILON *(Irish Ferries)*, ÉTRETAT, KERRY *(Brittany Ferries)*, SCOTTISH VIKING, STENA HORIZON, STENA LAGAN, STENA MERSEY, STENA FLAVIA *(Stena Line)*.

CÔTE D'ALBATRE, SEVEN SISTERS *(DFDS Seaways)*.

CÔTE DES DUNES, CÔTE DES FLANDRES *(DFDS Seaways)*.

CÔTE D'OPALE *(DFDS Seaways)*, GALICIA, SALAMANCA, SANTOÑA *(Brittany Ferries)*, STENA EDDA, STENA EMBLA, STENA ESTRID *(Stena Line)*.

CROWN SEAWAYS (DFDS Seaways), GABRIELLA *(Viking Line)*.

DAGALIEN, DAGGRI *(Shetland Islands Council)*.

DELFT SEAWAYS, DOVER SEAWAYS, DUNKERQUE SEAWAYS *(DFDS Seaways)*.

DEUTSCHLAND, SCHLESWIG-HOLSTEIN *(Scandlines)*.

DROTTEN, VISBY *(Destination Gotland)*.

EARL SIGURD, EARL THORFINN *(Orkney Ferries)*.

ECKERÖ *(Eckerö Linjen)*, POVL ANKER *(Molslinjen)*.

EUROPALINK, FINNLADY, FINNMAID, FINNSTAR, FINNSWAN *(Finnlines)*.

EUROPEAN CAUSEWAY, EUROPEAN HIGHLANDER *(P&O Ferries).*

FENJA, MENJA *(Molslinjen).*

FINNCLIPPER, FINNEAGLE, FINNFELLOW *(Finnlines)*, STENA GERMANICA *(Stena Line).*

FINNPARTNER, FINNTRADER *(Finnlines).*

FRIDTJOF NANSEN, ROALD AMUNDSEN (Hurtigruten)

FRISIA III, FRISIA V *(Reederei Norden-Frisia).*

GOTLAND, VISBORG *(Destination Gotland).*

HARILAID, KÖRGELAID *(Saaremaa Laevakompanii).*

HAVILA CAPELLA, HAVILA CASTOR, HAVILA POLARIS, HAVILA POLLUX *(Havila Kystruten).*

HJALTLAND, HROSSEY *(NorthLink Ferries).*

HUCKLEBERRY FINN, TOM SAWYER *(TT-Line).*

KING SEAWAYS, PRINCESS SEAWAYS *(DFDS Seaways).*

KONG HARALD, NORDLYS, RICHARD WITH *(Hurtigruten).*

KRONPRINS FREDERIK, PRINS JOACHIM *(Scandlines).*

LANGELAND, LOLLAND *(Molslinjen).*

LEIGER, PIRET, TIIU, TÕLL *(Praamid)*

LOCH DUNVEGAN, LOCH FYNE *(Caledonian MacBrayne).*

LOCH LINNHE, LOCH RANZA, LOCH RIDDON, LOCH STRIVEN *(Caledonian MacBrayne).*

LYNHER II, PLYM II, TAMAR II *(Torpoint Ferries).*

MARIELLA *(Viking Line)*, SPL PRINCESS ANASTASIA *(Moby SPL).*

MEGASTAR, MySTAR *(Tallink/Silja Line).*

MERCANDIA IV, MERCANDIA VIII *(ForSea).*

MIDNATSOL, TROLLFJORD *(Hurtigruten).*

MIDSLAND, WESTFALEN *(Rederij Doeksen).*

MONNIK, ROTTUM *(Wagenborg).*

MÜNSTERLAND, OSTFRIESLAND *(AG Ems).*

NILS DACKE, ROBIN HOOD *(TT-Line).*

NILS HOLGERSSON, PETER PAN *(TT-Line).*

NORBANK, NORBAY *(P&O Ferries).*

NORDKAPP, NORDNORGE, POLARLYS *(Hurtigruten).*

OERD, SIER *(Wagenborg).*

OILEAN NA H-OIGE, SANCTA MARIA *(Bere Island Ferries).*

PRIDE OF BRUGES, PRIDE OF YORK *(P&O Ferries).*

PRIDE OF CANTERBURY, PRIDE OF KENT *(P&O Ferries).*

PRIDE OF HULL, PRIDE OF ROTTERDAM *(P&O Ferries).*

PRINS RICHARD, PRINSESSE BENEDIKTE *(Scandlines).*

RED EAGLE, RED FALCON, RED OSPREY *(Red Funnel Ferries).*

RENFREW ROSE *(Highland Ferries)*, YOKER SWAN *(Sherkin Island Ferry).*

ROMANTIKA, VICTORIA I *(Tallink Silja Line).*

SILJA SERENADE, SILJA SYMPHONY *(Tallink Silja Line).*

SOUND OF SCARBA, SOUND OF SHUNA *(Western Ferries).*

SOUND OF SEIL, SOUND OF SOAY *(Western Ferries).*

SPIRIT OF BRITAIN, SPIRIT OF FRANCE *(P&O Ferries).*

STENA ADVENTURER, STENA SCANDINAVICA *(Stena Line).*

STENA BRITANNICA, STENA HOLLANDICA *(Stena Line).*

STENA GOTHICA, URD *(Stena Line).*

STENA SPIRIT, STENA VISION *(Stena Line).*

SUPERSPEED 1, SUPERSPEED 2 *(Color Line).*

WIGHT LIGHT, WIGHT SKY, WIGHT SUN *(Wightlink).*

WILLEM BARENTSZ, WILLEM DE VLAMINGH *(Rederij Doeksen).*

Fast Ferries

EXPRESS 1, EXPRESS 2, EXPRESS 3 *(Molslinjen).*

MAX *(Molslinjen),* SKANE JET *(FRS Baltic).*

RED JET 6, RED JET 7 *(Red Funnel Ferries).*

WIGHT RYDER I, WIGHT RYDER II *(Wightlink).*

Freight Ferries

ADELINE *(CLdN/Cobelfret Ferries)*, WILHELMINE *(Stena Line).*

AKRANES *(Smyril Line)*, BORE BANK *(Transfennica)*, BORE BAY *(Sea-Cargo)*, MYKINES *(Smyril Line)*

AMANDINE, OPALINE *(CLdN/Cobelfret Ferries).*

ANVIL POINT, EDDYSTONE *(Foreland Shipping),* FINNMERCHANT *(Finnlines),* HARTLAND POINT, HURST POINT*(Foreland Shipping).*

ARROW *(Isle of Man Steam Packet),* HELLIAR, HILDASAY *(NorthLink Ferries).*

AUTO ECO, AUTO ENERGY *(UECC)*

AUTOPREMIER, AUTOPRESTIGE, AUTOPRIDE, AUTOPROGRESS *(UECC).*

AUTOSKY, AUTOSTAR, AUTOSUN *(UECC).*

BALTICBORG, BOTHNIABORG *(Smurfit Kappa Group).*

BELGIA SEAWAYS, GOTHIA SEAWAYS *(DFDS Seaways),* SOMERSET *(Stena Line).*

BEGONIA SEAWAYS, FICARIA SEAWAYS, FREESIA SEAWAYS, PRIMULA SEAWAYS *(DFDS Seaways).*

BORE SEA *(Transfennica)*, BORE SONG *(P&O Ferries).*

BOTNIA SEAWAYS, FINLANDIA SEAWAYS *(DFDS Seaways),* FINNHAWK, FINNKRAFT *(Finnlines).*

BRITANNIA SEAWAYS, SELANDIA SEAWAYS, SUECIA SEAWAYS *(DFDS Seaways).*

CAPUCINE, SEVERINE *(CLdN/Cobelfret Ferries).*

CELANDINE, CELESTINE, CLEMENTINE, MELUSINE, VALENTINE, VICTORINE *(CLdN/Cobelfret Ferries).*

CELINE, DELPHINE *(CLdN/Cobelfret Ferries).*

CITY OF HAMBURG, CIUDAD DE CADIZ *(LD Seaplane).*

CLIPPER PENNANT *(P&O Ferries)*, CLIPPER POINT, SEATRUCK PACE, SEATRUCK PANORAMA *(Seatruck Ferries)*.

COLOR CARRIER *(Color Line)*, FINNMASTER *(Finnlines)*, MN PELICAN (*Brittany Ferries*), SC CONNECTOR *(Sea-Cargo)*.

COPERNICUS, GALILEUSZ *(Unity Line)*, MARCO POLO *(TT-Line)*

CORONA SEA *(Transfennica)*, FINNBREEZE, FINNMILL, FINNPULP, FINNSEA, FINNSKY, FINNSUN, FINNTIDE, FINNWAVE, FIONIA SEA *(Finnlines)*, HAFNIA SEA *(Transfennica)*.

EXPORTER, SHIPPER *(Wagenborg-Holmen Paper Shipping)*, SC ATHELA *(Sea-Cargo)*, TRADER *(DFDS Seaways)*.

FLANDRIA SEAWAYS, HOLLANDIA SEAWAYS, HUMBRIA SEAWAYS, SCANDIA SEAWAYS *(DFDS Seaways)*.

GARDENIA SEAWAYS *(DFDS Seaways)*, MELEQ *(CLdN/Cobelfret Ferries)*, TULIPA SEAWAYS *(DFDS Seaways)*.

GENCA, KRAFTCA, PLYCA, PULPCA, TIMCA, TRICA *(Transfennica)*.

HATCHE, QEZBAN *(Stena Line)*.

HERMINE, LAURELINE, SIXTINE, YSALINE *(CLdN/Cobelfret Ferries)*.

FLANDRIA SEAWAYS, HOLLANDIA SEAWAYS, HUMBRIA SEAWAYS, SCANDIA SEAWAYS *(DFDS Seaways)*.

L'AUDACE, LA SURPRISE *(Flota Suardiaz)*.

MAGNOLIA SEAWAYS, PETUNIA SEAWAYS *(DFDS Seaways)*.

MAZARINE, PALATINE, PEREGRINE, VESPERTINE *(CLdN/Cobelfret Ferries)*.

MISANA, MISIDA *(Sea-Cargo)*.

MISTRAL *(Smyril Line)*, SEAGARD *(Transfennica)*.

NEPTUNE AEGLI, NEPTUNE DYNAMIS *(Neptune Lines)*.

NEPTUNE GALENE NEPTUNE ILIAD, NEPTUNE ITHAKI, NEPTUNE KEFALONIA, NEPTUNE ODYSSEY, NEPTUNE THALASSA *(Neptune Lines)*

NORSKY, NORSTREAM *(P&O Ferries)*.

PAULINE, YASMINE *(CLdN/Cobelfret Ferries)*.

SCA OBBOLA, SCA ORTVIKEN, SCA ÖSTRAND *(SCA Transforest)*.

SEATRUCK PERFORMANCE, SEATRUCK POWER, SEATRUCK PRECISION, SEATRUCK PROGRESS *(Seatruck Ferries)*.

STENA HIBERNIA, STENA SCOTIA *(Stena Line)*.

STENA TRANSIT, STENA TRANSPORTER *(Stena Line)*.

TAVASTLAND, THULELAND, TUNDRALAND *(Wallenius SOL)*.

SECTION 10 – CHANGES SINCE FERRIES 2020 – BRITISH ISLES AND NORTHERN EUROPE

DISPOSALS

The following vessels, listed in *Ferries 2020 - British Isles and Northern Europe* have been disposed of – either to other companies listed in this book or others. Company names are as used in that publication.

BAIE DE SEINE *(Brittany Ferries)* In March 2020 returned to *DFDS* and renamed the SIRENA SEAWAYS. In April placed on the Klaipėda – Karlshamn route.

BALTICA *(Wallanius SOL)* In December 2019 charter ended.

BASTØ III *(Bastø Fosen)* In April 2020 sold to *Torghatten Nord AS* of Norway and renamed the BOMLO.

BORE BANK *(Transfennica)* In December 2019 sold to *Smyril Line* and renamed the AKRANES.

CITY OF OSLO *(UECC)* In March 2020 charter ended.

CLIPPER PENNANT *(Seatruck Ferries)* (In December 2019 chartered to *P&O Ferries).*

CLIPPER RANGER In December 2019 sold to *CTMA* of Canada and renamed the CTMA VOYAGEUR II.

CYMBELINE *(CLdN/Cobelfret)* In October 2019 sold to *Navigmag* of Chile and renamed the DALKA.

FIONIA SEAWAYS *(DFDS Seaways)* In February 2020 charter ended. Chartered to *Finnlines* and renamed the FIONIA SEA.

FJORD CAT (*Fjord Line*) In August 2020 sold to *FRS Baltic* and renamed the SKANE JET.

HONFLEUR *(Brittany Ferries)* In June 2020 contract to build this vessel was terminated. She is now listed in Section 8 under new owners, *Siem Industries* of Norway.

JUTLANDIA SEAWAYS *(DFDS Seaways)* At the end of March 2020 charter ended.

LIVERPOOL SEAWAYS *(DFDS Seaways)* In April 2020 withdrawn. Sold to *La Méridionale* of France and in May renamed the PELAGOS.

MALI ROSE *(Isles of Scilly Steamship Company)* In December 2019 sold to *Atloy Bat & Marina AS* of Norway.

MISANA *(Stena Line)* In March 2020 charter ended. Laid up. In August 2020 chartered to *Sea-Cargo*.

MISIDA *(Stena Line)* In January 2020 charter ended. Chartered to *DFDS Seaways* for two weeks In February chartered to *CoTuNav* of Tunisia Charter terminated in April. Laid up. In July 2020 chartered to *P&O Ferries* and in October to be chartered to *Sea-Cargo*.

MISTRAL *(P&O Ferries)* In December 2019 charter ended. Chartered to *Balieria* of Spain and used on the 'Canary Bridge' Huelva-Tenerife-Las Palmas service. In August 2020 chartered to *Smyril Line*.

NEWBUILDING *(Irish Ferries)* In June 2020 the order was cancelled. Construction had not started.

RUNGHOLT *(Wyker Dampfschiffs-Reederei)* In October 2019 sold to *Blue Cruises* of Greece and renamed the NISSOS CHRISI.

SAILOR *(DFDS Seaways)* In June 2020 sold to *Tallink*.

SASSNITZ *(Stena Line)* In April 2020 laid up and handed over to *Stena RoRo* following the ending of the Trelleborg – Sassnitz route.

STENA FORECASTER *(Stena Line)* In June 2020 charter from *Stena RoRo* ended. Laid up.

STENA FORETELLER *(DFDS Seaways)* In December 2019 charter ended. Chartered to *Irish Ferries* to cover during the overhaul of the ULYSSES operating Dublin – Holyhead and Dublin – Cherbourg. Charter ended April 2020, then laid up.

STENA SUPERFAST X *(Stena Line)* In March 2020 charter ended. In April chartered to *Corsica Linea* of France and, in June, renamed the A NEPITA.

TRANSFIGHTER *(Sea-Cargo)* In May 2020 charter ended.

VERONA *(Flota Suardiaz)* In March 2019 sold to *Anji Shipping Hong Kong Co Ltd* and renamed the SAIC ANJI PHOENIX.

Stena Saga *(Miles Cowsill)*

Bore Bank *(Frank Lose)*

VESSELS RENAMED

The following vessels have been renamed since the publication of *Ferries 2020 - British Isles and Northern Europe* without change of owner or operator.

GOTLAND *(Destination Gotland)*. In February 2020 renamed the DROTTEN.

THJELVAR *(Destination Gotland)* In May 2020 renamed the GOTLAND.

TRESFJORD *(Syltfähre)* In September 2019 renamed the RÖMÖ EXPRESS.

COMPANY CHANGES

Holmen Shipping The company has combined with Wagenborg to offer a twice weekly service between Sheerness and Terneuzen and Södertalje with a greater emphasis on attracting commercial traffic and has been moved to Section 7 under the heading *Wagenborg-Holmen Paper Shipping*.

MBNA Thames Clippers Following a change in sponsorship, the company now trades as *Uber Boat by Thames Clippers*.

Smurfit Kappa Paper Group *Wagenborg*, who operate the service, have formed a joint venture with *Holmen Shipping*. See above.

LATE NEWS

Seatruck Ferries/Stena Line In August 2020 the CLIPPER PANORAMA was chartered to *Stena Line* to operate between Birkenhead and Belfast and Heysham and Belfast.

Wallenius SOL Lines In August 2020 the VASALAND was chartered to *Anarres Shipping*, Cyprus to operate a new service between Marina di Carrara, Italy and Sousse, Tunisia. It is uncertain whether she will return to *Wallenius SOL Lines*.

FERRIES ILLUSTRATED

INDEX

Other books from Ferry Publications

NORTH SEA BRIDGE

For nearly two centuries, Denmark, Finland, Iceland, Norway and Sweden enjoyed direct passenger ferry connections to the UK. This book explores the development of the Scandinavia-UK ferry services from early 19th century to the final closure of the services during the first decades of the new millennia. Over 200 photos. 160 pages. Price £22.00 plus p&p.

COLOR LINE

Thirty years ago, Colo Line emerged as the inheritor of the great Norwegian maritime tradition of providing high-quality internatio ferry services to the country's nearest overs neighbours. Over 150 illustrations, many of which have never previously been published. 168 pages. Price £21.5 plus p&p.

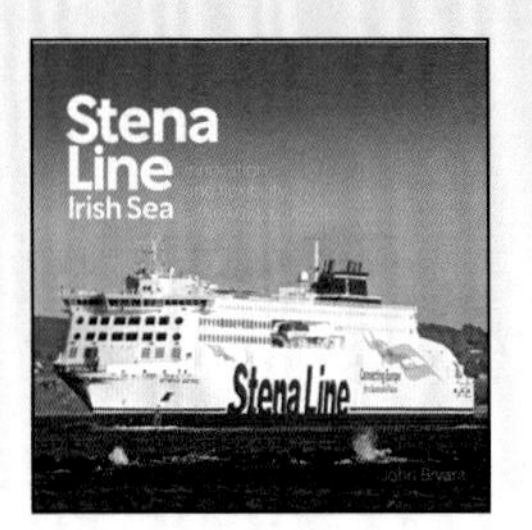

STENA LINE IRISH SEA – INNOVATION AND FLEXIBILITY THE KEY TO SUCCESS

This book takes a close look at Stena Line's Irish Sea shipping operations it inherited and to celebrate their achievements some 30 years on. Now the dominant operator on the Irish Sea, the company has long been at the heart of innovation and efficiency. The book traces the challenges it faced and the introduction today of the ground-breaking E-Flexer series of ro-pax vessels. 168 pages. Price £21.50 plus p&p.

BRITTANY FERRIE - THE FLEET - EDITION 2

This illustrated fleet publication encompass the entire fleet of Britt Ferries from the ***Keris*** to the companies latest ship currently under construction in Germany, the ***Galicia***. Detail information is given for each of the flee accompanied by a photograph or an illustration.The principal ships are illustrated by specially commissioned drawing by Marc-Antoine Bombail. The book also includes ships of the former fleet in their new waters si their sail. 96 pages. Price £16.95 plus p&p.

TRAVELLING TO THE CONTINENT

This nostalgic publication gives the reader an insight into the ferry operations from Britain to the Continent from the late 1950's to 2018. Each of the principle routes serving Holland, Belgium, France, Spain and Scandinavia are covered with a brief history, together with a wealth of photographs, brochures and other memorabilia. It includes the Night Ferry service via Dover and the other train ferry services to the Continent. 120 pages. Price £18.95 plus

FERRY & CRUISE REVIEW

Europe's best selling ferry anc cruise magazine published quarterly. High quality photo: leading articles and reports o both industries. Price £7.90 (UK)/£9.70 (Ireland and Europe) per issue including p

Order online from: www.ferrypubs.co.u
By telephone on
+44 (0)1624 898445
By post:
PO Box 33, Ramsey, Isle of Man IM99 4

Please telephone or email for current postage costs.